Lake Victoria: A Narrative Of Explorations In Search Of The Source Of The Nile

George Carless Swayne

Nzoe Antelopes. Little Windermere, Karague.—FRONTISPIECE.

LAKE VICTORIA

A NARRATIVE OF EXPLORATIONS IN SEARCH OF THE SOURCE OF THE NILE

COMPILED FROM THE

MEMOIRS OF CAPTAINS SPEKE AND GRANT

BY

GEORGE C. SWAYNE, M.A.

LATE FELLOW OF CORPUS CHRISTI COLLEGE, OXFORD

WILLIAM BLACKWOOD AND SONS
EDINBURGH AND LONDON
MDCCCLXVIII

CONTENTS.

PART II.

CHAPTER I.

FROM ZANZIBAR TO KAZÉ.

CHAPTER II.

FROM KAZÉ TO KARAGUÉ.

CHAPTER III.

KARAGUÉ.

CHAPTER IV.

UGANDA.

CHAPTER V.

UNYORO.

· CHAPTER VI.

UNYORO TO EGYPT.

ILLUSTRATIONS.

LAKE VICTORIA.

INTRODUCTORY CHAPTER.

IN spite of our Danish disgraces, and diplomatic defeats, and Jamaica Committees, and the thousand and one meannesses perpetrated by a generation deeply tainted with the worship of the " almighty dollar," the name of England is safe from contempt while she is still capable of producing men like those from whose diaries this narrative is compiled. While other countries are not unfruitful in the heroes of science, and France can boast of her Du Chaillu, her Maizan, her Jules Gerard—Germany of her Vogel, her Barth, her Von der Decken—America of her Kane,—England still stands pre-eminent in the number of self-devoted men who have carried the double cross of her standard, like the leading-star of religion and civilisation, into the most inhospitable regions of the earth. To mention names is invidious, because many will be omitted which deserve to be specified ; and yet it is impossible to think of African discovery without dwelling on the great name of Livingstone, the high priest and probably the martyr at once of faith and science ; and with-

A

out mentioning Speke and Grant's bold follower in the same regions, Sir Samuel Baker, who has enriched our maps by placing his great lake, called after "Albert the Good," by the side of that which Speke named after his beloved Sovereign — a happy combination, significative not of ambitious rivalry, but of harmonious union in a noble purpose. And the thought of African discovery suggests the valuable additions which have been made to knowledge by our Asiatic and American explorers, and by the pioneers of colonisation in the terrible deserts of Australia, amongst whom must not be forgotten the valiant Eyre, who has added to his fame as a discoverer that peculiar merit for which ancient Rome would have decreed her most honourable crown—the merit of having saved the lives of citizens. Though we may perhaps no longer possess the eyes to see heroism, it is a comfort to know that it still flourishes in our midst, if with little hope of adequate recognition; and that a soil where such salt is still found, is a long way off from utter moral putrefaction. Such are the class of men to whom England must always look for her leaders if her national existence or supremacy is imperilled by the bloated military establishments of other nations; men who have won victories of a higher character than those on the battle-field—victories over material nature and human ignorance — victories which have done great good and no harm to their kind, and where the lives of the victors have often been the only sacrifices, but won by an amount of personal courage, strategical skill, patience, perseverance, and fortitude, such as the greatest campaigns ever fought have scarcely demanded. It is more becoming to praise the dead than the living, and we may safely say that Speke was the *beau idéal* of a discoverer. In attempting to give, in a succinct form, the African experiences embodied in his notes and those of Captain Grant, it is necessary to confess that one great charm must be inevitably lost in the aroma of personal character that breathes from his own memoirs in numberless little touches and traits and anecdotes, which it would be impossible to reproduce in a limited space. Even Speke's weaknesses are evidences of the kind of power that was eminently suited to his task. When, for instance, he confesses that he rather likes than otherwise those Somali ruffians who pierced his body with eleven wounds, because they were always in high spirits and loved "a jolly row," some grave people might shake their heads, and wonder how a man of ten years' Indian service could still have preserved that thoughtless sympathy with exuberant life which is more appropriate to an Eton or Harrow boy; but it was just such a sympathy that enabled him to bear up against that depression of spirits which must be produced by long and exclusive contact with a race who combine the most violent passions and worst vices of adults with the mental constitution of children, and so saved him from utter despair in barbarian human nature. The worries he was subject to in his relations with the great black urchins who surrounded him were perhaps the greatest trial of his patience in his marvellous journeys, and could only be in a measure appreciated by those philanthropic gentlemen who have attempted to teach in a " ragged school." Even the most faithful of his men, such as Bombay and Baraka, gave Speke a world of trouble on the marches. The Wanguana or freedmen whom he took with him from Zanzibar were tolerably favourable specimens, yet he had to manage them like children, chiefly by humouring, tempered with a little fatherly severity. They used to say to him, when caught in some fault, " You ought to forgive and forget; for are you not a big man who should be above harbouring spite, though for a moment you may be angry ?   Flog me if you like, but don't keep count against me, else I shall run away ;˙ and what will you do then ? "

He mentions slavery and polygamy as the two chief curses of the African, which combine to keep him in a degraded condition.   But these two evils are doubtless the consequences no less than the causes of his relatively humble position in the scale of human races.   The man of a superior race, except under peculiar circumstances, will rather die than submit to slavery; the woman of a superior race will inevitably rebel against polygamy. Slavery, in that naked ugliness which reduces a human being to a saleable chattel, and stifles in him the germ of a diviner life, is, of course, utterly indefensible.   But there is a wide difference between such a slavery, as demoralising to the master as to the servant, and that degree of liberty which implies self-government.   How few nations, even among the *élite* of mankind, have proved themselves fit for this !   The utmost that can be said of most of them is, that with time they may possibly be educated up to it. The greatest possible happiness attainable at present by the unadulterated negro seems to be to fall under the just and mild dominion of some superior race.   An example of this was seen by Speke in the comparatively happy kingdom of Karagué, which was ruled by a prince in whom Semitic blood seemed to predominate—the good king Rumanika.   The tyrant of Uganda, Mtésa, on the other hand, though a Wahuma by extraction, was said to have come of a family which had been degraded in its type by repeated intermixture with slaves.   This prince is a fine specimen of a beggar on horseback—a spoilt child in a situation of absolute power.   Not incapable of warm affections, and fully able by natural acuteness to appreciate and submit to moral superiority, he indulges his animal propensities, and takes human life away, with an unconsciousness which, in a being not supposed to possess an immortal soul, would not be without a grim comicality. His vanity, his ferocity, his vulgarity, his capacity for being amused with trifles, his indifference to everything but the enjoyment of the moment—lastly, his unbounded good-nature and unmeasured generosity—all stamp him as the representative negro. Such lessons ought not to be lost on those who, like ourselves on a small scale, and the Americans on a large, have to deal with a population of emancipated black slaves. Nor are they to be lost on those excellent missionaries who, thinking solely of doing their duty in the service they have adopted, and the promotion of their peculiar views of Christian doctrine, may not always have had the leisure to study the natures of those who are the object of their labours.

As babes must be fed with natural and wholesome milk, so must these simple people be weaned from superstitions by the inculcation of clear and simple doctrine, instead of having their weak brains puzzled with some complicated modern system of developed theology. And in the name of all prudence, the family quarrels of the churches must remain as long as possible a dead letter to them. According to Speke's showing, the obstacles to missionary success are chiefly of an external character. As far as religion goes, the minds of the people in the interior of Africa would appear to be in the condition of a blank sheet of paper on which a few horrible caricatures have been scrawled by a haunting fear of the unknown supernatural. A message of universal love would appear to them almost too good news to be true. Yet there is little probability that the missionary can do much till the slave-hunter is put down. And this must be done, first, by shutting up

one after another of the slave-markets; secondly, by teach-
ing the selfish Arabs and native princes that legitimate
traffic will pay them much better, as well as introduce
them to a world of comforts and conveniences, of which,
under the present system, they must ever remain in ignorance.   Were the door thrown open to the missionary, it
is obvious that a mere preacher would make very little
way with the tribes of the interior.   Even a Wilberforce,
if obliged to express himself in Kisuahili, would find his
accustomed eloquence soon fail him.   A man bred in
some ingenious trade, such as turning, would at once
arrest their curiosity and arouse their intelligence; and a
good musician would at once find his way through their
correct ears to their hearts.   But nothing would make
a stronger impression upon them than a knowledge of
sleight-of-hand, learned from some professional wizard,
such as Robert Houdin, since the belief in magic is the
only belief that stands in the way of a better; and after
Aaron's rod had swallowed the wands of the magicians, it
would be easy to show that the apparent sorcery was all
produced by natural means.   It is really surprising, not
merely as looking to the possible regeneration of benighted
millions, but to the material gains which are sure to follow from opening up so vast and rich a garden as Equatorial Africa, that so little has been done by the principal
European Governments in forwarding exploring expeditions.   With us it has been considered far too much as
a matter of interest for the Geographical Society alone.
While money is forthcoming by hundreds of thousands of
pounds for enabling English products to make a creditable
show at the Paris Exhibition, how niggardly in proportion have been the doles dealt out to those brave men
who have gone forward into the wilderness to prepare a
vast virgin field for national enterprise; and with what,

perhaps unnecessary, sacrifices of their own resources, health, and often lives, have their labours been attended! It was a miracle that Speke was able with his scanty guard to push through the tribes on his road to the Nile; and probably Livingstone has perished—if he has—from the insufficient numbers as well as the untrustworthy nature of his defensive force. Yet all the narratives seem to show that a few hundred resolute and perfectly armed men, inured to similar climates, would be able to walk through Africa from one side to the other. It is only in the large kingdoms, such as Unyoro, Uganda, and Karagué, that large armies could be collected by the chiefs; and the kings of these two first countries appear to be perfectly manageable—the first through his avarice, the second through his vanity; while it seems to be the strongest wish of the exceptionally far-sighted Rumanika to open his gates to Europeans.

All the agricultural tribes on Speke's route seemed very glad to see him, though not averse to exacting as much black-mail as possible in a friendly way; and such exactions, though it might not be prudent altogether to resist them, might easily be kept within bounds by the presence of a strong armed force. The only tribes who keep up the true Ishmaelite character of hostility to all strangers appear to be the wandering pastorals, such as the Somali and Masai; and, of course, it would be necessary to keep them at arm's length. A careless confidence might lead to such a disaster as ruined the expedition which was to have started from Berbera; but, after all, these tribes do not appear to trust each other sufficiently to enable them to take common action in considerable numbers, and they appear to be very sparingly supplied with firearms. The mere employment of breech-loading guns would probably be equivalent to doubling the numbers of any expedition-

ary force.   Two valuable hints to future explorers seem
to be given by the account of Speke's rapid and most successful journey from Kazé to the Victoria Nyanza in 1858.
The first of these refers to the quality of the *guard*.   He
found he was faithfully and courageously served by some
Beluch volunteers from the Sultan of Zanzibar's mercen-
aries, and such men are to be found in abundance among
the Sikhs and in the northern provinces of India, who
have been used to British discipline, and would probably
bear well a climate not on an average more trying than
their own.   The other hint touches the advantage of flying
columns for purposes of exploration, unencumbered by
what the conquerors of the world, in just contempt, called
impedimenta.   Of course this implies the existence of
a central depot for the expedition : such, in this case, had
been formed in the Arab settlement of Kazé.   From
Speke's description, no region, from its fertility and resources, appears better suited for a base of future operations than that about Ujiji on the Tanganyika Lake.
Supposing such a depot established there, strongly posted,
of course, in an intrenched camp, the different points of
present geographical interest might be attacked at once
by different parties—one, for instance, might go to the
head of the lake, and see whether the river Speke heard
of, but did not see there, really exists—whether, if existing, it flows into or out of the lake, and whether there is
any communication between the Tanganyika, by it or otherwise, and Baker's Albert Nyanza ;   another might go to the
south of the lake, and ascertain in what direction the river
flows at that extremity, and whether the Tanganyika is
connected by it with Livingstone's Nyassa, and endeavour
to set the public mind at rest as to Livingstone's own fate;
while another might proceed to the south of the Victoria

Nyanza, and build boats, possibly of iron, in the lack of building-trees, by the help of the smiths in those parts, for the thorough exploration of the eastern shores of the Nyanza. It would now be generally admitted that Speke's great discoveries have gained in importance since those of Sir Samuel Baker have been published, confirming them in the most important particulars. Certainly Speke did not seem to have an idea of the great extent of the Luta Nzigé Lake, though he mentions native accounts which would have led him to infer it. On one subject only is he dogmatic—the physical impossibility of any of the great African rivers having their main sources anywhere except in the equatorial rainy zone; and as yet he has not been disproved. He was perhaps, too, a little confident that the head of the Tanganyika was completely shut in by mountains, for appearances in such cases are often delusive, and gaps and rents in hills by natural convulsions are often not seen except at their entrances. It would be strange if it should turn out that Speke was doubly right about the importance of the Victoria Nyanza, in the unexpected sense that water flows from his Nile into and out of Baker's lake, and, moreover, through Baker's lake into the Tanganyika, and so on into the Nyassa, forming a sort of southern Nile springing from the same reservoir as the northern. But, in the present state of facts, such speculations are simply amusing. When every corner of the country is known, and every principal source of the Nile has been visited, the real fountainhead of the river may still be a subject of controversy,—just as it is in the case of the best-known rivers, such as the Rhine and the Danube; but not the less for this has Speke rendered inestimable services to geographical science, and his name is quite worthy to be bracketed with that of Bruce, who discovered the source of the Blue Nile in the Abyssinian hills, which was long thought the most important branch, as having the greater influence on the inundations in Egypt. It may almost be disputed whether it is consistent with geographical accuracy to speak of *the* source of a river at all. A little brook may flow from a source, but a river has the configuration of a tree, its farthest source being, as it were, only the topmost of a multitude of branches.

It would be very difficult for any future explorers to achieve greater results than Speke and Grant effected with the means at their disposal; but a thoroughly well-found expedition, with a nucleus of Europeans eminent in different branches of science, might be able in the same time to gather much more multifarious information, as all work is more perfectly done by division of labour. It certainly speaks highly for the education of Englishmen, that two Indian officers were found able and willing to march into the heart of Africa, who were both more or less competent commanders, sportsmen, zoologists, geologists, land-surveyors, mathematicians, ethnologists, and philologists, besides being able to throw their observations on men and manners into language which proved what they might have done had they confined themselves to the province of pure literature. Amongst the scattered notices of the languages of the tribes through whom they travelled, one remark deserves particular notice—that the equator appears to be the boundary between two entirely different classes of languages. All the nations from Zanzibar to Unyoro appear to speak different dialects of the language of Unyamuézi, or the country of the Moon, which becomes at Zanzibar the Kisuahili or Coast dia-

lect; while the nations to the north of the equator speak
languages differing from it in some important particulars.
Speke says that the Coast language is based on euphony,
which introduces a great complexity of forms, but this is
a characteristic of many Indo-European tongues, such as
the Greek, and still more the Sanscrit; while it appears
to differ essentially from them in being not an inflexional
but an agglutinative language, like the Basque, the Mag-
yar, and the Osmanli in Europe. For instance, the syl-
lable *Wa* prefixed to the word signifying a country, means
men or people; *U*, in the same place, means locality, or
the country itself; *M* means a man or individual, and
Ki the language. As an example, we have Wagogo,
Mgogo, Ugogo, Kigogo—the people, man, country, and
language of Gogo respectively. It was only observed of
the people to the north of the equator—the Gani, for instance—that all their words had a guttural sound, and
they seemed to swallow them in speaking. Here, it may
be seen at a glance, is a wide field opened for investiga-
tion, and from the extensive area in which the Kisuahili
language is spoken, with certain modifications, it would
appear that an adequate knowledge of it would be a most
powerful instrument in the hands of any traveller whose
object it might be to bring these races into closer relations
with our civilisation.

One remark more in preface to this narrative. Whatever may be effected by subsequent travellers, however
great in a scientific point of view may be the results of
their labours, our heroes will always stand alone as having
performed the unparalleled feat of crossing from the south-
east of Africa to the north by a path unknown to civilised man before, with a courage and confidence equal to
that of Columbus when he discovered America. Courage

is not a rare virtue among British officers; but to judge of the amount of patience, self-command, and forbearance necessary to accomplish such a task, the narrative itself must be read; and indeed its perusal will not be without a moral bearing on the general relations of life.

GEORGE CARLESS SWAYNE.

BOSCOBEL HOUSE, CLIFTON.

PART I.

PRELIMINARY EXPLORATIONS

PART I.

CHAPTER I.

THE SOMALI EXPEDITION.

SPEKE'S PLANS OF EXPLORATION—HE IS APPOINTED TO ASSIST LIEU-
TENANT BURTON ON AN EXPEDITION TO THE SOMALI COUNTRY WITH
LIEUTENANTS HERNE AND STROYAN—HE CROSSES THE MOUNTAINS
INTO THE INTERIOR, WHILE BURTON GOES TO HARAR, AND THE
OTHERS COLLECT CATTLE AT BERBERA — HE RETURNS TO ADEN,
AND SAILS AGAIN TO THE SOMALI, LANDING AT KURRUM—HIS
MARCH TO BERBERA — NIGHT-ATTACK ON THE BRITISH CAMP—
STROYAN KILLED—BURTON, HERNE, AND SPEKE WOUNDED—MIRA-
CULOUS ESCAPE OF THE LATTER.

IT was in the year 1849 that Lieutenant Speke first
formed the idea of exploring Equatorial Africa. His only
object at first was to complete a museum of natural history that he had formed at his father's house, principally
from specimens collected on the slopes of the Himalayas,
and in Tibet, during service in India. He was obliged
to wait for the three years' furlough, granted to Indian
officers after ten years' service, before he would be able to
carry his plan into execution; and then he proposed, by
landing on the east coast of Africa, to strike the Nile at
its sources, and travel down its course to Egypt, expecting

to find the Mountains of the Moon stretching in a vast chain across the African continent, and the Nile rising in perpetual snows at some point in the chain, as the Ganges rises in the high region of the Himalayas.   On the very day following that on which his ten years' term of service had expired—namely, the 4th of September 1854—he sailed from the Indian shore for Aden, having bought various articles to the amount of £390 for distribution as presents among the natives of Africa.   His intention was to begin by endeavouring to pass through the Somali country opposite Aden ; but Colonel, afterwards Sir James, Outram, the British Political Resident, refused at first to countenance any such proceeding, not wishing to risk the life of a countryman among the impracticable savages of that region.

But as the Bombay Government, contrary to the advice of Colonel Outram—which the event proved to be sound —was at this time organising an expedition for the exploration of the Somali Land under the command of Lieutenant Burton, who, having succeeded in reaching Mecca, was thought most fit to be trusted with the conduct of an almost desperate enterprise, Colonel Outram suggested to Speke, that if he was determined to go at all hazards, he had better procure his appointment as an officer of this expedition, with which Lieutenants Stroyan and Herne had already been associated in an assistant capacity. This plan suited Speke admirably, as it would save him his furlough for another occasion ; and so he immediately obtained the consent of Burton, while Colonel Outram procured his appointment to the service.

The character of the inhabitants of the Somali country appears to be well, and not very favourably, known at Aden.   With a thousand vices they seem to combine the solitary virtue of being expert donkey-drivers.   They are notorious for cheating and lying, boasting of their exploits of this kind, and so boisterous and quarrelsome that it is found necessary to deprive them of arms. When first arrived, it was the habit of the different tribes to fight out their feuds with spear and shield on the hill-sides of the crater of Aden, and the same battles were afterwards carried on by means of sticks and stones. There were, in consequence, few of the men who did not bear scars, some of them so deep that it was a miracle how they could have recovered from the hurts inflicted on these occasions.

The simple costume of the men consists of a single sheet of long cloth, eight cubits long, thrown over the shoulder in the manner of a plaid. Some shave the head entirely, others wear the mane of a lion as a wig, which is supposed to add ferocity to the aspect of the wearer; while those who affect the exquisite let their hair grow, and adorn it with sticks resembling Chinese joss-sticks, which they also use as a comb to dress it. Their arms in their own country are a spear and shield, a club and a long two-edged knife. The women dress in a cloth which they fasten tightly round the body just under the arms, allowing it to fall evenly to the ground so as entirely to cover the legs. The married women encase their hair in blue cloth, gathering it up at the back of the head in a sort of *chignon*, while the virgins wear theirs loose, plaited in small plaits of three, which being parted in the centre, the hair falls evenly round the head like a well-arranged mop. They have a coquettish trick, when observed, of canting their heads backwards, which parts the locks in front, and discloses a pretty smiling face with white teeth and red lips. Their beauty soon fades after they have borne children, and their figures swell about the waist, as is common with the negro race, and acquire behind the development known as *steatopyga.* Though

B

of the Mussulman religion, the women do not wear the yachmac, or veil. In Aden the men are ashamed of their comparative nakedness, and assume the Arab garb, which they immediately put off on landing in their own country.

Almost all the Somali, in consequence of the nature of the land they inhabit, are pastoral nomads. Their government is patriarchal, and the chieftainship generally hereditary. The head of each clan is called the Gerad or sultan, who would have but little power were he not supported by the joint influence of all the royal family. On weighty occasions the sultan assembles his elders in parliament, and through them consults the people. Wars generally arise from cases of homicide, when a member of one clan kills one of another, and will neither pay the assessed valuation of the victim's life, nor give himself up to the avenger of blood. The whole tribe then marches out to enforce an execution in cattle supposed to correspond to the injury inflicted, and this being resisted, and new lives lost, the balance of blood-money remains unsettled, and the feud is kept open for generations. The sultans would be unable to command the co-operation of the clans in these wars, were it not that each individual hopes to enrich himself by plunder in the course of them; and, as a general rule, they only come to an end through the exhaustion of both sides. It is a point of honour to steal as many cattle with as little personal risk as possible, and those who expose themselves unnecessarily are only accounted foolhardy. The principles observed in their administration of justice, as far as they have any, are those of the Mosaic law, founded on strict retaliation. The northern Somali have no villages in the interior of the country, but move about with their flocks and herds wherever water is to be found, erecting temporary huts covered with grass mats, or throwing up loose stone walls for shelter, like dykes in Scotland. But on the coast they build primitive villages of huts with square mat walls supported by sticks, near which the chief of the place generally possesses a kind of stone box, which is used as a fort or store. It is usually built of blocks of coralline, cemented with mortar of the same material.

The Somali Land itself is in form a sort of elbow, lying between the equator and the eleventh degree of latitude north, and might be called the eastern horn of Africa. It is high in the north, with a general declination, corresponding to the river-system, to the south and eastward, but with less easting as the west is approached. A large and fertilising stream, the Jub, separates it from the mass of Africa. This river rises in the mountains of southern Abyssinia, and, leaving the territories of the Gallas on the west, falls into the Indian Ocean at the northern boundary of the Zanzibar coast. Besides this the only important streams are the Shebéli or Haines river, and another smaller one to the east, called the Wadi Nogal by Lieutenant Cruttenden, one of the chief branches of which is the Jid Ali Tug. This rises in some small hills on the north coast, and runs south-easterly into the Indian Ocean, dividing the country of Ugahden or Haud on the west from Nogal on the east.

The country of Ugahden is said to be a generally grassy plain, of red soil, nearly stoneless, and with water everywhere near the surface. It is considered to afford excellent pasture for the herds of the Somali, which consist of camels, ponies, cows, and fat-tailed Dumba sheep, besides being a favourite haunt of gazelles and antelopes. The Nogal country is of the opposite nature, being barren and stony. The prevailing formation is limestone of the purity and whiteness of marble. Here the Somali nomads are only enabled to keep cattle by following about the latest partial falls of rain, which give a temporary strength to the herbage.

According to traditional histories which Speke obtained from the natives, the present race of Somali have occupied the country for about four centuries and a half. About the year 1413 an Arab chieftain, Darud-ben-Ismail, was overpowered by an elder brother with whom he had some dispute about territorial rights, and driven southwards from Mecca, accompanied by a large band of followers, amongst whom was a beautiful Asyri damsel of gentle blood, whom he afterwards married. Arrived at Makallah on the southern shore of Arabia, the fugitives crossed the sea to Bunder Gori. Here they were hospitably received by the mixed Christian population of Gallas and Abyssinians who then held the land, and who appear, from archæological remains, to have been much more civilised than the present Somali. These were governed by one Sultan Kin, with whom the Arabs lived amicably until, by intermarriage and proselytising, they increased in number, and in the end succeeded in driving Kin and his Christian subjects back into the highlands of Ethiopia. Darud was left undisputed possessor of the land, and on his death his only son by the Asyri wife succeeded him. This man's son had three sons, called respectively, in order of birth, Warsingali, Dulbahanta, and Mijjertaine. Amongst these he divided his kingdom, and the tribes named after them occupy the respective portions to this day, the Mijjertaine being dispersed over the eastern country, the Warsingali holding the central, and the Dulbahantas the western territories. After this an Arab named Ishak came across the Gulf, and by forcible occupation founded the three nations who now occupy the coast-line, the country which he subdued having been divided between the three sons of his three wives. The names of these tribes are the Habr Gerhaji, the Habr Owel, and the Habr Teljala. In common with all places within the tropics and beyond the equatorial rainy zone, this country is subject to regular monsoons, or seasons of prevailing winds; consequently vessels can only enter the northern harbours during the five months of the year when the sun is in the south, from the 15th of November to the 15th of April, and then it is that the Somali come to settle on the coast, bringing their produce, such as sheep, cows, ghee, mats of grass and Daum palm, ostrich-feathers, and hides, to barter with the merchants from Arabia and Cutch, in exchange for the cloths, dates, rice, beads, and iron, which they bring over with them. The most important of these trading places is Berbera, which is in the same meridian as Aden. It is only inhabited during the five months open to trade, when great caravans come up from the rich provinces on the south and south-west, the principal being those from Ugahden and Harar.

In order to explore the most interesting part of the country, it was Burton's plan to wait till the breaking-up of the Berbera fair, and travel by the ordinary caravan route through the Ugahden country to the Webbe Shebéli, and on to Gananeh, and then to proceed by any favourable opportunity to the Zanzibar coast. To employ the fair months that must elapse before he could carry out this project, he determined to make an experimental tour to Harar, a place hitherto considered inaccessible to Europeans. In the mean time he directed Herne to go to Berbera, and, in case of his being forcibly detained by the Emir of Harar, to detain the Harar caravan until his party should be released. Herne was also to obtain all the information he could at Berbera about the caravans and the market, and to collect cattle for the final march, and Stroyan was to proceed to Berbera to assist him.

Speke, in the mean time, having nothing else to do, was to proceed to Bunder Gori on the Warsingali frontier, to go as far south as possible, passing over the maritime hill-range, and then turning westwards to inspect the Wadi Nogal, and march on Berbera so as to meet Stroyan and Herne at a date not later than January 15, 1855. On the march he was to make as many scientific observations as possible, and collect camels and ponies for the future expedition.

In making preparations for this journey, Speke engaged two men to assist him, one named Sumunter, who was to be his Abban or protector; and the other, named Ahmed, also a Warsingali, as interpreter. As everything depended on the honesty of the Abban, who is the universal go-between in all transactions with the natives, and holds a position like that of a courier in civilised countries, combined with that of a patron, the choice of Sumunter was a most unfortunate one, as he turned out a great scoundrel, and made the march miserable. Under these Speke also engaged a Hindustani butler called Imam, and a Seedi called Farhan, who did him good service. This man Speke describes as a kind of Hercules, with a large head, small eyes, squat nose, and prominent muzzle, with sharp-pointed teeth, in imitation of a crocodile. According to his own account, he was kidnapped when a child on the Zanzibar coast by the captain of an Arab vessel, who baited him with some dates, and as soon as his hands had closed on them, caught them and dragged him away. He then was employed as a "powder-monkey," till a fitting opportunity offered itself for running away, and he had been free ever since; and as he had served in the wars, he promised to be an efficient guard. Speke then, on the advice of Burton, adopted the Arab dress, which he found by no means pleasant to wear, and bought at Aden £120 worth of miscellaneous articles, consisting of sheetings, indigo, dyed fabrics, and a few coloured stuffs of greater value as presents to chiefs, with dates and rice in sacks, and a large quantity of salt. He also took with him an abundance of arms and ammunition, camel-boxes for carrying specimens, a sextant and artificial horizon, thermometers, and a roughly-made camera obscura.

Speke left Aden on the 18th of October 1854, in an Arab vessel, and, through the dilatory sailing of his nakoda or captain, did not arrive at his destination, Bunder Gori, on the Somali coast, till the 27th. He was much disappointed with what he had seen of the shore off which he had been cruising for some days. The maritime plain varied in breadth from a few hundred yards to one or two miles, till it reached some brown-looking hills in the background, and hills and plain alike seemed almost destitute of vegetation, while, excepting at a village where they had touched, no living creature was to be seen. Certain half-naked dignitaries who came off to welcome them to the shore asked a multitude of questions as to their business, and in return gave satisfactory information as to the state of the country. While waiting eleven days for an interview with the sultan, Gerad Mohamed Ali, until which no business could be done, Speke took walks about the plains, shooting a new variety of gazelle, called *Deza* by the Somali, and some of Salt's antelopes, and spent his time in fishing, bathing in the sea, or gossiping with the natives.

The Warsingali complained that their power had declined since the English had interfered in their fights with the Habr Teljala, and that their morals had deteriorated since we took possession of Aden, which they referred to our lax customs in prosecuting crime, requiring the evidence of an eyewitness before any accusation could be proved. They contrasted with English weakness the rough-and-ready proceedings of their own sultan, whose administration of justice was as accurate as it was stern and speedy. For instance, on one occasion a boy was brought before him for attempting to steal rice from a granary, and he confessed to having thrust his hand through the door and got his finger up to the second joint in the grain, on which the sultan adjudged that exactly that portion of the finger should be cut off. At the end of a long conference, including much consultation between the sultan and his elders, it was decided that Speke might go anywhere within the sultan's dominions, but that he must not presume to cross the frontier, especially into the Dulbahanta country, as the English would hold him responsible for any disaster that might befall their countryman. After this decision, the sultan in due time visited Speke in person. He wore a dirty-coloured Somali robe or *tobe*, hanging down to his sandalled feet, and looked like an ancient patriarch. First he marched past in silence in the centre of a double line of men, sloping their arms, evidently in imitation of European order, after which he received a thundering salute from Speke's men, who had crammed their guns with powder, which is the black man's way of showing the excellence of his weapon. Speke found the sultan with his followers in great agitation, huddled and squatted on the ground in front of the fort, while he approached and tried to dissipate their nervousness by engaging them in conversation, but with very little success. Having left them, he afterwards found them all absorbed in prayer, prostrating themselves and rising by turns, and muttering for hours together. He then ordered them a banquet of rice swimming in ghee, with dates unlimited; and it was perfectly astonishing to see what they consumed, in spite of their previous alarm; for in fact, according to Somali custom, they had prepared themselves for the feast by several days' fasting. A

man's superiority is supposed by the Somali to be shown
by his capacity to take in food, in the same way as a
gun's is by its being able to stand large charges of powder.
Finding in a subsequent conversation the sultan inex-
orable about his going among the Dulbahantas, Speke
asked him simply to assist him in procuring camels,
thinking that he might feel his way when once in the
interior. This he agreed to do, but not without a large
present of cloth, made not only to him, but in lots to his
wives, children, and akils. The measurements were made
by the primitive standard of the length of the fore-arm, and
much delay was occasioned by the sultan's measuring his
fore-arm with that of every one else in the room, and then
measuring and remeasuring, for fear of mistake, every cloth
in turn. Speke was also coaxed by the sultan out of his
silk turban and a gun, but when asked for powder to feed
it with, made a stand at last against the extortion, and the
sultan walked doggedly away, as if injured. This was
his first experience of African rapacity. In the purchase
of camels the sultan exacted a large tithe for himself as
agent, and the inhabitants having been used to handle
dollars, Speke found his cloths at a discount, so that his
purchases were unsatisfactory, and he was obliged after
great delays to start with an insufficient number of
beasts of burden, while a series of disputes began between Sumunter and himself, in consequence of the
frauds and peculations of the former, which continued
during the whole of the journey. His only method of
getting his lazy and reluctant men to move forward was
to stop in uncomfortable spots exposed to the sun, not
allowing a tent to be pitched. With the sultan's son
as guide, the track first led them across the maritime
plain, about two miles broad, and composed of sand over-
lying limestone, with boulders in the dry shallow water-

courses, and no vegetable life but a few scrub acacias and certain salsola. Then they wound up the deep bed of a dry river lying between the lower spurs of the mountain-range, and began a straight ascent up its cracked uneven passage till they reached a halting-place about five miles from Bunder Gori. Here some interesting rock-pigeons, similar to the Indian painted bird, were shot by Speke as they lit at some pools in the bed of the ravine. As they got on, very slowly in consequence of the interminable delays, the ground became more woody; tall slender trees with thick green foliage grew in the bed of the ravine, and the, brown rocky hill-sides were decorated with budding bush acacias, which afforded a good repast to the camels, weary with their journey through the boulders. Then the camels were whipped up a winding steep ridge which formed one of the buttresses of the mountain, and the tent was pitched for the first and last time during the journey at the end of a three days' march, which ought to have occupied only one. The higher the hill was ascended, the more abundant the wooding became, and green grass appeared at this altitude, 4577 feet, among the stones. The temperature was pleasant, the average at noon being only 79°. The rocks were observed to be full of fossil shells. Speke killed a new snake, a variety of *Psammophis sibilans*, and an interesting little antelope, *Oreotragus saltatrix*, the "klip springer" of the Cape, as well as hyraxes and small birds. Having heard here that his scapegrace Abban, whom he had sent back to Bunder Gori on a commission, was arrested for theft there, Speke sent to see what had become of him, and was meanwhile left alone with the young prince and two or three camel-drivers. At this juncture a number of disagreeable visitors in the shape of hungry savages came up the hills, and settled themselves on the date-bags in the camp and

clamoured for food, being supported by the young prince
and the camel-men. Speke, however, stood by the stores
with his gun while they all danced round him and vocife-
rated with savage delight at his helplessness. Suddenly, as
if a new thought had struck them, they darted away down
the hill, and seizing a goat from a neighbouring flock,
killed and quartered it without loss of time. Then came
up the goat-herd clamouring for the price of his animal,
and insisting that Speke ought to pay him, and his persecutors seized the mussacks or water-skins and carried
them off, all but one. Having successfully intimidated
Imam, whom he sent to fill this from a spring down the
hill, they then tried to prevent Speke from filling it himself, flourishing their spears and bows, and saying they
would kill him. At this disagreeable crisis the sultan's
eldest son, Mohammed Aul, arrived, and rebuked his
younger brother and the rest of the party into decent
behaviour. The day after this scene the sultan arrived,
and then Sumunter, whom Speke at once arraigned before
the sultan for his manifold villanies. After hearing the
case for the prosecution and the defence, the sultan coolly
decided that Sumunter, being Speke's Abban, had a right
to do what he liked with his property; but on Speke's
threatening to go back to Aden and lay the case before
the police-court there, the sultan was brought to reason,
and promised his protection for the future. While waiting at this place Speke found a new species of lizard,
called *Tiloqua Burtoni*, after the commander of the expedition; and a leopard was brought into the camp
which the Somali had destroyed with sticks and stones
in a cave. He saw the *Saltiana* antelope besides the
species mentioned already, and tracks of a few of the
rarer sorts. Rhinoceroses formerly abounded, but had
been killed off by the Somali, who value their hides as a

material for shields.   Amongst the bush were found the frankincense and several gum-producing trees, the germs of which, picked by the women, are transported to Aden. The natives chew the bark of the acacia into small fibres, and then twist it with their hands into a strong cordage.   Its bark also makes a good tan for leather, but is surpassed in valuable qualities by that of a squat stunted tree like the "elephant's foot," called *mohur* by the Somali, with smooth skin and knotty warts upon it resembling a huge turnip, reddish inside, with a yellowish green exterior. It is highly aromatic and astringent.   To make mussacks, the Somali pull a sheep or goat out of his skin, tie up the legs, and fill it with bits of this bark, chopped and mixed with water. They then hang it in a tree to dry, and manipulate it into pliability.   It is considered as a corrective to bad water, and when washed with water is also used in the rude surgery of the Somali as a poultice for wounds.   During his rambles about this place Speke had dropped very innocently several bits of paper about; these were destined to give him a great deal of trouble, as some of them were picked up by wandering Dulbahantas who did not know what to make of them, and thought that they were evidence of some design to mark out the country for sinister purposes.

The whole party being now together, a short march was made to relieve the one beyond, as the water they were now drinking was the last on this side the range. The way led up a gradual but tortuous ascent, thickly clad with strong bushes, to a kraal or ring-fence of prickly acacias, evidently made to protect sheep from the sudden attacks of wild beasts or freebooters. They remained here three days at an altitude of 5052 feet, sending relays of goods across the mountain, and allowing the stragglers in the rear to come up.   Here the sultan turned back, having got fresh presents out of Speke, including a razor to shave his head. At dawn on the 4th of December 1854, they set out to clamber over the range to the first watering-place in the interior. It was a double march, very stiff for the camels. In front lay an easily traversed, densely wooded, undulating ground; but three miles from the camp beyond it the face of the mountain frowned like a bluff wall, which seemed impossible for any camel to surmount. The stiffest and last ascent on reaching this was up a winding, narrow goat-path, with sharp turns at the end of every zigzag, and huge projecting stones set in it. It was wonderful that the camels with their splay feet and spindle-legs, with awkward boxes on their backs, which struck against every projection, did not tumble headlong; and many times at the corners they fell on their chests, with their legs dangling over the steep, and were only pulled into their places by the combined exertions of all the men. Like the Tibet ponies when in danger, they seized everything within reach, and held on with their teeth. However, the glorious view from the summit of the pass, called Yafir, repaid all the trouble of the ascent. The altitude was 6704, it being almost the highest point on the range. From a cedar-tree under which he cooked his breakfast, Speke saw to the north the Gulf like a mill-pond, the village of Bunder Gori, and two buggalows (Arab vessels) lying in the anchorage like dots of nut-shells, just as it were below the steep face of the mountain. Unlike this grand view to the north — a deep rugged hill covered with verdure, and the sea like a large lake below — the southern scene was tame; the land dropped gently to hardly more than half the depth, and scarcely a tree was visible, while from the foot of the hill to the far horizon there was nothing visible but a hot, arid, and hideous wilderness: very different from the glowing

descriptions which the Somali had given of this, their land
of promise.   On the hill-top several piles of stones were
observed—much like those raised by the Tibet Tartars to
the memory of their Lhama saints—which the Somali said
were Christian tombs left by their predecessors.   Once
over the brow, they descended the southern slopes, which
fell gently in terraces, and encamped at dark, after a march
of seventeen miles in a deep nullah, at an altitude of 3660
feet.   Here a halt of two days was made, which Speke
spent in shooting and collecting while the cattle rested.

Gazelles and antelopes, bustards, florikan, and partridges,
as well as other interesting birds and reptiles, were found,
mostly in ravines at the foot of the hills, or amongst
acacia and jujube trees, with patches of heather in places.
Speke decided here that it would be useless to attempt
proceeding through the Southern Dulbahantas, as there
appeared to be nothing but waterless desert in that direction, and decided on returning to Berbera through the
Northern Dulbahantas; but hearing of some old Christian
ruins left by Sultan Kin only a day's march to the eastward, he determined to go and see them first.   The route
lay down a broad shallow valley, in which meandered
a nullah called Rhut Tug.   All the wood in this country
is found in depressions similar to this one, near the base
of hill-ranges, where there is water near the surface, and
shelter from the winds that blow over the higher ground
of the great plateau of Nogal.   The trees, however, were
much stunted in this spot, which had been much lauded
by Speke's followers; there was but a sign of grass and
one flock of sheep, though gazelles were numerous; and
amongst the highly-plumaged birds, one of striking
beauty was observed, the *Lamprotornis superba*, a kind
of maina, called " cow-bird " in the language of the Somali,
because it follows cows to their pastures.

Speke was very much disappointed with the " Christian ruins," and strongly suspected them of being of more recent origin than was alleged, judging from the appearance of the walls of a church, which he thought was just as likely to have been a mosque. Beside this church there was the site of a village, a hole in the ground denoting a limekiln, a cemetery, and the ground-lines of a fort. The site of the ruins was certainly remarkable, as the nearest water was now at some distance, which could not have been the case when they were occupied. In the cemetery the Somali still bury their dead, and erect in the Christian fashion, probably in traditional imitation of them, crosses at the head of the tombs. Here Speke was detained some time by a strike among his men, headed by his refractory Abban, who was temporarily brought to reason by the sultan's brother, Hassan, who, however, demanded a gun as his fee. During his detention he shot a female *Hyæna crocuta* in the act of robbing. They now marched westward from Rhut Tug, and emerged from the low valley to the usual level of the plateau, on whose bare face large troops of ostriches and gazelles were observed. They travelled on without seeing any habitations or people, and came to a nullah, where were several pools of bitter spring-water with Egyptian geese swimming on them. This place was called Barham. The scenery was noteworthy. On the north of the line of march, about ten miles distant, was the hill-range, at the foot of which, in small ravines, grew some belts of jujube trees and hardy acacias ; but to the south the monotonous desert stretched away in a succession of little flat plains, bounded by bosses of white limestone, which appear to have been left standing while atmospheric influences wore down the plains lying between them. Again these little plains sank in gentle gradation to their centres, in which nullahs drained the land to the south and eastward, possibly to join eventually the Rhut Tug.

At a parting between the watercourses of Rhut Tug and Yubbi Tug, they came on the tomb of the great founder of the Somali nation, Darud-ben-Ismail. The tomb itself appeared insignificant, nor did it attract the veneration of the Somali. But there was an excavated tumulus near, where the interpreter said a Somali, wishing to bury his wife, found a hollow compartment propped with beams of timber, at the bottom of which were several earthenware pots, some leaden coins, a ring of gold such as are worn in the noses of Indian Mussulman women, and much other miscellaneous property. There were many flocks about this place, and Speke was struck by the sleek appearance of the Dumba sheep, and told it was the result of their feeding on a little green pulpy-looking weed, an ice-plant called Bustube, succulent and highly nutritious. But the fat-tailed breed of sheep, having a reservoir of nutrition in their tails, appear to be able to thrive on less food than other kinds. Crossing this high land, they began descending to the westward, and having put up a kraal for protection, spent the night in a plain called Libbahdile (the haunt of lions). These animals are only said to frequent the Nogal in the rainy season. They now came into a broad valley, down the centre of which wound the Yubbi Tug, forming a natural boundary-line, separating the Warsingali from the Northern Dulbahantas. The steepness of the sides of the nullah obliged them to follow its left bank till they turned its head, which ended abruptly. During this march the interpreter related some circumstances connected with a raid of the Dulbahantas on the Warsingali, who finally tantalised the former into retreat, by exposing their flocks and herds to their view on the wrong side of the impassable nullah, at the same time guarding its head, and protecting their own flank with a strong armed party. Detained on the Dulbahanta frontier by difficulties created by the Abban, Speke employed himself with shooting; and besides gazelles, antelopes, a lynx, florikans, and partridges, killed some beautiful little honeybirds and others, the most beautiful specimen of all being the *Nectarinia Habessinica.* It is a small bird of gaudy plumage, with metallic lustre as the light strikes its feathers, which is most remarkable on a warm sunny day when it inserts its sharp curved bill into the flowers to drink the honey, buzzing like a bee the whole time, so that its wings are undistinguishable. Water being rare in this land, it is strange how long many of the beasts of burden can do without it even under hard work. The Somali generally only water camels twice a-month, donkeys four times, sheep every fourth day, and ponies once in two days, and object to doing it oftener lest the animals should learn to require it. The antelopes may not be able to get at water for months together, as every drop of it is jealously guarded by the people.

The bees, too, of this country have their peculiar habits: instead of settling in trees, they burrow in the ground like wasps, so that honey has to be dug for; and during Speke's stay the people often came to borrow his pickaxes for that purpose. The honey was very acceptable to modify the brackish water of the interior. While out shooting, Speke repeatedly saw the Somali chasing Salt's antelopes on foot, which he himself was accustomed to kill like hares with common shot. They had a way of tiring down the little creatures by disturbing them from their resting-places under bushes in succession, as they cannot stand the mid-day sun. With larger game they are also keen sportsmen, and kill the elephant by teasing

C

him into repeated fruitless charges by means of a man
mounted on a white horse, till the crowd of confederates
are able to hamstring the fatigued beast with their double-
edged knives, and then finish him with their spears and
bows. Ostriches, again, are killed either by poisonous
herbs thrown in their haunts, or by being ridden down,
which is a more difficult operation. The ostrich is known
to be a shy bird, and so blind at night that it cannot feed.
The Somali pony, again, though hardy and enduring, is
not swift. The hunter, knowing their peculiarities, pro-
vides himself with a pony and two or three days' provisions. He pursues the ostrich that he marks, but so cautiously as not to scare it out of sight during the day; and
at night, when the ostrich cannot feed, rests to refresh
himself and pony. At length the bird becomes weak from
hunger, and falls an easy victim.

The natives have also two ways of killing gazelles.
One is for two men to walk slowly round a herd, diminishing the circles, till one of them finds a convenient ambush; the other continues his walk until the herd are
slowly moved to the spot where his friend is lying in
wait. The other method is to ride them down on their
slow ponies, taking advantage of the habit fleet animals
have of heading their pursuers. By riding at the leading
gazelle they make up for the difference in speed by the
shorter distance the pony has to traverse, and so tire out
the game.

There being great difficulties about penetrating into
the country of the Dulbahantas, which were increased by
the roguishness of his retinue, Speke continued his westward march down the valley, until in due time they rose
again to the bare and stony level. Each of the eleva-
tions and depressions resembled the other, while the
mountain-range was still at an even distance to the north.

At a place called Jid Ali the Abban was at home; and Speke discovered that he had been leading him thither for his own purposes, while the Abban's mother endeavoured to persuade him to advance no farther. After a time, however, he got away and arrived near the watercourse of Jid Ali Tug. The water in this nullah extended for about half a mile, when it became absorbed in the thirsty soil. It consisted of a chain of pools connected by runnels, produced by bitter springs, which served, however, to make the country green. The hungry Dulbahantas, attracted by the dates and rice, were here very troublesome; they forgot their intestine wars, and came flocking up begging and bullying. As the Abban was loitering at home, this state of things was especially disagreeable, and continued for days together. Meanwhile Speke went out shooting, and had good sport, animals being abundant from the exceptional supply of water. In one spot he found an old man who, having made a pilgrimage to Mecca, had learned the art of husbandry, and had succeeded in establishing a small farm in the wilderness, growing *jowari*, a kind of millet, by means of irrigation from the nullah. The people here were very religious Mussulmans. They abused Speke's interpreter for never saying his prayers; and if he cut the deer's throats a little lower down than the canonical place, in order to save the specimen, they spat on the ground to show their contempt. To throw date-stones in the fire, as they are supposed to be the seeds of the fruit of Paradise, was sacrilege in their eyes. If Speke walked up and down, they held councils of war on his motives, imagining that no man in his senses would take unnecessary exercise. Considering that the northern Dulbahantas were all said to have been driven up here by the southerns, Speke was surprised to find so few dwellings or flocks in the valley. But they change their ground from patch to patch of vegetation with great ease. All their worldly goods are packed on a camel, while the wife, with perhaps a baby, is seated on a donkey, and so they move house. Their fare is very hard, except in the rainy season, when they have plenty of milk. The poorer classes are said to pass their lives without tasting flesh or grain, living on sour milk, wild honey, or gums; and yet they seem to enjoy a singular immunity from disease, endemic ophthalmia forming the principal exception. Speke himself found the climate at this season (Christmas) very delightful. The nights were so cool that he had to wrap himself in flannels, and yet he slept on the ground without a bedstead, never pitching a tent once in the interior, and never wore hat or shoe throughout the journey, except once or twice when he put on a sandal as a protection against thorns. With all this roughing he never knew a moment's illness. There was considerable danger, however, in his position at this stage. The Dulbahantas, who only bowed to the law of the strongest, and did every man what was right in his own eyes, objected altogether to his being in the country; and whenever he came home from his solitary shooting excursions, surprise was expressed in the camp that he had not been murdered. In fact, his life was repeatedly threatened, because he would not give up all his property. The camp, being near a watering-place, was a point of attraction to all the loose ruffians in the country; and at last Speke, finding it getting too hot to remain any longer, moved to a place somewhat nearer the Abban's home, who still managed to detain him on various pretexts, taking part with the Dulbahantas against him, in order to plunder him. He had to bribe them to let him get away by the sacrifice of a considerable amount of property. At last, on the 11th of January, the westward journey was recommenced. The track led across a flat alluvial plain, which was covered with a thick growth of acacias, and dry grass nipped short by cattle. At the next camping-ground Speke was again stopped by the Abban's manœuvres, and the Dulbahantas became more troublesome than ever. At last he ascertained that, the southern Dulbahantas having gained a victory, the road to Berbera would be thronged with people, so that further advance in that direction was impossible. He now determined to turn northwards and march over the hills to Bunder Héis, where he could either embark or march along the coast to Berbera. Still there were difficulties about the new route, as the tribe that held it could be brought to no terms ; and at last, in despair, he faced about and marched in a north-easterly direction, intending to cross the hills occupied by the Habr Gerhajis, so close to the Warsingali frontier that the robber tribes would not have power enough to enforce any demand. As the Abban was always slipping away, Speke tried to engage his mother as a guide to Bunder Gori, where she wished to go, but the Abban peremptorily ordered her home again. They ascended the hill-range by a steep winding footpath up one of its ridges, which resembled the descent from Yafir. The caravan crossed the hill opposite the headland of Galwéni, travelled a short distance on the flat summit, and encamped amongst some thick jungle on its north or seaward side. As they were preparing to unload, a number of the Urus Sagé section of the Habr Gerhajis seized the camels by the heads and demanded, with violent gesticulations, the customary fees. Speke's men, however, knowing their power, made such demonstrations that the Urus Sagé skulked off, threatening to return in stronger force.

On the top of the range they came on a most interest-

ing and novel scene. They stepped in a moment from
constant sunshine into constant clouds, and saw what
accounted for the dense verdure of the north, as well as
the extreme barrenness of the south side of the hills. For
two months they had not seen a cloud or felt a drop of
rain, and now they were launched into the middle of the
" Dairti " or north-east monsoon, which had been pouring
for some time previously against the north face of the
mountain, and was arrested by it. The same phenomenon is observed in the Himalaya Mountains, where those
who go to Chini, on the Sutleje, during the hot season,
see the clouds of the Indian monsoon enveloping all the
mountain-chains for months together on the north-west
side, and hanging suspended on the top of a high hill in
front of that place, but never passing over to the dry
plateau of Tibet. The view below was now obscured by
the successive volumes of rolling cloud. While the camp
was detained here, the Urus Sagé came again and tried
to interfere with the loading of the camels. They were
at last brought to reason, and consented to act as guides
down the steep and slippery descent, whose difficulties
were increased by thick strong green jungle-bushes, as
well as rocks and other obstacles especially adverse to
camels. In a cave under a rock, where they put up for
the night, the ground was brown with fleas, sheep having
been kept there. By burning certain boughs, however,
which the Somali recommended as a specific, they were
summarily expelled. They finally arrived, by a tortuous
track, in the hollow of a watercourse which divides the
Warsingali from the Habr Gerhaji, flowing into the Gulf
at Ras Galwéni. During the journey some of the trees
were pointed out, the gum of which is used by the native
women for fumigation. They sit over it, when ignited,
as the Cashmere people sit over their little charcoal-pots

when resting during a journey, enshrouded in a large wrapper, so as to allow the fumes to reach every part of the body. On the 28th of January Speke records the great delight that he felt in breathing the sea-air again, and feeling himself comparatively free from the persecutions of his tyrant Sumunter. He was impatient to end this comparatively objectless journey, and join his friends on the larger and more promising one, and he was even now behind time. The Habr Gerhajis gave some little trouble, but the march was continued over the foot of some low spurs to a broad watercourse on the maritime plain. Here Speke shot and stuffed a very interesting rat, much resembling the little gilléri squirrel of the Indian plains, but plumper in face and body, like a new-born rabbit. This has been named *Pectinator Spekii* by Mr Blyth, curator of the Asiatic Society of Calcutta. He also saw some nondescript black canine animals with white-tipped tails, one of which he had seen on the other side of the range. They more resembled a wolf than a hyena, and there were three hunting together, like jungle-dogs in India. On the 29th of January the expedition marched into Bunder Gori, where Speke found the buggalow waiting which had brought him over, and returned in it to Aden, where he arrived after a five days' sail; and in joy at his release from annoyances, and the prospect of meeting old friends, threw himself into the sea, after the fashion of the Somali, and swam ashore.

Sumunter the Abban, regarding whom Speke had sent a written complaint to Aden, was now summoned to appear in the police-court, and punished by a sentence of two months' imprisonment, a fine of 200 rupees, or in default six months' more detention, with hard labour, and banishment after his imprisonment had expired. Thus ended Speke's first excursion in Africa.

Meanwhile Stroyan and Herne had been employed in Berbera or its vicinity. The former had been shooting in the interior, and had killed three elephants, while the latter was purchasing cattle for the transport of the expedition. Speke was anxious, after a little repose, to be employed again, so Burton requested him to cross the Gulf again to Kurrum, to keep in communication with Herne, and assist him in completing his complement of animals, by collecting what he could, and marching with them along the sea-shore to Berbera. This, Speke thought, would employ him until the breaking-up of the Berbera fair. He was accompanied now by a man of the Mijjertaine tribe as interpreter, nicknamed El Balyuz, or "the Ambassador," who, from his honesty and straightforwardness of character, proved a perfect treasure after Sumunter and Ahmed. Being unable to procure the services of any of the Somali policemen from the Government, Speke engaged a dozen men of various races (Egyptians, Nubians, Arabs, and Seedis) as an escort, and armed them with his sabres and muskets. Having provided himself with money and provisions, and added to his suite his old servants Imam the butler and Farhan the gamekeeper, he was ready for a second start by the 20th of March 1855. They reached Kurrum, on the Somali shore, on the 24th, the Somali sailors quarrelling during the passage as to who should be Speke's Abban, and becoming very uproarious; but Speke, who had had enough of Abbans, and refused to have any more, brought them to reason by threatening to put back. The negotiation for camels at Kurrum was not very satisfactory, as the people asked high prices for poor animals; but, as a set-off, it was here that Speke first heard of the existence of the Victoria Nyanza.

The Somali said that it was as large as the Gulf of

Aden, and navigated by white men, though their accounts were corroborated by no eyewitness. Speke supposed them then to allude to the Atlantic Ocean, but mentions that Colonel Rigby, H.B.M. Consul at Zanzibar—Colonel Hamerton's successor—afterwards told him that he had heard of this lake when he was previously travelling in the country. The white navigators were evidently the expeditionists sent up the Nile as far as Gondokoro by Mehemet Ali twelve or fourteen years before, the lake and the Nile having been confounded in the transmission of the intelligence.

The village of Kurrum was made up of a single fort and a large collection of mat huts grouped together close to the shore. The plain, about half a mile broad, consisted of a sandy-brown soil almost bare of vegetation. The hills in the background were small, dull, and brown, like those seen in going down the Red Sea. Acacias and other gum-trees were said to grow in the recesses as elsewhere. Gums could only be collected in the dry season, and then the gum-pickers were said to become deaf from the close air of the ravines. Speke bought twenty-five camels at Kurrum, and then stopped his purchases, as he heard from Herné that they were to be procured more cheaply at Berbera; and as he had no reason for delay any longer, set out for that place. The farther they travelled westwards, the broader became the maritime plain, and the richer its clothing of shrubs and grass. Besides the ordinary acacias, which were finer and more numerous, there were many clumps of the bastard cypress and tall rank grasses growing on sandy hillocks, as in India. This country is considered as a paradise by the Somali, who will not believe that the English possess any equal to it as pasture-ground.

There was little adventure on this march, except that

the Somali stole a pony and a camel, which was a most
impudent proceeding so close to the seaboard. The pony
was recovered, but not the camel. The caravan arrived at
Berbera on the 3d of April, this little march having served
to show the stamina of the soldiers to the advantage of
the Seedis as compared with the Egyptians. Speke was
warmly welcomed at Berbera by Herne and Stroyan, and
thoroughly enjoyed the society he found there, where all
was now life and movement. The market was thronged
with traders, and the harbour swarmed with native Orien-
tal craft. Their camp was on a rising ground facing the
east and overlooking the fair. The three tents were pitched
in line about a dozen yards apart—Stroyan's on the right,
Herne's in the centre, and Speke's on the left flank nearest
the sea. About forty or fifty camels and some ponies and
mules that they had collected were tethered in front of
the tents by night and guarded by a sentry. By day they
were sent out to graze under an escort, with Somali
archers to look after them. The whole company mustered in all about forty souls, amongst which were the
two Abbans of Stroyan and Herne, who, it was eventually
decided, could not be dispensed with; but Speke's Balyuz
was considered the chief, or Ras Cafila. The market-
place was crowded with people, whose numbers were
variously estimated from 20,000 to 60,000, who had been
flocking in since the middle of November, and as they
came erected mat huts to carry on their bartering trade.
At sunrise on the morning of the 7th of April a very interesting scene took place. The great annual Harar caravan arrived. It was made up of a number of small caravans which had joined company for mutual support.
Down the whole breadth of the plain, like a stream of
working ants, they came on in single file, each camel's
nose being tied to his leader's tail. Close to their sides

were Somali men with spear and bow, who tended them
and looked after the loads. Outside these again were
squads of armed guards mounted on ponies. There were
about 3000 people in this caravan alone, as many head
of cattle, and 500 or more slaves all driven chained together for sale. A little later the same morning the camp
was again enlivened by the approach of a man-of-war,
which came up the coast in full sail, looking like a swan
among the ducks of native shipping. It was the East
India Company's schooner Mahi, commanded by Lieutenant King, bringing Lieutenant Burton and the rest of the
expedition. They were saluted with small-arms, and the
officers went on board and brought off their friends. The
Mahi departed in the evening, having given a thundering
salute, to show the Somali that the expedition was under
the protection of the British Government. Burton now
took possession of the central tent with Herne, and the
officers were appointed to their respective duties. Burton
was to command; Stroyan to be chief surveyor; Herne,
photographer, geologist, and assistant-surveyor; while
Speke was to make himself generally useful, looking after
the men, setting the guards, and collecting specimens of
natural history. The central tent was fixed upon as the
rendezvous in case of alarm. Here Speke hung up his
guns and sword, while his revolver and dirk were placed
in his belt by day and under his pillow by night. In the
rear of the camp the whole guard slept under arms. As
so many men were on duty by day two sentries only were
posted by night—one with the guard in the rear, and the
other over the cattle in front; whilst the English and
Balyuz occasionally patrolled to see that the sentries were
on the alert.

Two days after this there was a change in the direction
of the monsoon in the hills behind the camp from south-

west to north-east. This was a warning that they would soon have to start for the south. The fair had begun to break up. The plain was alive with the ant-like caravans now streaming away in the reverse direction. But a vessel was daily expected from Aden which should bring letters and instruments, and a fatal indecision was the result. The great Ugahden caravan was allowed to depart without the expedition.

On the 15th of April the shore and harbour were seen deserted by every living thing except some diseased cattle and one forlorn girl who had caught smallpox, and, with two or three days' provisions, had been mercilessly abandoned by her parents. Speke took care of this child and placed her under shelter, but she ultimately wandered away into the desert and was never heard of more. Even the matting and sticks which formed the booths had been carried away on the backs of the camels. The two Abbans had left on leave with the caravans to visit their families at home, with the intention of being afterwards picked up as the expedition passed, leaving their sons as substitutes. However, the officers felt little anxiety, as the shore was near, and they did not think the Somali would have the face to attack them in a place of such consequence and so exposed to retribution as Berbera. Their confidence was so great that they did not even think it necessary to do sentinel duty themselves at night. Most providentially, as matters turned out, an Arab vessel, late for the fair, came into the harbour on the 18th. She had on board several Somali men and four women, who were going home. They petitioned the officers to take them with them for safety; but having so many mouths to feed already, they could only consent in the case of the women, on the condition that they should make themselves useful in the camp. In the evening the captain and crew were invited to dine in the camp, which was again a fortunate circumstance.

Shortly after sunset, as they were sitting as usual on an extemporised divan in front of the tents drinking coffee, telling stories, and enjoying the cool evening sea-breeze, a challenge was heard from the sentinel placed on the rear right of the camp, followed by a sudden and rapid discharge of musketry.

As strict orders had been given that there should be no unnecessary firing, Speke went to see what was the matter, and found three men leading ponies quietly walking into the camp, while the guard were firing bullets over their heads to intimidate them. In great wrath Speke rebuked the men for their disobedience to orders, directing that, in case of opposition to a challenge on another occasion, they should fire into and not over the offending object. The three men were then brought up before Burton and the other officers to be questioned, as they were suspected of being spies. They managed, however, to make out a good story, saying that they were Habr Owel men, of the same tribe as the Abbans, and had only come to see whether the newly-arrived vessel contained building materials, as an old enemy of theirs, the chief of Zeylah, was watching his opportunity to build forts on their coast. They were regaled with dates, and allowed to depart at their leisure.

All now turned in to sleep at the usual hour, and there was silence in the camp. A little after midnight there suddenly arose a furious noise, as though the world were coming to an end. There was a terrible rush and hurry; sticks and stones came flying like hail, followed by volleys of firearms, and Speke's tent shook as if it would come down. He jumped up with pistol and dirk in hand, and ran to the central tent to see what was the matter.

Burton, who was trying to load his revolver, said, "Be sharp, and arm to defend the camp;" while Herne, who was guarding the rear, was seen firing away resolutely at a host of foes, on whom he must have inflicted considerable damage. Speke was armed in a moment, and stepped out in front of the tent, but from the darkness could not see whether the dusky forms before him were friends or foes. He ran under the lee of the fly of the tent to take a better view, and stooping low, perceived some heads of men peeping like monkeys over the boxes. Burton then said, "Don't step back, or they will think we are retiring." Nettled at this mistaken rebuke, Speke went forward again, and fired at close quarters at the nearest man, who was stooping to get a sight of his figure in relief against the sky. He fell, and was seen no more. Then he shot a second and a third, who were crouching in the same way. He now found himself on the brink of the rising ground, entirely surrounded, and he placed the muzzle of the Dean-and-Adams against the breast of the largest man, but for some reason or other his revolver refused to revolve. He was raising it to dash its butt in the fellow's face, when he felt his legs paralysed, and found himself falling, grasping for support and gasping for breath. He afterwards discovered that he had received a heavy blow on the lungs. In another instant he was on the ground with a dozen Somali upon him. The man he had tried to shoot disarmed him, and then felt him to see if he carried a dagger between his legs, as the Arabs sometimes do, to rip up a foe when they are laid prostrate. Speke was naked, all but a few rags. They tied his hands behind him, and began to address him in Arabic. He replied in broken Somali, and heard them say that they had not killed any of the English, and would not kill him. It was apparently the captain of the gang whom he had tried to kill, and into whose hands he had fallen. This man now made him rise, and holding the other end of the rope that bound his hands, led him round to the rear of the camp, avoiding groups of men, lest they should take the law into their own hands and despatch his prisoner. Indeed, on arriving at the rear, men kept flocking round him, threatening to stab him with their spears, as if anxious for the honour of drawing the white man's blood, but overawed by the presence of the captain. Speke was now becoming very weak and faint, and scarcely able to breathe; for his whole frame had been stunned to insensibility by the blow of the club on the lung breast, and now respiration was hindered by the swelling that had set in, combined with the tightness of the skin, produced by his hands being tied behind him. His captor obliged him, at his request, by fastening his hands in front, and gave him water, and something to lie upon. Feeling a little revived, he began to chat with this person, who sat by his side holding the cord, while others came up and began mocking and jeering at him. They then went off to plunder the property. Several wounded men were now brought, and laid in a line before Speke. They groaned and rolled and stretched themselves, as if in agony, with repeated cries for water, which was supplied them. In the rear there was a murmuring of voices, a sound of breaking of boxes and ripping of bales of cloth, as though a band of robbers were dividing their spoil in silence and fear of detection. The day had now begun to dawn, and the mischief was brought to light. The tents were down, the property was lying in order on the ground, the camels and ponies were picketed in their places, and the robbers were standing looking on. Speke's captor and protector now consigned him to the charge of another man of less prepossessing appearance, and selecting two stalwart men of his own proportions, came again to the front. The two then, linking arms and sloping spears over their shoulders, began a slow march to a deep, full-measured tune, till they had completed the circuit of the camp and arrived at the same place again. This kind of pæan of victory greatly amused Speke in the midst of his troubles, and he even felt a desire to " encore" it. It was, at all events, an evidence of the method and order with which plundering parties were conducted. After this an indescribable confusion began. Every man except the one in charge of Speke fell upon the property. Some darted on the camels and began pulling them along, others seized the ponies, others caught up anything they could carry away. The whole ground was a scene of pull devil, pull baker, and might was right. As one fellow was trailing his cloth behind, another would rush at it and pull him back. Clubs were liberally used, and spears flourished.. What could not be torn was stabbed or cut asunder. The camels and ponies were for ever changing hands. It reminded Speke of an Indian poultry-yard, and the fowls fighting for entrails thrown among them. In the middle of this scramble an alarm was given that another party were coming down from the hills to rob the robbers. In an instant there was the deadest silence; and then, except forty or fifty of the oldest hands, the whole crowd dispersed in a panic, flying in long jumps, and making for the hills. Speke afterwards heard that this was a common occurrence, there being no honour among Somali thieves. While the multitude were away, three fine fellows, who had stolen the soldiers' sabres, came on, one of whom, with ferocious gestures, threatened to cut Speke in two. Twice he lifted his sword over his head and brought it down with force within an inch or two of his side, while his intended victim stared him in the face without flinching. He thought that this was done to test his courage, and had he cried for mercy, he would have been sacrificed on the spot. But worse was yet to come. Speke's jailer, probably vexed at having been kept away from the pillage, stepped up close, and coolly stabbed him with his spear. He raised his body a little in defence, when his assailant knocked him down by jobbing the spear violently on his shoulder, almost cutting the jugular arteries. Speke rose again as he poised his spear and caught the next prod, intended for his heart, on the back of one of his shackled hands, the flesh of which was gouged to the bone. The villain now stepped back, as if to get him off his guard, and dashed his spear down to the bone of his left thigh. Speke seized the spear with both hands, but his tormentor drew a club from his girdle and nearly broke his left arm with a blow which caused him to drop the spear. Finding now that the spear was too blunt to finish the business at once while he was standing still, he dropped the rope-end, walked back a dozen paces, and rushing at him with savage fury, plunged the spear through the thick part of his right thigh to the ground. With the quickness of lightning, seeing that death was inevitable if he hesitated an instant, Speke sprang on his legs and gave the miscreant such a sharp back-hander in the face with his bound fists that he staggered him for a moment. That moment was enough for a start, and he ran for his life, taking care, by holding his hands on one side, not to be tripped up by the dangling rope. He was barefoot and almost naked as he darted over the shingly beach towards the sea. His persecutor followed for a short distance, then threw his spear like a javelin after him. Speke dodged it by stooping, and his pursuer gave up the chase. Still he had to run the gauntlet of about forty thieves, who all tried to cut off his retreat. He

D

bobbed as they threw their spears after him, until he reached the shore, where he had the satisfaction of seeing that
he was followed no longer.   Fainting from loss of blood, he
sat down on a mound of sand, picked open with his teeth
the knots that bound his hands, and opened his breast to
the pleasant sea-breeze of sunrise.   The prospect, however,
was gloomy.   There was probably no help nearer than
Ain Tarad.   He could not walk the distance ; and it
seemed as if he must inevitably perish in the desert,
when, gazing on the few remaining huts of Berbera, he
saw some female figures beckoning to him.   In desperation
he hobbled towards them, his right leg being drawn up
nearly double, and so weak that it would only support
the weight of his body for an instant at a time.   The
women turned out to be the four who the evening before
had been permitted to join the camp.

Just then he saw some men hurrying to meet him
along the shore.   These were the old Balyuz and several
of the servants.   He learned from them what had happened.   Immediately on the alarm, the soldiers had fired
their guns, and all but one or two made off.   Stroyan
had been killed, probably at the beginning of the affair.
Burton and Herne had fled just after Speke had left
the central tent.   Burton had been speared in the
face, Herne much bruised with war-clubs, and some of
the men of the expedition had received severe sword-
cuts.   Speke's companions were safely on board the Ain
Tarad vessel, which had come in so providentially the
previous evening, and they had sent the Balyuz and
the other men to search for him.   He was carried to the
vessel, and stretched on the poop, thankful for his miraculous escape, but bitterly grieving for the loss of his
excellent friend, poor Stroyan.   Burton now despatched
a boat's crew to the site of the camp, where they only

found such things left as were too cumbersome to carry away. The Somali had destroyed about £1500 worth of property, but had spoilt in the scramble almost everything which could have been of value to them. The boat's crew, however, succeeded in bringing back Stroyan's body. The survivors weighed anchor on the 20th, and in two days arrived at Aden. Speke lost in this unfortunate expedition, which failed from inexperience, about £510 worth of his private property, which he never recovered. He had, he says, nothing to show for it but eleven artificial holes in his body. When he arrived at Aden he was a miserable-looking cripple; but during his residence of three weeks, in which every attention was paid him by his friends, his wounds healed so rapidly that he was able to walk abroad before he left. They closed, he says, like the cuts in an India-rubber ball when pricked by a penknife, in spite of the unfavourable climate of Aden. He attributes this to the healthy and abstemious life he had previously led. He left Aden on " sick certificate," and arrived in England in the early part of June 1855. But as the Crimean war was then at its height, though suffering from blindness, he could not resist the call to active service, and got appointed as Captain in a regiment of Turks, with whom he remained till the close of the war.

As for the Somali, they brought on themselves the vengeance of the British Government. A blockade of their coast-line was established, the condition of the raising of which was the surrender of the authors of the outrageous attack on the camp, the chief of whom was Ou Ali, the murderer of Stroyan. The Habr Owel believed the matter serious when they found that a British man-of-war was the only vessel present at the next Berbera fair, and they petitioned for a treaty of friendship,

sending for trial to Aden a man who showed the scar of
a gun-shot wound in his back, and promising to send
forward all other suspicious characters as soon as they
could catch them. It does not, however, appear from
Speke's narrative whether the most guilty parties ever
suffered condign punishment.

CHAPTER II.

DISCOVERY OF THE TANGANYIKA LAKE.

PROJECTED EXPEDITION INTO THE INTERIOR OF EASTERN EQUATORIAL
AFRICA—THE ROYAL GEOGRAPHICAL SOCIETY AND THE MISSIONARIES'
MAP—CAPTAINS BURTON AND SPEKE GO TO ZANZIBAR—AN EXCURSION
ALONG THE COAST, AND TO FUGA—THEY START FOR THE INTERIOR—
HEADQUARTERS AT KAZÉ, AN ARAB DEPOT—DISCOVERY OF THE TAN-
GANYIKA OR UJIJI LAKE—SPEKE CROSSES THE LAKE—BURTON AND
SPEKE EXPLORE IT NORTHWARDS—RETURN TO KAZÉ.

CAPTAIN SPEKE, finding himself in the East without occupation, as the Crimean war was over, was planning an
excursion, for purposes of natural history, to the Caucasus,
and had already made considerable preparations, when he
was again invited to join Captain Burton in exploring
Africa, with the understanding that he should be put to no
expense, as the Home and Indian Governments had promised to contribute £1000 each. This decided him to
take the first mail to England, and give up the Caucasian
scheme. He thought, as at first, that he had better nurse
his furlough for a future occasion, being, as he observes,
more of a sportsman and traveller than a soldier, and
only caring for his profession when he had the sport of
fighting. Arrived in England, he was introduced to the
Royal Geographical Society by Burton, and made acquainted with the special objects of the projected expedition. On the walls of the Society's rooms hung a large

map of a section of Eastern Africa, extending from the equator to the fourteenth degree of south latitude, and from Zanzibar sixteen degrees inland, which had been made by Messrs Erhardt and Rebmann, missionaries at Zanzibar. About half the area of this map was taken up by a lake of portentous size and unseemly shape—something like that of a gigantic slug or salamander. It professed to represent a single sheet of fresh water eight hundred miles long by three hundred broad—as large as, if not larger than, the Caspian Sea. The great Arctic explorer, Admiral Sir George Back, could not rest till the mystery of this lake was solved; and it struck him that the very man to do it was Captain Burton, who had just returned from Constantinople, where he had been engaged with the Bashi-Bazuks. After many preliminary difficulties, which were only surmounted by Speke taking with Burton the overland route to India, and conferring with the authorities at Bombay, they set sail together to Zanzibar on the 3d of December 1856, in the East India Company's sloop-of-war Elphinstone, commanded by Captain Frushard, I.N., this ship having been detached on the service in order to give importance to the expedition in the eyes of the Sultan of Zanzibar and the natives of that coast generally. At Zanzibar they were hospitably received by the consul, Colonel Hamerton, whose influence had been unbounded over the old and faithful ally of his nation, the Imaum of Muscat. Zanzibar was now ruled by the son of the Imaum, Sultan Majid, whose qualities much resembled those of his father. They found that they had arrived at the worst season for a long inland journey, and that it would take more than a month to organise an expedition. It was the height of the dry season, when there was no water to be had in the interior, and just before the beginning of the vernal monsoon or greater

rainy season, when there would be a deluge. So Captain
Burton determined to while away the time in visiting
interesting spots on the coast, proposing, if possible, to
have a look at the snowy Kilimandjaro Mountain, of
which reports had been sent home by the Rev. Mr
Rebmann, which had furnished a considerable bone of
contention to carpet-geographers. To communicate with
this Mr Rebmann, who was now at his station-house on
a high hill at the back of Mombas, was one of the instructions given them by the Geographical Society.

They hired a small beden, or half-decked Arab vessel,
by the month; and having engaged a respectable half-
caste Arab Sheikh, named Said, to be guide and interpreter, set sail and steered northwards, coasting along
the aromatic shore of the island of Zanzibar till they left
it, and soon after came in sight of the still more lovely
island of Pemba, the "Emerald Isle" of the Arabs.
Putting in here, and starting the next morning, they
arrived in three days in the Mombas creek after a rough
passage, which was almost too much for the crank vessel,
and which frightened the Arab Sheikh out of his wits.
Mombas on the north, and Kilwa on the south, are the
two largest garrison towns on the mainland belonging
to the Sultan of Zanzibar. They each have a Wali or
governor, custom officers, and a Beluch guard, and certain
attractions to the antiquarian in the shape of Portuguese
ruins. They left their traps here in charge of a Banyan
called Lakshmidos, the collector of customs, and started
on the 17th of January to visit Mr Rebmann. It was a
good day's work to row up the creek and walk over the
hills to his residence. The inlet was so fringed with
dense masses of the mangrove shrub, which were covered
by small tree-oysters in countless numbers, that the only
view was of the hills towering to some ten or twelve

hundred feet above. Then they ascended the Rabbai, and crossing it by a steep slope came among the Wanyika, the first negro tribe that Speke had seen ; and going down a decline through quiet villages, entered the peaceful retreat of the Kisuludini mission-house, where they found Mr Rebmann and his English wife, and were received by them with the most generous hospitality, though there was a famine in the land. The times, indeed, were so hard with the poor negroes that the only way they had of supporting their families was to sell some of the junior members of them. In addition to the famine, an attack was expected from the barbarous pastoral Masai ; but as these freebooters only cared for beef, Mr and Mrs Rebmann evinced no great anxiety, and went on with their packing for a change of residence with the greatest composure. On returning to Mombas, the English officers heard that some Beluch troops had been sent against the Masai, and that fighting had taken place. Taking all circumstances into consideration, Captain Burton decided on trying to get to the Kilimandjaro by another route. He had heard of some attractive Portuguese ruins on the coast, on some spots whence the followers of Vasco de Gama had been driven southwards by the Arabs ; and Speke was inclined to spend any leisure time in shooting. Speke considered Mombas as an excellent starting-point for excursions into the interior. Dr Krapf had already been as far as Kitui, in Ukambani, only fourteen marches from Mombas, and there heard of a snowy mountain called Kenia, lying somewhere north of Kilimandjaro, on the same range, which probably separates the river-systems of the east from those which flow westward into the Nile. Indeed, whilst they were stopping at Mombas, a well-appointed caravan of some two hundred men arrived from Kitui laden with ivories, bought in the

district of Ukambani, and they described the country in
the most glowing terms; they had, moreover, camels
and donkeys, a sign of travelling facilities in a country
where men usually take the place of beasts of burden.
Burton and Speke left Mombas on the 24th of January,
and sailed south, touching at villages on the coast-line,
where Speke had what he calls his first flirtations with
hippopotami. The coast-line was one continuous scene
of tropical beauty, with green aquatic mangroves growing
out everywhere into the tidal waves, with the beetal,
palmyra, and other palms overtopping this fringe; and in
the background a confused jungle of every tree, shrub,
and grass that characterises the richest grounds on the
central shores of Africa. The little islands they passed
amongst, and all the great and small reefs, dangerous to
navigation, were the produce of the coral insect, the lime
of whose cells is particularly favourable to vegetable
growth. Nothing could exceed the hospitality of the
Banyans in the villages, who treated them with the
greatest respect as Indian officers. They are a class of
men who come over from India to pass their solitary
lives among savages in these remote parts as accountants,
&c., that they may save a little money for their old age.
Tanga, the most considerable of the villages, was the
terminus of the caravans which, passing south of the
Kilimandjaro, traverse the Masai country to Burgenei,
near the south-east corner of the Victoria Nyanza. It
would appear that caravans have also reached the shore
of the Nyanza at one degree south latitude, and entered
Usoga round its north-east corner.

They now made for the mouth of the Pangani river,
where, on landing, they met with a warm welcome, and
were greeted by a band of real Ethiopian serenaders.
There were, however, so many difficulties, real and artifi-

cial, in going to Kilimandjaro, that they decided on giving
the mountain up altogether, and thought it best to make
a flying trip inland to Fuga, to whose king, Kimuéri, they
had introductions from Sultan Majid. Finding the inhabitants of the place they were at excessively extortionate,
the English officers resolved to steal a march upon them,
and get on without their assistance. It so happened that
the captain of a small Beluch garrison at Chogué, up the
river, came to pay his respects. They easily engaged
this man to wait at Chogué for them, and give them there
some of his men as a guard. In the mean time they pretended to have given up their plans, and, leaving the
Sheikh and a boy to take care of the property, set sail in
a small canoe, as if on a shooting excursion, and made for
Chogué. The hippopotami played about them in the
tortuous course of the river, looking as if they meant to
dispute the passage, and for ever popping up their heads
and inviting a shot. Speke found it difficult to ascertain
if he had killed any or not, as they sank immediately
when fired at, whether wounded or not. The only way
to get their bodies is to wait till they are left by the
receding tide, or until they float from the buoyancy of
engendered gases. They sailed through the night, and
arrived at Chogué at dawn, where they were greeted by a
discharge of matchlocks. Out of the little garrison of
twenty-five men they found no difficulty in securing five
as guards, as the men are miserably paid; they furnished
also four slave-servants, and two men as guides. They
mounted in the morning, after a scrambling march, the
hill of Tongué, and put up in its fort. This is an outlying
eminence, detached from the massive clusters of Usumbara by a deep rolling valley of broken forest ground,
which, as shown by tracks, must contain in the rainy
season vast herds of elephants and buffaloes, besides ante-

lopes and lions, although at present few animals appeared
to tenant it. Looking south-west over the broad valley
of the Pangani, Speke was able to take compass bearings
on some cones in the Uzégura country, belonging to the
Nguru hills. The whole country appeared to be covered
with the richest vegetation, and the sound of a waterfall
was heard, said by the Beluches to be a barrier to the
navigation of the river farther inland. They descended
the Tongué hill by its northern slopes, and threaded the
forest inland, arching round by north to westward. Then
they passed to the north of the Khombora hill by a depression between it and the much larger hill of Sagama,
forming the south-eastern buttress of the Usumbara; and
opening into the valley of the Pangani again, they put up
at a Wazégura village on its right bank, crossing by a
ferry. A compass had been left some fifteen miles behind,
and the only man who could be got to volunteer to walk
back for it with Speke was a Seedi soldier, one Mabarak
Bombay, whose obliging nature was shown by this incident, and who became Speke's right-hand man in his subsequent travels. On the bank of the river, which they
recrossed, Speke saw a dead hippopotamus, which the
savages had stalked, bristling all over with arrows; and in
the bed of the nullah, by following which they found the
instrument at their last bivouac, observed how the little
pools were gradually drying up, the fish perishing in them
and falling an easy prey to the unsightly green-and-brown-
striped iguanas. Those reptiles, some bearing fish in
their mouths and some dropping them, scuttled off to
their hiding-places as soon as they came in view, their
excessive fear of man being accounted for by the eagerness with which the negroes pursue them for food. The
thirty miles' walk was enlivened by Bombay's yarns; and
Speke found him an indefatigable walker, and a most

agreeable companion. Returning to the Pangani, and crossing it, they now followed the beaten track up the valley, and passed the Luangéra river, near its junction with the Pangani, by means of a tree thrown across it. This stream, though not broad, is deep and sullen, and seems to be infested with crocodiles. They now continued the march on the alluvial plain round a spur of the Vugiri hills, which overhung their right like a bluff wall decked with bush and tree, while the Pangani roared away on the left, in many places here divided by inhabited islands. Leaving the river still coming from the northwest, they then took a sharp turn round the extreme west of the Vugiri, and entered on a cultivated plain leading direct to Fuga. Overtaken by a fierce storm, they here put up in some sheds outside a village. Except three small cones close to them to the north-west, there was nothing but dense uninterrupted jungle as far as the Makumbara mountains, ten miles off. The village was in the midst of a dense thicket, entered by a very narrow passage cut through the branches, and protected, moreover, by piles and stakes. Still more secure from attack are the villages built on the islands, the divided river forming a natural moat which is too much for African engineering. The first half of the journey from this place to Fuga led by well-beaten paths through fields of sugar-cane and bananas, tamarind-trees, papaws, and various jungle shrubs filling up the non-arable area; then began an ascent by zigzags up the steep hills on which the capital is situated. The face of the steep was clothed with large timber trees, over which climbed the delicate sarsaparilla vine; and below them flourished the universal plantain, regarded in this country as the staff of life. At length they worked up to a bare eminence, commanding the whole plain they had left behind. To the north

was the Makumbara range, a dense mass of solid-looking
hills joined on to, but much higher than, the spur they
stood on, the other extremity of which looked as if suddenly cut off by the Pangani river.   Beyond the river,
farther back than the western extremity of this range, were
other large hills which, bedimmed by distance, could be seen
tending in a south-westerly direction, being probably a link
of the longitudinal chain which fringes the whole of the
southern African continent.   In this region they would
form what would be called the East Coast Range, there being three main features in African topography—a belt of
low land, a belt of mountains, and a high interior plateau.

The country beyond the valley of the Pangani rose into
gentle undulations; but on the near side all was flat and
densely wooded, save in one little spot to the north-west
of the Mbara cones, where a sheet of water made a conspicuous bald place—and here it was that, according to
the natives, there was an abundance of elephants and
other game.   The inhabitants of Fuga were taken by surprise by their visitors, who were requested to remain outside.   The king, Kimuéri, was at least a hundred years
old, and suspicious in proportion; and it was in vain that
Captain Burton tried to cajole him, by promising to find
him some herbs that would insure longevity.   Whilst
they were waiting, some negroes were seen chasing down
an antelope.   This was a rufous-brown animal, like the
Kakur deer of the Himalayas; but, unlike known African
species, it had four points of horns.   Speke tried to purchase its head, but its captors were too greedy for the
flesh to let him have it, and he did not see another specimen.   The king, though suspicious, was civil, sent his
compliments, with a present, and allowed them to depart
as they came.

On the 16th of February they descended from the fresh

air, at an elevation of between 4000 or 5000 feet, to the close jungly plain, and then to the Pangani by the old route. They then followed the course of the river down to Chogué. The valley, though varied, was generally contracted by the closing in of the rolling terminal abutments of the Tongué hill on the one side—with rising land almost joined to conical hills, which overhung the river on the other or Uzégura side. Scarcely any life was observed on the line of march, and all was silence but the rumbling and gurgling sound of the river among the boulders and at the rapids. Opposite Tongué Fort they saw the cataract which they had heard from its summit. It was then a considerable cascade, but is doubtless at its grandest when the river is full. Burton dropped down the river in a canoe from Chogué to Pangani, while Speke surveyed the banks with Bombay. He had now become thoroughly attached to this man, and made an arrangement with the jemadar of the Beluches by which he was to quit the service he was in and attach himself to Speke. After an attack of yellow fever at Pangani, from which both Speke and Burton suffered, they returned to Zanzibar, reaching it on the 6th of March. They now waited for the end of the Masika, or great vernal rainy season, which follows the sun to the north, and generally lasts forty days. It was highly interesting to observe the regular procession of the wind and rain in the wake of the sun as he went north. The atmosphere being heated and rarefied by the vertical rays, a vacuum is produced, which the cold airs of the south rush up to fill, condensing the heated vapours drawn daily from the ocean, and precipitating them back to the earth. The constant occurrence of this phenomenon at the same time and in the same place fills the air with electricity, so that thunder and lightning accompany nearly every storm. Under these conditions of the atmosphere Speke confesses that he felt an extraordinary nervous irritability.

The delay at Zanzibar was rendered very agreeable by the hospitalities of the place and the varieties of its scenery, though its slave-market merited strong reprobation. They had now leisure to prepare for the serious expedition into the interior. The orders of the Geographical Society to Captain Burton were: To penetrate inland from Kilwa, or some other place on the east coast, and make the best of his way to the reputed lake of Nyassa; to determine its position and limits; to ascertain the depth and nature of its tributaries; to explore the country round it, &c. Having obtained all requisite information in that quarter, he was then to proceed northwards towards the chain of mountains marked on the Society's maps as containing the probable sources of the Bahr el Abiad or White Nile, which it would be his next object to discover. Captain Burton accordingly thought at first of starting from Kilwa, to attack the missionaries' slug-shaped lake in the tail. He gave this plan up on account of the reported hostility of neighbouring tribes—though the route from Kilwa to Nyassa was afterwards safely performed by Dr Roscher *—and decided by going by the caravan route to Ujiji. Sheikh Said, who went with them to Mombas, was engaged as cafila-bashi, or caravan-leader. The escort were enlisted from volunteers from the Sultan of Zanzibar's Beluch guard, and a Banyan named Ramji added some slaves. Everybody at Zanzibar did his best to forward the expedition, and Colonel Hamerton obtained from the Sultan the use of the corvette Artemise to take them over

---

* Dr Roscher was afterwards murdered by robbers in Uhiyow. The chief of their tribe sent them to Zanzibar, where they were executed by the Sultan's orders.

to Kaolé on the mainland.   The journey inland was commenced on the 27th of June 1857, there having been
some delay in procuring a sufficient number of donkeys.
The districts passed through on the road to Kazé will be
noticed in the narrative of Captains Speke and Grant's
last expedition, which passed over the same ground.
When they arrived at Ugogi, on the west of the East
Coast Range, they would have been stopped by exhaustion of the cattle, had not they found some pagazis
or porters, who had been left behind by a caravan, desirous of going to their homes in Unyamuézi.   The tedious
march to Kazé only ended on the 7th of November 1857.
Kazé is a place in the centre of Unyamuézi, the Land of
the Moon, in south latitude 5°, and east longitude 33°.
It is a trading depot of the Arab merchants, fast expand-
ing into a colony.   This they did not know when they
started, but expected to find a depot of that sort at Ujiji.
On the way they had both contracted fevers in the country of Uzaramo.   Speke's occurred at intervals, but Burton's stuck to him throughout the journey, and even
lasted for some time after he had returned home.   The
Arabs at Kazé were found to be extremely obliging,
especially their host, one Sheikh Snay, who supplied them,
moreover, with some very valuable information.   When
Speke opened the missionaries' map, and asked him where
Nyassa was, he said it was a distinct lake from Ujiji,
lying to the southward, and then that Ukéréwé was a
lake to the northward, much larger than Ujiji.   This
solved the mystery at once.   The missionaries had run
three lakes into one.   Snay, moreover, said that he thought
the Ukéréwé Lake was the source of the Jub river; but
Speke and Burton argued that it was more likely to prove
the source of the Nile, because they knew the Jub
to be separated from the interior plateau by the East

Coast Range. Snay and his associates also said that the Kitangulé and Katonga rivers ran out of the Ukéréwé Lake, and that another river, supposed to be the Jub, but really the Nile, ran into it, which of course was inconsistent with the lake being its source. On their being cross-questioned, it appeared that they had no clear ideas as to whether the rivers in question ran into or out of the lake, but they only knew that they were connected with it. Speke also heard from Snay that vessels frequented some waters to the north of the equator, which confirmed the statement he had heard when travelling in 1855 in the Somali country. Excited by this information, he wished to go at once to the Ukéréwé Lake (afterwards the Victoria Nyanza), instead of to Ujiji; but Burton preferred going west, as he heard that they were likely to be stripped of all their property in Usui—an apprehension which subsequent experience went far to verify.

They had been now more than a month at Kazé, and Burton was so ill that he allowed Speke to assume the command of the expedition for a time. They pushed on by degrees to Mséné by Christmas. This was a small colony occupied by Wasuahili. The country was very rich, and under rice cultivation. They were now on a great decline of country draining to the westward. As they went on the soil became deeper and richer, and the vegetation more luxuriant. After crossing the Malagarazi river in a bark canoe at the Mpété ferry, they found that, having travelled about a hundred and fifty miles along the slope from Kazé, they began to ascend at the eastern horn of a large crescent-shaped mass of mountains overhanging the northern half of the Tanganyika Lake. This crescent is large and deep in the body to the north, and tapers to horns as the mountains stretch southwards down the east and west sides of the lake. Speke recognised in this mountain

mass the famous and half-fabulous Mountains of the
Moon, so called anciently because all information respecting them came from the Wanyamuézi, or " people of the
Moon," just as the great indefinite lake which had resolved
itself into three was called the Sea of the Moon. It is
strange that Ptolemy should have heard of two lakes
east and west of each other, which he considered were the
respective sources of the two branches of the Nile. Speke
thinks that he must have got the information through
some of the people of the interior who had wandered to
the eastern coast, since the Anthropophagi would have
barred all communication by the channel of the Nile
itself. The line of march had been nearly due west from
Zanzibar for about six hundred rectilinear geographical
miles. From the summit of the eastern horn of the
mountain, the lovely Tanganyika Lake could be seen in
all its glory. But Speke, after having toiled through so
many leagues of country inhabited by savages, and suffered much illness and privation to attain to this point, was
destined to see nothing before his eyes but mist and glare.
Inflammation had attacked them, resulting from fevers
and the influence of a vertical sun, and brought on almost
total blindness. They now proceeded down the western
slopes of the hill, and soon arrived at the margin of the
lake, and hired a canoe at Ukaranga to go to Ujiji, the place
most frequented by the Arabs, who, after their custom,
apply its name to the lake. The Tanganyika Lake, lying
between 3° and 8° south latitude, and in 29° east longitude,
has a length of three hundred miles, by from thirty to
forty broad at its centre. The surface-level, as ascertained
by the temperature of boiling water, was only 1800 feet,
and it appears quite sunk in the mountains. Its waters
are very sweet, and abound with a great variety of delicious fish. In the northern part, which was of surpassing

fertility, the hills, instead of being, like those on the plateau they had left, outcrops of granite, were composed of
argillaceous sandstone. Rains lasted all the year round,
and this at a considerable temperature. The sides of the
lake were inhabited by numerous tribes of the true negro
breed, some of the most conspicuous being the Wabembé
cannibals, whose territory was shunned by the Arabs.
Bombay described them as being very terrible, and
" always on the look-out for some of our sort."

On pulling up at Kawélé, a small village in the Ujiji
district, they found themselves in the hands of an extortionate chief named Kannina, who fleeced them to the
best of his power.

Their first object on arriving was to get boats for the
survey of the lake, but this was a difficult matter. Nearly
all the border tribes were at war, and the little cockle-
shell canoes were not only unseaworthy, but there was
no proper stowage-room in them. The only vessel that
would suit them was a dhow or sailing-vessel belonging
to a sheikh living at Kasengé Island, on the western
shore. But as this dhow was said to be on the wrong
side of the lake, it was necessary to send or go to bargain
for it. Kannina being impracticable, they obtained a
boat and crew from another chief at the extortionate
charge of four *kitindis* and four *dhotis merikani*, besides
the usual sailors' fees. The dhoti is a piece of American
sheeting measuring eight cubits, the measure being from
a man's elbow to the top of the middle finger. The kitindis are a sort of brass-wire bracelets worn on the lower
arms by the negro females, coiled from the wrist to the
elbow, like a wax taper encircling a stem. Sometimes
this wire is wound flat round the neck to a breadth of
about eight inches, giving the wearer's head the appearance of that of John the Baptist in a charger. Such neck-

laces are never taken off, so at night, or when the wearer rests, a block of wood or stone is placed beneath the head, to prevent the wire from galling.

After this preliminary arrangement, there was a delay of no less than eighteen days before all could be got ready. Though vexatious in itself, this enabled Speke to recruit his health for the trip across the lake, which he proposed making in person. In the mornings and evenings he used to refresh himself by bathing in the lake, in spite of the crocodiles. These animals, however, were supposed by the natives to obey a certain charm, which consisted in placing the boughs of a particular tree about fifty yards from the shore, within which they would not venture. At noon, protected by an umbrella and stained-glass spectacles, he usually visited the market to obtain daily supplies. The commodities brought for sale to the huts of grass and branches in which the market was held were fish, flesh, tobacco, palm oil, and spirits, potatoes of different kinds, artichokes, various beans, plantains, melons, cotton, sugar-cane, pulse and vegetables, ivories, and sometimes slaves. On the 3d of March 1858 he set out in a long narrow canoe, hollowed out of the trunk of a single tree. The party was composed of Bombay as interpreter, a Goanese cook-boy, by name Gaetano, two Beluch soldiers, and twenty stark-naked savage sailors, commanded by a captain, who sometimes wore a goat-skin. But the man of quaintest aspect in the whole party was Sidi Mabarak Bombay. His breed was that of the true woolly-headed negro, though physically he was not a fine specimen, being somewhat smaller in general proportions than those often seen as stokers in the steamers that ply in the Indian Ocean. His head, though it looked as if carved of wood, like a barber's block, was lit by a humorous pair of little pig-like eyes, set in a generous benign countenance, which told the truth as to his honesty and good conduct. His projecting baboon-like muzzle was adorned with a set of sharp-pointed alligator teeth, which were shown to advantage when he grinned, which he often did on the slightest provocation. He was the very personification of the "jolly nigger" at the corner of a tobacconist's shop. The few facts of history which he knew were as follows: His father lived in a village in the country of Uhiyow, a large district situated between the east coast and the Nyassa, in latitude 11° S. His mother died when he was an infant, so that he scarcely remembered her. When he was about the age of twelve, a large body of Wasuahili merchants and their slaves, equipped with sword and gun, came to the quiet village, and, surrounding it, demanded of the inhabitants instant payment of their debt in cloth and beads, which represented sums formerly advanced in times of dearth. This was the usual system of these slave-hunters. The demand was known to be legal, but the villagers could not pay, and as resistance was hopeless, they all took to flight. Most of them, including Bombay, were captured, and he never heard more of his relatives. Then the captives were all grouped together, tethered with chains or ropes, and marched off to Kilwa, on the east coast, and from thence transported in dhows to Zanzibar. Bombay was bought by an Arab merchant in the slave-market there and taken off to India. By the death of this master, whom he served for several years, he became free. Then he enlisted in the late Imaum's army, and passed his days in half-starved idleness till he was fortunate enough to be engaged by Speke at Chogué.

Whilst they were encamped under a tree, where, by appointment, some of the party who were late were to join, some villagers brought ivories for sale, and were

much disappointed at finding that the Wazungu (white
men) were not come for purposes of traffic. In the night
they experienced the full fury of a tropical storm. The
rain came down in a deluge, and the surcharged earth
poured a regular stream of water over the beds, baggage,
and everything alike. The tent—a small gable-shaped
affair, six feet high, and seven by six square, made of
American sheeting—had to be kept upright by the main
strength of the men. Even the hippopotami seemed
angry at the unusual severity of the weather, to judge by
the frequency of their snorts and grunts, as they indulged
in devastating excursions among the crops. Since the
15th of November, when the rainy season commenced,
there had not been such a violent downpour. They
waited till the storm subsided on the 5th, and then put
to sea. It was very close packing. Speke littered down
amidships, with his bedding spread on reeds, in so short
a compass that his legs kept slipping off and dangling in
the bilge-water. The cook and bailsman sat on the first
bar, facing him ; and behind them, to the stern, one-half
of the sailors sat in couples ; whilst on the first bar behind
were Bombay and one Beluch, and beyond them to the
bow, in pairs, the remaining crew. The captain posted
himself in the bows, and all hands on both sides paddled
in stroke together. The fuel, cooking-apparatus, food,
and baggage were thrown promiscuously under the seats ;
and the sailors' blankets, of grass matting, were placed on
the bars to make them soft. When all was arranged, the
seventeen paddles dashed vigorously off, and soon crossed
the mouth of the Ruché river. Next Ukaranga, a village
lying in a bay, with a low range of densely-wooded hills,
about three miles in the rear, was passed, and then the
bay itself. The tired crew now hugged a bluff shore,
crowned with dense jungle, until a nook familiar to the

men was entered under plea of breakfasting. Here all hands landed, fires were kindled, and the cooking-pots arranged. Some prepared their rods and nets for fishing, some went hunting for fungi (a favourite food), and some collected fuel. The cook-boy Gaetano, who was always doing something wrong, dipped his pot in the sea for water, which, according to the local notions, was just the right proceeding to attract the crocodiles, and was thought generally unlucky.

While all hands were quietly breakfasting there was a sudden alarm of enemies, and all rushed to the boat, some with one thing, some with another, but the greater part of the kit was left behind. For some minutes there was breathless silence. Then one man, gaining courage, jumped off and secured his pot; another followed: at last a search was made to see if there was any ground for the panic. They stole along, sneaking and crawling through the bush in various directions, till at length a single man, with his arrow poised, probably in self-defence, was pounced upon. His story was not believed by the sailors, who proclaimed him and his party, who were some eight or ten men squabbling in the jungle at a distance, to be indisputable marauders, as no one could be in such a wild place on any good errand; so they broke his bow and arrows, and let him go. The sailors were as proud of this exploit as if they had won a great battle. They now coasted along till the Malagarazi's mouth was passed, often resting and mooring the boat with ropes or creepers. This river is the largest on the eastern shore, and was formerly crossed by the caravan on its road to Kazé in small bark canoes, each of which contained a man and his load. They had still the same tree-clad hilly view to the eastward, beautiful but monotonous. The eternal green of the trees and blue of the lake were painful, from the absence of all life and habitation. Speke thought that the country must have been inhabited at some time or other, and have been swept clear of all its population by slave-hunting parties; but still there might have been villages hid away among the nooks of the hills. After they had left Mgéti Khambi, a beautiful little harbour amongst the hills, out of sight of the lake, on the 6th of March, the gathering of clouds in the south cautioned the weather-wise among the sailors to halt. As they rested on their oars, the glimmer of lightning illuminated the distant hills, while low heavy rolling clouds of pitchy darkness, preceded by a heavy gale and foaming sea, spread over the whole southern waters, rapidly advanced. It was an ocean-tempest in miniature. When it had blown over, having occupied their spare time in fishing, they left their berth again and proceeded. A change of scenery at last took place. The chain of hills parallel with the shore was broken, and in its stead they saw small detached and irregular lines of hills, separated by plains of forest, thickly clad in verdure, like all the rest of the country. They passed the Riguvu and Hebué rivers. Were it not for the gaps in the hills suggesting the courses of rivers, such streams might be passed without notice, the mouths being choked by bulrushes and aquatic reeds, and the inland channels closely hidden by forest vegetation. At a small nook called Riguvu Khambi, where they rested for the night, Speke picked up four varieties of shells new to conchology. The day after they had to put back again, and Speke went after some buffaloes horned like the Cape variety, but could not get a shot; he also sprang some antelopes, and saw fresh tracks of elephants. They now hugged the bluff shore till they came near the usual cross-ing-place, to a point whence the island of Kivira on the opposite shore, with the Uguhha heights in the background,

was distinctly visible. The comparative narrowness of
the lake here caused it to be considered the most favourable spot for crossing. Speke naturally wished to obtain
all the information he could about the lake, but the superstition of the captain and crew prevented his getting any.
To answer questions at sea was contrary to their *uganga*
or religious principle, and they thought it particularly
unlucky to speak of the places of departure or arrival.
On the 8th of March they arrived among some islands,
the principal of which and the only inhabited are Kivira,
Kabizia, and Kasengé. Having replied satisfactorily to
a challenge from Sultan Kasanga's watch-boat, they proceeded to the largest island, Kivira. Whilst at Kivira, a
storm attacked them and upset everything, while the tent
itself was only kept upright by force. When it abated, and
a candle was lighted to rearrange the kit, the whole inside
of the tent became covered in a moment, as by magic, with
a swarm of black beetles. Tired of vain endeavours to
brush them away, Speke put out the candle, tried to
overcome the annoyance they gave him by crawling all
over him, and fell asleep. He was awoke by one of
these horrid insects trying to penetrate into his ear, but
too late ; for trying to extract it, he pushed it farther in.
The creature went on up the channel of the ear till it
came to the drum. It seemed enraged by the obstacle,
and began burrowing away at it like a rabbit. Speke
compares the worry this caused him to the situation of
the camp's donkeys when once attacked by a swarm of
bees. Neither tobacco, oil, nor salt could be found : he
tried melted butter, but it did no good ; then he applied
the point of a penknife. A few thrusts quieted the beetle,
but wounded his ear so badly that inflammation and
suppuration set in, and all his features were distorted on
that side. The affection was indescribably painful, and

for several days, being unable to masticate, he had to live on broth alone. He was afflicted with deafness for many months in consequence of this accident, and bits of the beetle came away for a long time afterwards; but it was not entirely an unmixed evil, for it acted as a seton on the inflammation in his eyes.

Kivira Island is a massive hill, about five miles long by two or three broad, and of irregular shape. In places there are high flats formed in terraces, but generally the steeps are abrupt and thickly wooded. The mainland immediately west is a promontory at the southern end of the Uguhha Mountains, and the island is separated from it by so narrow a strip of water that, except on a profile view, it might be taken for a headland. The relatively large population live in mushroom-shaped huts on the high flats and easier slopes, cultivating manioc, sweet potato, maize, millet, pulse, and all the common vegetables; and poultry is abundant in the villages. Their simple dress consists of small black monkey-skins, cat-skins, and the furs of any available vermin. These are tucked under a belt, and, according to number, go quite or partly round the body, the heads hanging in front and the tails depending gracefully below. The monkeys are driven by the people into small square nets when engaged in robbing the ripe maize, and so caught. Speke found these people most unpleasantly inquisitive, and was obliged to take refuge from their impertinences in the boat; for the tent was the worst place of all, as they would pull up the sides and peer in, and if he turned his head away to be quiet, make all kinds of uncouth noises to rouse him.

In the island of Kabizia, which they visited next, they breakfasted on a freshly-caught fish, the *singa*, a large, ugly, black-backed monster, with white belly, small fins, and long barbs, but no scales. In appearance a sluggish ground-fish, it was always grossly fat, and at this season full of roe. Its flesh was held in high esteem by the natives. Kabizia is very small, with a gradual slope from the north-west, and at the south-east end assumes the form of an Indian bull's hump. There is a village of some twenty huts, whose inhabitants live by fishing, and are in other respects like those of Kivira. Though their destination was in sight, the crew could not be got off for a long time, until they were quite surfeited with the fish, which they thought so delicious, and had secured a supply to carry away. On the mainland opposite this island was seen the western horn of the concavely-disposed mountains, which increase in height as they extend northwards. The seaward slopes were well wooded from near the summit to the water's edge; but on the tops, perhaps from the prevalence of strong winds, grass only was visible. Westward, behind Kasengé Island, and away to the southward, the country was of an undulating formation and uninteresting. Arrived at Kasengé after a pull of ninety minutes, Speke was welcomed by the Arab merchant, Sheikh Hamed bin Sulayyim, and a host of natives. The sheikh hospitably entertained him in his commodious house, built of mud and roofed with rafters and brushwood. The dhow Speke had come for was then lying at Ukaranga, on the eastern shore, but the sheikh said it would be at his service in a few days. There was, however, a difficulty about the crew, as he wanted his own men for a march to a territory called Uruwa, a hundred miles to the south-west. He gave Speke a description of the lake; and what he said was very important, as bearing on the question of the Nile in connection with Sir Samuel Baker's survey of the Little Luta Nzigé Lake, or "Albert Nyanza." There were no islands, he said, in the middle of the sea, but several in various places near the shore,

divided from the mainland by shoals and narrow channels.
A large river called Marungu supplied the lake at its
southern extremity; and on a visit to the northern end,
he had seen a much larger river, which he was sure flowed
out of the lake; for though he did not venture on it in
consequence of its banks being occupied by desperate
savages, he went so near its outlet that he could see and
feel the outward drift of the water.   He also described an
adventure he had had with a tribe to the north called
Warundi, who tried to surprise him in his dhow.   Speke's
opinion of his story was that in all probability his rivers
ran the reverse way, and that the Marungu ran out of the
Tanganyika into the Nyassa, forming a chain of lakes
draining into the Zambézé, while the river to the north
ran out of the Moon Mountains into the lake.   It was to
solve this problem that the world-renowned Dr Livingstone was on his way when, as is now reported, he was
murdered by the natives in the neighbourhood of the
Nyassa in the summer of 1866.   It was Speke's firm
opinion that the Nile could not rise far south of the
equator, because there would be no rain-supply to feed its
sources; and he argued that Hamed must be wrong, not
only because the north of the Tanganyika is encircled by
lofty mountains, but because the lake's level is so much
lower than that of the adjacent plateau.   Indeed he might
have thought that the lake had been formed in a volcanic
trough had not Livingstone determined the level of the
Nyassa to be nearly the same; and the Babisa, who live
on the west of the Nyassa, in crossing the country between the two lakes to Luwemba, pass the Marungu
river, but no mountain-range.   Hamed said it would take
eight days for Speke to go to the north of the lake, and
fifteen to go to the south.   Considering the present state
of the Nile question, it is much to be regretted that

circumstances prevented him from going to either extremity.

The island of Kasengé is a narrow ridge of high land, about a mile long, running north and south, devoid of trees, and only partially cultivated. All but its north-western end, where it abuts on the lake, is encircled by a girdle of water about eighty yards broad, so that it is quite imbedded in the land. It contains a more numerous population than the other parts. The people are filthy, very inquisitive, and easily amused. They have the large lips, flattish nose, and frizzly wool of the Kaffir race. The women wear a cloth round the body, fastened under the arms and reaching below the knees, and generally beads, brass necklaces, or other ornaments; while the men only hang, in the fashion of a game-bag, a single goat-skin over the shoulder, and gird themselves with a short kilt if they possess one. They lie about the huts on a warm day like pigs basking in the sun. The women of these people are so unnatural that they sell their children into slavery for a cloth or two. The slave-trade appears to be the universal blight of the interior of Africa, preventing it from being one of the finest countries in the world.

The village was large and straggling, consisting of a number of haycock-looking huts, framed of wood or boughs and covered with grass. The most pretentious house belonged to the Sultan Kasanga. This potentate received Speke kindly, giving him a goat and some grain, and receiving as usual a present in return. There appeared to be an abundance of all kinds of provisions in these parts, the surrounding country being highly cultivated, and in fact exporting its produce to Ujiji and other distant markets.

On the 13th of March the desired dhow sailed up, look-

ing very graceful in her white sails, like a swan on a garden reach. She only came, however, to tantalise Speke;
for sailors could not be procured, and Speke regretted
much that he had induced Burton to let Ramji's slaves,
whom they had brought from Zanzibar, return home, as
they were all good sailors. Speke nearly prevailed on
Hamed, by offering him £100, to give up his journey to
Uruwa, and accompany him round the lake. Had he
succeeded, he would have saved his life, for Hamed, with
all his suite, was afterwards murdered in Uruwa. Speke,
however, would have probably shared his fate had he
accompanied him to Uruwa, which he was half inclined
to do, in order to connect the line from Zanzibar with the
Portuguese and Dr Livingstone's routes to Loando on the
eastern coast. He was curious about the copper mines
at Katata, from which copper comes to Uruwa. Hamed
described the roads as easy, lying through an undulating
country, fertilised by small streams, presenting no impediment to travellers. The ivory trade brings the Arabs
continually farther and farther inland, as the nearer
countries become so overstocked with beads that ivory
rises to so high a price as not to pay for transport.
Uruwa is half-way across the continent, and in a few
years the Zanzibar Arabs must unite their labours with
the people who come from Loando on the opposite coast.
After a twelve days' stay at Kasengé, Speke took leave
of his generous host Hamed, and, obliged to give up the
dhow in despair, proceeded to return in his canoe as fast
as the weather and the superstitious fears of the crew
would permit. He wished to bring over the sultan's
goat, which had just borne a kid, to supply milk to his
sick companion Burton at Ujiji; but the crew pretending
that the elements were angry at his doing so, he was
obliged to kill the goat and kid, taking care to disappoint

them of the flesh, a longing for which, he surmised, was at
the bottom of their scruples. On the 27th of March they
took their final departure from Kivira and crossed the
breadth of the lake again in fourteen hours; the voyage
home, with its incidents of stopping to picnic on the land
and taking refuge from storms, being very nearly the
counterpart of the voyage out.

Being disappointed about the dhow, Speke and Burton
now tried what they could do with Kannina in the way
of inducing him to give them the means of completing the
survey of the lake. It so happened that he wished to go as
far as Uvira on a commission of his own, and promised to
take them on to the lake-head, they paying all expenses in
return for his protection. Two canoes started; Burton,
with Kannina, in the large one manned by forty rowers,
and Speke in one considerably smaller. When they got to
Uvira, however, Kannina, to their intense disgust, declined
to fulfil his part of the bargain on the ground of the hostility of the Warundi, who lived at the head of the lake,
which he must of course have been acquainted with before.
The only advantage that Speke gained from this excursion
was a corroboration of his theory as opposed to Hamed's,
since the sultan's son at Uvira told him that the river
named Rusizi drained the high mountains in the north
and flowed *into* the lake. His own observation of the
mountains from some neighbouring heights confirmed this
statement, as they seemed to close the lake entirely. On
coming up the lake, they travelled the first half of the
way up the east coast, then crossed over to the end of a
long island called Ubwari, made for the western shore,
and coasted it to Uvira. The two canoes raced together
in a very spirited fashion. Their naked crews, in untiring
emulation, would paddle away like so many black devils,
dashing up the water whenever they neared each other,

and delighting in drenching with spray their clothed passengers. These fellows only go naked in bad weather and when working—in fine weather and on shore they strut about in their goat-skins; and it is an amusing sight to see them, on the coming on of a shower, carefully wrap up their skins, put them in their loads, and stand cowering and shivering like a dog which has just come out of a cold pond.

Speke found, by accurate and repeated measurements, that the lake of Tanganyika was twenty-six miles broad at the place of crossing from Kivira, which is its narrowest central part. He could not exactly estimate its average breadth in consequence of the numberless bays and promontories that break the coast-line, but he guessed it to be from thirty to forty miles. Having unfortunately forgotten to take a sounding-line, he was unable to ascertain its depth, but thought it must be considerable, both from the trough-like formation of the land in which it lies, and also from having seen fishing-baskets hauled up from great depths close to the shore, by long ropes with trimmers attached. The fertility of the banks was amazing, and he had as yet seen such splendid vegetation in no part of Africa that he had visited. To the northward rain falls in frequent showers all the year round, but on the southern portion only during the six months when the sun is in his southern declination. Hence the northern part was naturally richer than the southern, and hence he argued the lake must be kept up by a constant inflow from the north.

On returning to Ujiji, after a long compulsory sojourn at Uvira on Kannina's business, they found their stock of beads and cloth, the currency of Africa, nearly exhausted. The ras-cafila, Sheikh Said, volunteered to go back to Kazé and get another supply, and Speke much wished to com-

plete the survey of the lake; but in consequence of his
companion's broken health it was finally resolved that
they should return at once to Kazé. They would have
found great difficulty, however, in getting away, had not
some supplies been fortunately brought by an Arab ivory-
trader called Mohinna, an old friend that they had left
at Kazé. As it was, all went well. The whole party
had got into condition by the excellent fare at Ujiji,
which seems to have possessed a market teeming with
every delicacy, though sometimes Kannina, who was the
only cow-keeper, was very troublesome in stopping their
supply of milk on various pretexts. One day he took
offence because they turned his mendicant wives out of
the house, mistaking them for casual paupers. Another
day he was absurdly frightened at a cheese they had
made, thinking they must have done it by magic, and
that such tampering with the natural uses of milk made
the cows dry. They found this a common superstition in
other regions, the natives having a special objection to
the boiling of milk. The cattle which supplied the milk
were of a uniform red colour, like the Devon breed;
they attain to a great height and size, and have stupen-
dous horns.

The weather being now fine, as the rainy season had
ceased by the 15th of May, they marched rapidly across the
eastern horn of the mountains to the Malagarazi ferry,
but by a more northernly route than that by which they
had come. The river, which they reached in early June,
was found to be in a state of flood, overflowing its valley
to the extent of a mile or more. The last time they had
seen it was at the beginning of the monsoon, when it was
contained in its banks. The rains about 5° south latitude
had just lasted for the six months that the sun was in the
south, and were now gone to the north with the sun.

Speke thought this an important fact in its relation to the rise of the Nile on the other side of this mountain-axis, proving that whilst the rain falls most where the sun is vertical, it is greatly augmented by these mountains, lying as they do exactly on the rainy zone of the world.   They reached Kazé by the latter end of June 1858, by a more northernly and straighter road than that by which they had previously travelled, a twelvemonth having elapsed since they had left Zanzibar.

CHAPTER III.

DISCOVERY OF THE VICTORIA NYANZA.

ARAB INFORMATION AT KAZÉ—SPEKE MARCHES TO THE NORTH—THE COUNTRY, PEOPLE, AND SULTANS—WARS AND RUMOURS OF THEM—FIRST SIGHT OF THE GREAT LAKE—SPEKE NAMES IT THE VICTORIA NYANZA—SPECULATIONS ABOUT IT AND ITS NEIGHBOURHOOD—ADVENTURES ON THE RETURN MARCH—THE GREAT RESOURCES OF THE COUNTRY—TRIUMPHAL RETURN TO KAZÉ.

CAPTAINS Burton and Speke were the honoured guests of Sheikh Snay at Kazé, and felt as if they were living in a civilised country, from the pleasant manners and society of the Arab community which surrounded them. It was from this sheikh that Speke had first heard of the Ukéréwé Sea (now the Victoria Nyanza), and he now received from him his first information respecting the wonderful kingdom of Uganda. He said that he had been once on a visit to Sunna, the king of that country. Starting from Kazé, it took him thirty-five marches to reach Kitangulé (bearing N.N.W.), and twenty more marches north by east to reach Kibuga, the capital of Uganda. The only troublesome people on the way were the natives of Usui, bordering on the kingdom of Karagué, which was a mountainous land to the west of the lake, bounded on the north by the Kitangulé river. Beyond this lay the Unyoro territory, enclosing the kingdom of Uganda in the direction of the lake. He thought that, by the assistance of the King of Uganda, boats might be constructed to survey the lake, or rather the Nile, which he confounded with it. He gave an account, which turned out to be substantially correct, of the Kitangulé and Katonga rivers; but in speaking of the great sailing-craft on the lake, must have alluded to the Nile at Gondokoro. Another man named Musa, a Hindi merchant, who appeared very straightforward, described in minute detail his journey to the north, and told of a third river north of the equator, beyond Uganda, much larger than the Katonga, and generally called the Usoga river, as watering that district. He produced a negro slave who had been to Usoga, and seen this river, which he called Kivira, coming out of the lake and intersecting stony hilly ground on its passage to the north-west. This river Kivira was evidently the Jub of Snay, and the Nile of Speke. A Suahili merchant, Abdullah bin Nasib, had, moreover, heard of sailors who keep logs and use sextants on the N'yanza (the Nile), and of the Kidi and Bari people living on the Kivira. These people were plainly the same who became known by the Egyptian expeditions sent up the Nile to discover its source. M. Ferdinand Werne, who was with the second of these expeditions, which got up higher than any of the others, states, on Dr Beke's authority, that according to Lacono, King of Bari, the course of the river continued southwards for thirty days' journey. This, Speke observes, would place the source of the Nile exactly at the Victoria Nyanza's southern extremity—in 2° south latitude, lying in the Unyamuézi country. It appears that the Arabs, in the course of their trade, had better opportunities of obtaining information formerly than at the time of Speke's stay at Kazé, the King of Uganda having broken up their station on finding that they interfered too much with his subjects; but they had still establishments in the kingdom of Karagué, the sultan of which was said to be a most respectable man.

Though the way was reported to be unsafe, in consequence of civil wars, Speke now wished to form a caravan for exploring Northern Unyamuézi as soon as possible. There were great delays and difficulties before he could get men together. The Beluches had to be paid very highly for volunteering on extra service. The only man who knew the coast language had to be engaged with great persuasion as kirangozi or leader, and then porters had to be found. Bombay himself turned unexpectedly restive and extortionate. His motives, however, when known, in a measure excused him. He had bought, to be his adopted brother, a fine athletic slave of the Wahha tribe; and it was for this poor relation, and not himself, that he made such excessive demands for cloth. Bombay never wanted anything for himself, but he had a good-natured weakness for spoiling adopted brothers. He characteristically shared the wearing of his fez cap with another of these, an ill-favoured lout named Mabruki, as well as with a little slave-child, whom he had bought for light services, such as carrying his sleeping-hide and water-gourd on the march.

The caravan left Kazé on the 9th of July 1858. It consisted of the kirangozi, twenty pagazis or porters, ten Beluches, armed with their own guns, as guard, Bombay, Mabruki, and Gaetano, with a kit sufficient for six weeks. Speke took with him one large elephant-gun of Burton's, and two rifles and a smooth-bore double gun of his own, manufactured by Blissett of Holborn. Burton remained behind to recruit his health, and make observations at Kazé. The Beluches were very sulky at starting, and seemed to repent of their bargain, and the road was not

calculated to raise their spirits. It lay through fields of
jowari (holcus), across the plain of Unyanyembé. When
it was dark, the stalks, lying across the path, tripped up
the traveller at every step; and if he extended his hands
to keep himself from falling, the heavy bowing ears, ripe
and ready to drop, would bang against his eyes. The
deep sandy soil was an additional inconvenience. Then
the pagazis all stole away on the first day to have a car-
ouse on pombé (African beer), which was their universal
custom before starting on a march, and this did not im-
prove the temper of the guard. After passing the cultivated plain, the track went down a broad valley with a
gentle slope, full of tall and slender forest trees, with low
hills on either side. They passed one dry nullah, the
Gombé, a tributary of the Malagarazi, some pools of water,
also two caravans, one of ivory for the coast, the other
bringing cattle to the Unyanyembé markets. No game
was seen but a troop of very wild zebras. They halted at
a village in the district of Ulikampuri. The villages in
central Unyamuézi form a large hollow square, the walls
of which are the huts, ranged on all sides of it in a
kind of street in two walls, the breadth of an ordinary
room, which is partitioned off by interior walls of earth
like the outer ones, and resembling the sepoys' lines in
India. The flat roof serves as a store for firewood, and
for drying grain or vegetables. Most of the compartments
contain the families, with poultry, brewing and cooking
apparatus, stores of grain, &c. The rest are devoted to
the goats and cows. What few sheep there are seem to
be of the Persian stock, but are scraggy, and bear but
slight signs of the " blue blood " of the fat-rumped breed.
The cows are small and short-horned, with humps like
Brahminy bulls, and of many colours. In front of every
house is a granite slab for grinding jowari. The women,

kneeling before these, rub the grain to powder with a smaller stone, swaying their bodies, and keeping time to a monotonous tune.

They now marched to a village at the southern extremity of the Unyambéwa district, the Beluches having by this time quite recovered their tempers. The first five miles lay over flattish ground, winding among low straggling hills of the same formation as the whole surface of Unyamuézi, diversified with granite outcrops. The country now opened into an extensive plain, covered, as at first, with rich cultivation, which was succeeded by a slender tree-forest, amongst which were seen some shy antelopes. Here a curious scene took place on meeting an ivory caravan of Wasukuma. On nearing each other, the two kirangozis or leaders advanced, with the distrustful look of dogs who do not know each other, with heads awry and eyes steadfastly fixed on each other, and with bodies motionless and strictly poised, like rams preparing for a fight, and then rushed in with their heads down, and butted amain till one gave way. A general mêlée of the caravans followed. Speke, in his ignorance, thought the matter serious, and was going to interfere with his knobbed stick, but he reflected that in the blackness of both parties it would be difficult to distinguish friend from foe, and whilst he was hesitating accordingly both sides stopped and broke into hearty laughter at his excitement. He found out that the struggle was only the custom of the country when two caravans met, to determine the rule of the road in passing. After passing the forest, they came upon villages well supplied with provisions; but as yet the white beads which Speke had brought with him were not good currency, as the natives of these parts happened to have a passion for coloured. Eight miles more over an open, waving, well-cultivated country brought them to the boundary of Unyambéwa. The district was governed by a sultana called Ungugu, who requested the pleasure of Speke's company. Speke was obliged to comply with this virtual command, though he had to go far out of his way to get to the royal residence. He entered it by an aperture in the tall slender stakes surrounding the dwellings, and after following a passage constructed like the outer fence, was suddenly ushered into a yard full of cows, which served as an antechamber. There a couple of drums, shaped like beer-barrels, with a cow-skin stretched over them, were beaten as a royal salute. After a delay, they were ushered into the sultana's establishment—a small court, in which the common mushroom huts, with their ample eaves, afforded a grateful shelter from the sun. A cow-skin was spread for Speke, and a wooden stool set that he might assume a better state than his suite; and then he was received not as yet by the sultana in person, but by her maid-of-honour, a lady of unattractive but good-natured countenance. From her he obtained eggs and milk, of which he was greatly in need. Speke having been reported by the maid as not dangerous, the sultana at last appeared, a short stumpy old lady of about sixty. Her nose was short, squat, and flabby at the end, and her eyes were bald of brows or lashes; but she had great energy of manner, and her face wore a perpetual smile. The dress she had on was an old barsati, presented by some Arab merchant, and was if anything dirtier than her maid's. The large joints of all her fingers were bound with small copper wire, and her legs staggered under immense anklets made of brass wire wound round elephant's tail or zebra's hair. She wore huge solid brass rings on her arms, and from her bracelets of thin brass wire there hung various charms made of wooden, brazen, horn, and ivory ornaments. The sultana squatted at Speke's side, and first shook hands. Then she manipulated his shoes (always a marvel in these barefooted regions), his overalls, his waistcoat, especially the buttons, and his coat. The latter article she wished him to give her for her own wear. His hands and fingers were pronounced as soft as a child's, and his hair was likened to a lion's mane. To her question where he was going, a dozen voices answered, " He is going to the lake, to barter cloth for large hippopotamus teeth." This satisfied her, and she retired into privacy. Still he could not get away without being kept waiting for a bullock which the queen insisted on his receiving in return for his presents. The palace was a type of all the common villages beyond Unyamuézi proper. The mushroom-shaped grass huts are surrounded by a slender palisading, having streets or passages of the same construction, with outlets at intervals leading into the different courts, each containing five or six huts similarly partitioned with poles. If the village happens to be on soft or moist ground, it is often fortified with a moat or evergreen fence in addition to the palisading.

They next reached a village in the Ibanda district by a good road over flat ground covered partly with fine crops, partly with trees as before, and then came to Ukamba, in the country of Msalala. After more plain, they then passed a ridge of hills which crossed the road, gradually closing from the right and running into highlands passing round the west of the level, then descended into a district studded with the same little hills as before. This country was so beautiful, and the markets were so well supplied, that the pagazis could not be got on ; and Speke himself would gladly have lingered, had he not been obliged to make the most of his time and resources. A son of the Sultan of Mséné, between Unyanyembé and Ujiji, who came on a visit, seeing Speke busy with his

instruments, took him for a magician, and begged him to
cast his horoscope, tell the length of his father's life, divine
the weather and crops, the probabilities of wars, and the
future history of the country. Bombay shrewdly replied
that such a mighty business would require more days of
study than his master could afford to give. As the people
here dispensed with the loin-cloths which Speke brought
as currency, and white beads were not the fashion, he
found everything very dear. If he had brought coloured
beads, he might have bought a hen with a necklace.
Among a cloth-wearing tribe, one kilt (worth a dollar at
Zanzibar) would have bought forty fowls; here it only
purchased four fowls and nine eggs. The weather at this
time was delightful, and the air was so bracing in the
morning that it made the fingers tingle.

They were obliged to diverge now from the regular road
to get out of the way of a war between two young chiefs,
brothers of the Wamanda tribe. The new way led from
the Msalala to the Uyombo district, governed by a chief
called Mihambo. He was not powerful enough to exact
the customary " hongo " or tribute, but gave a sheep in return for a present. His people were busy with the harvest, cutting the jowari, and thrashing it with long sticks.
The country here lay in long waves, clad with trees and
brushwood, with rich cultivation in the hollows. It was
the same, with an unvarying temperature, as far as Ukuni.
On the road they met a party of Wanyombo who had
taken advantage of the difficulty among the Wamanda to
lift some forty or fifty head of cattle. Two albinos were
seen in the village, one an old woman with greyish eyes,
and the other a young one, who ran away and hid herself,
and could not be bribed into permitting a peep. The
old lady's skin was of an unwholesome pink, her hair,
eyebrows, and eyelashes of a yellowish white. Two por-

ters fell ill from eating too much beef on this march, but the natives thought their illness caused by the butcher having put out his tongue and clenched it with his teeth while slaughtering. On the 19th of July they re-entered the Msalala district. The country was now divided between large cultivated plains, interspersed with fine trees, and the small hills of outcropping granite. There being no direct route to the northward here, they had to make lines from village to village, which caused much trouble and delay. Speke witnessed the operation of brother-making. Two men desirous of forming the tie of blood seat themselves face to face on a cow-hide with outstretched legs, one pair overlapping the other. They then place their bows and arrows across their thighs, and each holds a leaf; then a third, holding a pot of oil or butter, makes an incision above their knees, and requires each to put his blood on the other's leaf, and mix a little grease with it. This is the salve of fraternity, with which each then proceeds to anoint himself. Finally the two brothers bawl out the names of all their relatives, and swear by the blood to stand by each other till death.

Ugogo, which lies between the coast and Ujiji, is quoted as a marvel of population, but in these parts the road literally swarmed with black humanity. The people were so inquisitive that nothing but the stick would keep them at a respectful distance from the "Mzungu." They were now stopped by a guard of the Sultan Kurua, who told them that his eldest brother, who was at feud with him, held the line on which they were marching, and that they must consequently diverge to Mgogua, the sultan's village. Kurua was a plain young man, with two pretty young wives. They received Speke kindly, and sent him a bowl of fresh milk, the extreme of attention. In the evening the sultan sent the inevitable bullock, always an expen-

sive present.   But he was more easily satisfied than most
of the chiefs, and after receiving his "hongo," swore that
he was Speke's brother.   This civility was perhaps in part
owing to his expressed wish to ultimately get some gunpowder to fight his big brother with.   This country was
peculiar, in being sprinkled over with an efflorescence of
salt.   The quantity of cattle in Msalala was astonishing,
large droves, tended by a few men, covering the plains and
filling the villages at night; and its crops were as fine as
its herds.   The climate was so temperate that it was a
luxury to walk till 9 A.M., and then to ride till noon ; but
the next three hours were too warm for exertion.   The
evenings and mornings were calm, and after 10 P.M. a
blanket was agreeable.   It must, however, be borne in
mind, that the land in these latitudes, on the meridian 33°
east longitude, lies at a very considerable height.   The cot-
ton-plant flourished here as in Unyanyembé or Ujiji, and
everything would grow by simply strewing the seed.   The
sultans have no regular civil list, but are maintained by
their slaves tilling the ground, tending cattle, or trading
for them in slaves or ivory, besides occasional perquisites
from travellers, a percentage on all plunder, or a share of
the game-bag of hunters.

They now came to Senagongo, the village of Kanoni,
Kurua's second brother, and confederate in arms against
their senior.   Their fraternal feuds were the natural
result of polygamy, as the brothers were born of different mothers.   The track pursued here was rather tortuous, to avoid the seat of war.   To the east the country
was open, with a spacious view ; to the west this was
limited by an irregular series of low hills, cultivation
and scrub-jungle alternating.   Kanoni's subjects were
a most uproarious set.   They appeared to keep every
day a kind of wild festival, which lasted, with all sort of

noises, from early in the afternoon till midnight. But Kanoni himself, more complaisant even than Kurua, excused their taking the bullock, showed them the road for a short distance, and even offered them a guide to the lake and back, which offer Speke would have accepted gladly, but that the arrangement was bungled by Bombay. They proceeded on to a deserted village named Khahama, and then to one in the district of Nindo, first passing a belt of jungle, then some cultivated land, then a large waste of thorn and bush, with broad grassy flats lying about the road. A herd of hartebeests, giraffes, and other animals gave a truly African character to the scenery, and the tracks of elephants and other large game were also seen. The village passed, they were received by a waterless wilderness of forest, intersected by some long and broad plains covered with tall grass. These flats much resembled some crossed while travelling parallel to the Malagarazi river, the cracked nature of the now parched soil being an evidence of occasional inundation. Everywhere in Africa this kind of ground suggests the neighbourhood of a river, as was in fact the case here. Another kind of evidence is furnished by the abundance of animal life, for elephants and buffaloes must drink every day.

Passing a small conical hill which assisted Speke's mapping, the caravan now rested in the plain of Salawé. The harvesters, when they saw them, all struck work and followed them to the village. As an illustration of the natural greed of the people here, Speke mentions that a child to whom he gave some beads clutched them with the eagerness of a monkey, and then ran away and hid them, instead of showing them with pride to his playmates. The road ahead was now said to be unsafe, but on they went, after delays and wranglings among the men. Several kinds of antelopes were seen, and the Beluches fired at an

ostrich. Their route appeared, from the general nakedness
and destitution of the people, to be one little frequented
by merchants. The district was occupied by the Wasemba
tribe, lying between the Wanatiya on the east and the
Wazinza on the west. On the 27th of July, on crawling
through the opening in the palisading of one of the villages, they saw a tall narrow pillar of granite, higher than
Pompey's at Alexandria, or the Nelson Monument at
Charing Cross, with huge boulders of the same rock
standing round its base, so as to bring to mind Stone-
henge on Salisbury Plain. There was another similar
but much higher column five miles farther on, which
overtopped the trees and all other surrounding objects.
These pillars were good landmarks, the latter being
visible at eight miles' distance. From the cultivated plain
of Salawé they went through another wilderness lying in
a long broad valley between low hills, and arrived at
length at the northern boundary of the district. The
country was diversified in hills and dells, while brown
granite rocks, overgrown above, gave variety to the colour-
ing; and numerous herds, grazing about the fields and
villages, animated the whole. The palm was conspicuous
among the trees. The only drawback to perfect enjoyment in this divine scenery were the howling inquisitive
savages, who made the traveller feel like a bear baited by
a pack of curs. As they crossed some hills, a covey of
guinea-fowl was sprung, and Speke shot near some springs
several couple of sand-grouse of unusually dark plumage,
and not quite so large as the Tibet bird.

The sandstone here is rich in iron; and, in fact, the
iron used in the manufacture of nearly all the tools of
this part of the continent is found, smelted, and wrought
in this tropical "black country." On the 30th of July
1858 Speke saw, at about four miles' distance to the left,

a sheet of water, which ultimately proved to be a creek, and the most southern part of that Nyanza which was known to the Arabs as the Ukéréwé Sea. At this moment he discovered, according to his own conviction, the source of the Nile! And it would have been discovered ages ago, he maintained, but that the ancients knew nothing about the rainy zone on the equator.

They now went down a grassy and jungly depression into a deep, dirty, viscid nullah, which communicated with the southern end of the creek. This he named the Jordan. After it had been forded with difficulty, they put up at the nearest village in the Urima district. The country to the east appeared open and wavy, but to the north and far west very hilly. Flocks and herds abounded on the fertile land. Hippopotami frequented the nullah at night, and lived there during the rains, but during the dry season migrated to the larger waters. The fields round the villages were said to suffer from the nocturnal ravages of the rhinoceros. While this nullah drains the land to the south-east, a river which, as Speke heard, rises in the Msalala country, draws off the water from the strata they had recently been crossing to the westward of their track, and empties it into the creek on the side opposite to the mouth of the nullah. On the last day of July, hearing that a shorter route than that by Sukuma frequented by the Arabs led to Muanza, where Sheikh Snay advised him to go, Speke followed the nullah's right bank a few miles to the westward, then turned northwards, and went along the creek to a village at the end of the Urima district. Here lived, in the flats and bottoms among the scattered hills, a large motley population of smiths, husbandmen, and herdsmen. All travelling is suspended in these parts during the rainy season, in consequence of the inundations of the lake and the general saturation of the country. As they followed the creek, which increased in breadth as it extended northwards, they saw many little islands, well wooded, standing boldly out of the water, which, in conjunction with the hill-dotted country round, formed a very pleasing landscape. With his naked eyes, however, Speke was only able to see it dimly; and his French grey spectacles, or "double eyes," as the natives called them, excited too much curiosity to allow him to use them conveniently. They now passed along a jungly depression, where they saw florikans, ostriches, and Saltiana antelopes, and Speke shot some partridges; and then threaded between villages and fields lying in small valleys, or crossed over low hills, till they came to Ukumbi, a village of the Walaswanda. The next day's march followed a tortuous route—sometimes along the creek, sometimes through a diversified populous country as before. Some small perennial streams, rising in the base of the hills, meander in the valleys here, and keep up an evergreen freshness of vegetation. The creek grew wider to the north, and was studded with rocky island-hills covered with brushwood, which, as they stood out of the dark-blue waters, reminded Speke of the Greek Archipelago. These became, from their variety, more attractive at every turn, and he was now able to enjoy the view better, as the people here were too much engrossed with their harvesting to plague him. The village of Isamiro, and the long hill which the caravan mounted on quitting it, and which Speke named Somerset, are worthy of especial record, since it was from the summit of the latter that he first gazed on the pale-blue expanse of the Victoria Nyanza. The distant sea-line of its horizon was defined in the calm atmosphere between north and west, but this did not convey a just idea of the breadth of the lake, as the islands composing the Bengal Archipelago of the map,

rising from 200 to 300 feet above the water, interfered
with the line of vision to the left; while on the right the
western horn of the Ukéréwé Island cut off the view of
the distant water to the north-east. An elbow of the
lake, however, stretched out far to the eastward, at the
base of the low range on which he stood, to where a hummock of the mainland marked what he thought was its
south-east angle.

At twenty or thirty miles the more considerable islands
of Ukéréwé and Mazita formed the apparent northern shore
of this firth. The former of these, from which the lake
was generally named, was reported not to be large; and
though evidently of no great height, Speke could descry
several spurs stretching down to the water's edge from its
central ridge of hills. Mazita was higher, of a hog-backed
shape, but from the distance its physical features were
less distinguishable. In consequence of the obstruction
offered by the northern islands of the Bengal Archipelago,
it was only possible to see that in the west a series of
low hill-tops stretched as far as the eye could reach, while
nearly close below the spectator was the mouth of the
creek which comes from the south, and along whose shores
they had marched for the last three days. Even in a well-
known country the view would have attracted attention
from its placid beauty. Each island, swelling to a rounded
summit, clothed with wood between the rugged angular
closely-outcropping granite rocks, was perfectly reflected
in the glassy surface, on which here and there a black spot
could be detected, the tiny canoe of some Muanza fisher-
man. On the gentle shelving plain below, the smoke curled
above the trees, which here and there just disclosed villages and hamlets, their brown thatched roofs contrasting
with the emerald of the beautiful milk-bush, the coral
branches of which clustered round the cottages, and formed

G

alleys and hedgerows equal to the choicest of English
shrubberies. But the view was nothing as compared
with its associations. Speke felt sure that he had at last
solved the great old riddle. The Arabs' account was substantially true, and the map he had sent home on their
testimony required but trifling alterations. He had found
a lake worthy to be called by the name of his sovereign,
and he called it the Victoria Nyanza. Muanza, his
journey's end, now lay at his feet. This was a happy-
looking secluded nook. Its plain, well cultivated to the
north, lay almost flush with the lake. Here they came
on one Mahaya, whom the Arabs had cautioned them to
avoid, at his own palace, but did not recognise him.
When inquiry was made about him, no one knew his
name, the reason being that great men in these parts go
by a number of *aliases*, partly to keep up their grandeur,
partly to mystify travellers. On the way to the quarters
of an Arab, by name Mansur bin Salim, Speke shot several red Egyptian geese of the same kind that he had
seen in the Somali country. He saw another, black all
over, except a patch of white beneath the lower mandible,
and standing as high as the Canadian species. The Arab
received him gladly, and contradicted the reports about
Mahaya. The northward journey was completed on the
3d of August. They had come 226 miles in twenty-five
days from Kazé, which, including stoppages, makes an
average of nine miles a-day. From his observations from
an eminence here, which he named Observatory Hill,
aided by information, Speke was inclined to think that
the islands Ukéréwé and Mazita were in the dry season
connected by a tongue of land with the eastern shore.
There was a sultan called Machunda in Ukéréwé who
trafficked in ivory. It seems strange that trade should
go round by Unyanyembé, considering the nearness of

the lake to Zanzibar; but the way as the crow flies is through the Masai and other tribes notorious for inhospitality.

From Observatory Hill the little hummock which marked the south-east corner of the lake was again visible due east, but though the air was clear it was indistinct. From this circumstance, as well as from the fact that all the hills about here had an even height of 200 to 300 feet, Speke judged it to be forty miles off at least. On facing N.N.W., he could only see a sea-horizon, and was told that the breadth of the lake beyond Ukéréwé was twice the distance to the hummock. He subsequently calculated its breadth at more than a hundred miles. As to its length to the north, his informant denoted immeasurable distance by repeated snaps of his fingers, adding that nobody knew, but he thought that it went to the end of the world. From the village of Sukuma, to the east of Observatory Hill, Ukéréwé is reached by six hours' paddling due north, which would make the arm of the lake about fifteen miles broad. On his way back Speke shot two red geese and a florikan, a great boon to poor Mansur, who, having been fleeced of all his worldly goods by the Sultan of Ukéréwé, had been living for nine months on jowari porridge, the food of slaves, accorded him by the charity of Mahaya. As Speke's train was coming through Muanza, one of his Beluch soldiers was taken for him, as, being sick, the man rode his donkey. The subject of the ovation took it with great composure, but from his not wearing "double eyes" he was less fêted than Speke would have been under similar circumstances. Speke was generally taken for an Arab merchant during this journey, from the dress he wore by the advice of his friends, though his suite would sometimes betray him by singing the song of "the White Man" (Mzungu).

Sultan Mahaya now sent a messenger to say that he was offended by being passed by the day before, and forbade his subjects to supply provisions. Presents, however, and an apology, followed by a visit from Speke in person, made matters right. The palace was a rural-looking place, shrouded in trees, perched on a small rocky promontory facing the north-west side of the lake. The reception was most courteous. Mahaya was a man of about fifty years old, of great stature, with massive but symmetrical limbs. His dress was the usual *barsati;* his arms were set off by heavy brass and copper bracelets, and by numerous thin circles made of twisted fibres of the aloe, on each of which was strung a white porcelain bead resembling a bit of tobacco-pipe, ranging down the whole of his upper arm, while his elbows were decorated with a pair of huge ivory rings. On his forehead were fastened two small horns by thin ornaments of thong, which were charms against the evil eye; and he wore a necklace of two strings of coarse blue beads. He was said to be the justest and kindest chief in these parts, and his countenance in conversation sustained this character, though another impression might have been conveyed by the dark, broad, massive face, still more darkened by a matting of close, short, and crisped ringlets. He said he was of Wahinda extraction, or from the princes of the Wahuma, but his features led Speke to doubt this. In deference to his advice and that of Mansur, Speke gave up an intended visit to Ukéréwé and Mazita, but was able to collect certain information from some notables that Mahaya assembled. Mahaya's pretty little wife, a woman from Unyoro, had come from farther north than any one else present, and knew about many places in the district of Uganda. She, like Speke's former informant, had never heard of the lake having an end. Canoes never went right across it, though the Waganda once tried to send boats for salt along the shore to the Lake Ngo, at its north-eastern corner.

From various geographical considerations Speke now felt quite sure that the Victoria Nyanza must be the head of the Nile. The reasons why the expeditions sent up the Nile had failed to discover it, was doubtless the existence of important rapids, consequent on the variation of altitude between the north end of the Nyanza near the equator, and the farthest limit of the expeditions at 4° 44' north latitude, the rise of the river being 2000 feet in 300 miles. The two districts about the Palace of Uganda and Gondokoro on the Nile might be described as two landings, the falls between them representing a staircase, and the whole country between latitudes 2° and 5° north might be compared to the terraces of a hanging garden. The Nyanza is now known as a great sheet of water, flush with the basial surface of the country, with the Mountains of the Moon on its western side, and, according to Dr Krapf, the snowy Kenia on its eastern flank. Krapf tells of a large river flowing from this snowy peak in a north-westerly direction, which would lead right into Speke's lake. As the streams from the Moon Mountains enter the lake at the opposite side, these, added to the flow of water from Mount Kenia, must serve to feed it considerably. From its character being rather that of a vast surface-flood than of a lake included by mountains, Speke judged that the Nyanza could not be very deep. The islands, which stood like paps in the water, were exactly similar in character to the hills on his overland journey, so that the adjoining country, if flooded, would wear the same aspect. The water of the lake was sweet and good, though, from the disturbance of the winds, it had a dirty-white colour; but Speke, unlike the natives, found that of the Tanganyika more to his taste. Fish and crocodiles were said to abound in the Nyanza; but only two species of the former were observed—one of perch-like form, like those taken at Ujiji, and the other, unknown to the market there, resembling a minnow. Mosquitoes of a light dun-brown colour covered in swarms the grass and bushes on the shore, and rose in clouds against the hands and face whenever the vegetation was disturbed. The dogs of Muanza, though but twenty inches high, were the largest Speke had seen in Africa; but Mahaya told him that those of Ukéréwé were of a peculiar breed, and very fine indeed. The only canoes he saw were fit for nothing but fishing close to the shore. The want of building materials might account for the small size of the boats. The only tree of any girth on the route from Kazé was the calabash, whose wood is too soft for boat-building. Ukéréwé was said to be very fertile and populous, having two sultans besides the notorious Machunda. All the tribes, according to Mahaya, from the Northern Wanyamuézi, along the south and east of the lake, were so inhospitable that it would be impossible to visit them without a large and expensive escort.

Having gained all the information he could, Speke bade adieu to Mahaya and Mansur, and then, with great regret, retraced his steps, being tied to time, and having no resources to prosecute the journey farther north. The fauna of the country disappointed him: he had been led to expect to see more wild animals; but as he travelled by a fertile and populous track, this may have accounted for their scarcity. The elephants were remarkably fine, and known to carry tusks of more than 500 lb. the pair in weight. Besides these there were lions, leopards, hyenas, foxes, pigs, Cape buffaloes, gnu, kudu, hartebeest, pallah, steinboc, and the little Saltiana gazelles. The chief game-birds were the bustard, florikan, guinea-fowl,

CHARACTER OF THE NATIVES.

partridge, quail, snipe, various geese and ducks, and a very dark-coloured rock-pigeon or sand-grouse. The birds were scarce, and generally of sober plumage. In these agricultural districts the traveller is generally better received than among the pastoral Somali, Gallas, Masai, &c. The people hail his coming as a good omen, and allow him to see and do what he likes. They appreciate commercial relations, and are not suspicious like the nomads. The Somali, who were about the worst specimens of the pastorals, as Speke had experienced on his first expedition, would never admit a traveller unless accompanied by a man of their own tribe, and even then watched him with the eyes of Argus. Not that the agricultural tribes were models of perfection; individually they were very bad, but the chiefs had the sense to see that it was their interest to keep the people in order. Speke always found the lighter-coloured tribes, such as the Wazaramo and Wagogo, more troublesome and pugnacious than those of a dingier hue. He took his farewell view of the Nyanza on the 9th of August from the point where he had first sighted it. The exhilaration of his escort, who now stepped out cheerily, knowing they were going home, atoned in a measure for his own feelings of chagrin. Not only the Beluches, who, except just at first, had behaved well throughout, but even the sullen pagazis, seemed transformed.

They now left behind the Wasukuma, or Northerners, whose articulation was peculiarly disagreeable, and produced an effect like that of spitting at an offensive object, as every word seemed to begin with a T'hu or a T'ha. About the country of Néra the women were very imperfectly clad, the younger ones satisfying themselves with a string of aloe fibres round the waist, with white beads at the end, which soon, from wear and butter rubbed in, get to look like India-rubber. Whenever they ran, the waving motion of the appendage suggested the fly-puzzlers attached to horses' head-stalls. A few of them wore no costume but a bunch of leafy twigs. Some of the neighbouring tribes went more naked still, and held all wearers of clothes in contempt. The Watuta and these tribes Speke seemed to consider as of common origin with the Zulu Kafirs and the Masai, having migrated originally from the shores of the Caspian across the Red Sea to Abyssinia; while the Wahuma or Watusi were a branch of the same stock less mixed with the negro, and retaining a purer type. Several of the princes of the equatorial regions appear to be of this last family.

On the further march Bombay had the misfortune to break Captain Burton's elephant-gun, as he was pitched off a donkey which Speke had lent him to ride. This was the more annoying to his master, as it reminded him of a misadventure with another gun of Burton's when he was hippopotamus-shooting on the Tanga river. On that occasion he had made the hippopotami very savage by firing at them when the tide had run out, and only some pools and reaches were left them to develop their energies in. A large female glided under water to the stern of the canoe, and gave it such a lusty cant with her head or withers that the end of the boat shot up into the air, and sent Speke sprawling on his back, with his legs forced up by the seat, while the polesman and the big double gun were driven like shuttlecocks right and left into the air. The gun plumped into the middle of the stream, while the man lighted stern foremost on the back of the excited pachyderm, but soon scrambled back into the canoe. The she-hippopotamus charged again, but was quieted by the reserve gun. Captain Burton's unlucky elephant-gun lay on the sandy bottom all night, but was fished up by divers in the morning. Many other anecdotes of hippopotamus-hunting were told to Bombay to beguile the way, and he told his stories in return. He was very inquisitive as to the origin of the Seedis, the caste to which he belonged; and he told Speke what he had heard from his master, when he was made a Mussulman, to account for their degradation. "Mahomet, whilst travelling from Mecca to Medina, one day happened to see a widow woman sitting before her house, and asked her how she and her three sons were, upon which she was troubled, for she had hidden one of them, lest Mahomet, as is customary when there are three males of a family present, should seize him to do porterage. 'Very well,' she said; 'but I have only two sons.' To which Mahomet replied, 'Woman, thou liest; thou hast three sons, and for trying to conceal it, this is my decree: The two boys thou hast not hidden shall increase and multiply, have fair faces, and rule over the earth; but the progeny of the third shall be Seedis as black as darkness, who will be sold in the market like cattle, and remain in perpetual bondage to the descendants of the other two.'"

As they returned to their old quarters in the village of Salawé, the people being in their cups were unusually troublesome, and Speke had to send his boots at the head of an old fellow who wanted to pull his pillow from under him. They saw some large game again in repassing the Nindo Wilderness, but none were killed. Though many men and women wore ostrich-feathers, and skulls and skins were seen in every house, these were said to have been obtained where the animals had died a natural death. On comparing this part of his journey with that from the east coast and to the north, Speke remarks that the sickliness which prevailed in the

expedition during the first eight months was perfectly
unaccountable to him, as all physical conditions appeared
favourable. On the journey to the north he complained
of sleeplessness, which he thinks was partly induced
by his anxiety to take the altitude of the stars as the
clouds swept over them, yet without a corresponding
fatigue or drowsiness in the day. On the return journey
he enjoyed cooler nights and perfect rest.

Having got to Kanoni's again, they were warmly welcomed, Bombay and the Beluches undergoing a total
eclipse in the embraces of dusky damsels. Then Kanoni
asked Speke to let the Beluches fire their guns to adver-
tise his elder brother of the honour done him; and after
that there was a sham fight, with immense brandishing of spears and shields, and pointing of arrows, and
throwing about of sticks and stones, and advancing and
retreating, until the whole foreground swarmed with
moving and hopping objects, like a legion of frogs making
for a pond after the first burst of rain. The one principle
in the tactics of these people appears to be perpetual
motion. The butcher's bill was, to all appearance, most
portentous. The slayers made believe to kneel on the slain,
to hack and hew them, and worry them with the malice of
ferocious dogs. After this Kanoni gave a spread of sour
curd. He was a dark, square, heavily-built man, very
much given to pombé, and overflowing with kindness
—when full. Speke tried hard, with little success, to get
geographical information out of him and others. Reflec-
tion is a torture to the weak brains of negroes, and after
a little questioning they become rambling and evasive.
Bombay, however, was an honourable exception, and delighted in passing examinations. At Kurua's the field-
day was repeated, the Beluches acting the enemy. The
forces, though not numerous, were gay : some were decked

with cock-tail plumes, others with bunches of feathers from a guinea-fowl shot by Speke, which, in consequence of some superstition, pretended or real, could only come into the village in a plucked state; while chiefs and nobles were clad in long baize mantles. Their spears and bows were of the usual kind, and the shield, something like a Kafir's, was made from a long strip of bull-hide painted with ochre. When the conflict was over, all hands rushed to the big drums in the cow-yard, and set to work drubbing them as if they had deserved it. This set every one on wires in a moment, and dancing was kept up till the sun went down, and cows usurped the ball-room.

On the road to Kanoni's and Kurua's great trouble was taken by the kirangozi to lead the caravan out of the path of the elder brother. This Speke surmised to have been unnecessary, as he would have been equally glad to see him with the others; and Bombay thought that Kurua's excessive civility was prompted by his wish to seem in the right by being countenanced by Speke. It has been mentioned before that he had a great desire to get gunpowder. Some time back the elder brother had made a tool of an Arab merchant, on the strength of whose friendship he threatened his two juniors with extermination unless they resigned to him the whole government as his birthright. As the drinking of pombé seemed to be the great business of the men in these parts, the brewing of it took up most of the time of the women. It is prepared from bajéri and jowari (common millets). The grain is first malted, then they set a double row of sticks, generally in the middle of the village, fill a number of pots with the malt mixed with water, and place them in a line down the middle of the street of sticks, or in two lines outside it; the sticks are then set on fire, and the wort is boiled till fit to put aside for refining; then the pots are left to stand three days to ferment, and the liquor is ready for use. It has the strength of labourers' beer, but the taste of pig's wash. Being drunk with the dregs it is supposed to be both meat and drink, so that many people live on it entirely. Without it the slave-master could hardly get the labourers to till the ground. While they are working he sits in judgment, generally under a tree, and watches to see who has deserved his pint.

In the evening Speke's attention was arrested by small processions of men and women, supposed to be possessed of the Phépo or demon, passing up the streets, turning into the different courts, and paying visits to all the houses in turn. They advanced at a slow funereal pace, with starting, mincing, jogging action, some holding up twigs, others balancing open baskets of grain or tools on their heads, with bodies, arms, and heads wagging in harmony to a low, confused, droning, humming chorus. When they came to the sultan's door he rose and joined in their antics. This ceremony is thought to be efficacious in casting out the devils, and prevails also at Zanzibar. The notion, common in Europe, that freaks of nature may result from frights in pregnancy, is improved on here, for it is thought that the wife may be affected by a shock to the husband's feelings. On one occasion, when Speke had shot a doe waterboc, he directed his native huntsman, whose wife was *enceinte* at the time, to dissect the uterus and expose the embryo, but he refused, fearing lest the sight of the kid might give his own unborn progeny the shape of a fawn.

After marching fifty-eight miles in four days, they arrived at their old quarters in Ulikampuri. Speke compares the surface of the high land they went over to the long sweeping waves of the Atlantic Ocean; and where the hills were fewest and in lines, they reminded him of small breakers curling on the tops of the rollers, their irregularities being represented by those of waves disturbed by puffs of wind. Where the hills were thick, he thought of the chopping sea in the Bristol Channel. The absence of rivers along this line to the lake proved that the hills were nowhere very high, and in fact they met with no passes that impeded the march. The stone, soil, and general aspect of the tract were uniform. The rock is chiefly granite, the rugged blocks of which lie like knobs of sugar over the surface of the little hills, intermingled with ferruginous sandstone; whilst the soil is made of a light brownish-grey sand of the colour of the stone, plainly resulting from its disintegration. The outcropping hills are all covered with brushwood; and palms on the plains, though few and far between, proved water to be near the surface, while the springs are numerous and evenly distributed. The mean level of the country between Unyanyembé and the lake is 3767 feet, and of the lake itself 3750. The people, as has been seen, are not badly affected to strangers. Their government is a half-patriarchal feudalism, and all stand by their chief for mutual support. The large fields of iron to the south of the lake were supposed by Speke to be continued under the lake itself. Cotton from a perennial tree, different from the Indian variety, abounds; and indigo, the sugar-cane, coffee, tobacco, sesamum, rice, and indeed all tropical products, grow, or might be grown, to judge from the luxuriance of existing species, within 3° of the equator, without fear of the periodical droughts which affect the lands beyond that zone. To the east of the lake ivory is abundant and cheap, and its western regions appear to have many advantages. The

hills of Karagué are high, cool, and healthy, and depastured
by vast droves of large-horned cattle—ivory, fine timber,
and all the necessaries of life being also found there in
abundance.   Of the kingdom of Uganda to the north of
the equator Speke heard a most glowing account.   It
was said to swarm with people, cultivating coffee and all
common grains, with greater flocks and herds than he
had yet seen.   If only by proving the Nyanza to be the
Nile's head he could open up this country to commerce,
what incalculable good he might effect!   Even the coast
people, so miserably harried by slave-hunts, were being
gradually tamed; and envy of the comforts of civilised
men was working, with other influences, to mitigate their
barbarism.   The caravans were penetrating the inner
regions farther every year, and these were reported as in
general remarkably healthy.   At present the staple products from the interior are ivory, hides, and horns; while
the chief exports from the coast countries are the clove,
the gum-copal, textile materials from the banana, and
oleaginous plants, such as the ground-nut and cocoa-nut.
A species of palm growing on the borders of the Tanganyika Lake yields a concrete oil similar to, if not the
same as, the palm-oil of Western Africa, but its limited
quantity deducts from its commercial value.   The same
cause which Dr Livingstone describes as operating on
the western side of Africa has prevented these regions
from sooner becoming known—viz., the jealousy of the
coast people, who wish to keep in their hands the mono-
poly of the ivory trade.   These shortsighted churls would
double or treble their receipts if they could be persuaded
to adopt a more liberal course.

By way of acknowledging his great obligations to the missionaries for the valuable aid they had given him, Speke
wished to point out, from information and experience

gained during this and his final journey, as the most favourable countries for missionary enterprise, the kingdoms of Karagué, Uganda, and Unyoro. With magnificent natural conditions, these regions, being ruled by kings of the Abyssinian type, might even retain a latent germ of Christianity. He found these princes, on later personal acquaintance, extremely intelligent, and desirous of giving their children a good education. At first they objected to his passing through their territories to the Nile, but gave way on his promising to do his best to open a communication with Europe by its channel. To do this it would be necessary to put the trade of the White Nile, which had fallen into bad hands, on a more legitimate footing. Speke considered that the kingdoms of Karagué, Uganda, and Unyoro were only average specimens of a general region of fertility, in all probability stretching from east to west across the African continent, and corresponding to the zone of perennial rains. In a westerly direction he assumed that this zone gave birth to the head-waters of the Zambesi, as to the Nile and Tanganyika Lake on the east, as well as, farther west still, to the Chadda branch of the Niger and the Gaboon river. The most important exploring expedition which could be undertaken would be one intended to cross Africa from east to west, close to the first degree of north latitude, to ascertain the geognosy of that parallel. Within the coast-ranges the temperature is always moderate, from the elevation of the table-land; and the climate has been ascertained to be much more healthy than that of tropical countries subject to periodical seasons. The fertile zone might also be attacked from Gondokoro on the Nile, or from the French port of Gaboon on the equator. The former line is already partially explored and ready for working, only requiring protection from the Egyptian Government; the latter would require to be first inspected by a scientific expedition.

This most satisfactory excursion to the Victoria Nyanza was concluded on the 25th of August 1858, when, under the pleasant influences of a cool night and full moon, the caravan returned to Kazé. The whole population came out to meet them, and conducted them in triumph to their quarters. Burton greeted Speke on arrival at his former dwelling, and said that, in consequence of the rumours of war, considerable apprehension had been entertained as to his safety. His geography he accepted with qualifications, still maintaining that *his* Mountains of the Moon must sever the great lake from the Nile. All returned in high spirits, delighted with the climate, the country, the sultans, and the good cheer. The Beluches had proved an efficient and trustworthy guard, and Bombay had earned golden opinions from every one. The lake had been reached in sixteen marches, though by a zigzag route, which corresponded with the computations of the Arabs; and the supplies for six weeks had just held out. The total to-and-fro distance performed was 452 miles. Though the temperature was at this time at its highest, still the register showed, during the first seven days of September 1858, that the climate of the Unyamuézi plateau is by no means unbearably hot.

PART II.

THE VICTORIA LAKE AND THE NILE

PART II.

CHAPTER I.

FROM ZANZIBAR TO KAZÉ.

CAPTAIN SPEKE AND SIR R. MURCHISON—PLANS FOR ANOTHER EXPEDITION—PREPARATIONS AT ZANZIBAR—MARCH THROUGH UZARAMO—USAGARA AND UGOGO, WITH NOTICES OF THE PEOPLE OF THOSE COUNTRIES — SPORTING — ADVENTURES WITH BUFFALOES — THE WILDERNESS—ARRIVAL IN UNYAMUÉZI—NATURAL HISTORY.

THE years 1857 and 1858, while attention at home was engrossed with the Indian mutiny and its suppression, were quietly adding two glorious pages to the annals of African discovery. In the early spring of the latter year Captains Burton and Speke discovered the Tanganyika Lake; in the middle of the summer Speke alone, while his companion was recruiting his health at Kazé, discovered the Victoria Nyanza. That famous lake is entirely his own, and will be associated with his memory to the end of time. There is no doubt that it is one of the chief sources of the Nile, and the one which in all probability contributes most to its bulk; whether it is the source most remote from the mouth of the mighty river, is a problem which science has yet to solve. From want of time and means, Speke had not as yet been able to verify the connection of his lake with the Nile, but he was naturally most anxious to do so at the first opportunity. In May 1859 he was in London, showing his map to Sir Roderick Murchison, the President of the Geographical Society, who said at once that the Society must send him to Africa again. A grant was obtained from Government of £2500, and the Indian department put at his disposal a supply of arms and ammunition, scientific instruments, and presents for the natives and Arab merchants. Captain Grant, an old friend and brother sportsman of Speke's, hearing that he was bound on the journey, applied to be associated with him, and received his appointment in due form from the Geographical Society. About the same time, Mr Petherick, an ivory merchant, arrived in England, and offered to place boats at Gondokoro on the Nile, sending men up the White River to collect ivory in the meanwhile, in order eventually to assist the expedition in coming down. If possible, he was also to ascertain at the same time if the branch called the Usua river had any connection with Speke's lake.

On the 27th of April 1860, Speke and Grant embarked on board the new steam-frigate Forte, commanded by Captain Turnour, at Portsmouth, and arrived, by way of Madeira and Rio de Janeiro, at the Cape of Good Hope on the 4th of July. Here Sir George Grey, the governor, took up the scheme of the expedition warmly, and gave most valuable assistance. He had himself been wounded by savages in Australia, much as Speke had been among the Somali. Speke recruited here ten volunteers from the Cape Mounted Rifles (Hottentots), and with them and twelve mules, given him by the Cape Government, embarked on board the steam-corvette Brisk, and touching at Delagoa Bay and Mozambique, arrived at Zanzibar on the 15th of August, the Brisk catching a slaver on the way. Speke was welcomed by his old friend Colonel Rigby, the consul, successor of Colonel Hamerton, deceased, who told him all the news of Zanzibar. Dr Roscher, as has been told, had made a successful journey to the Nyinyézi Nyassa, or Star Lake, but had been afterwards murdered in Uhiyow. The Baron von der Decken was organising an expedition to search for the relics of his German country-man, and if possible complete his project.* The interior of the continent had been long in a disturbed state, in conse-quence of feuds between the ivory merchants and the na-tives. Hopes were, however, entertained that peace would shortly be restored. What was most important to Speke was that Colonel Rigby had sent on to Kazé, for his use, thirteen days before, fifty-six loads of cloth and beads.

Speke next called on Sultan Majid, as in duty bound, was received very affably, and promised every assistance that lay in his power. After some delay, during which Speke cruised about the coast, the expedition was formed. Bombay and his adopted brother Mabruki had been among the first to greet Speke on his arrival, and were immediately re-engaged; but his old friends the Beluches, who wished him to take them, had been superseded by the Hottentots. Bombay prevailed on Baraka, Frij, and Rahan—old sailors who, like himself, knew Hindustani— to join. Then thirty-six Wanguana, or freedmen, were en-listed to carry loads, or do any other work, and follow the expedition to Egypt. Each was to receive a year's pay in advance, the remainder when their work was done, and they were to be sent back to Zanzibar. The sultan added

---

* This heroic traveller, after ascending the Kilimandjaro Mountain to a certain distance, and fixing its height at 22,000 feet, ascended the Jub in 1865, with a party of his countrymen and Speke's man Baraka, in two iron steamers. He was murdered, with his friend Dr Link, at Berdera, a town on the Jub, in the Somali country.

thirty-four labourers, taken from his own gardens. A hundred pagazis, or Wanyamuézi porters, were next sought

Said Majid, Sultan of Zanzibar.

for, to carry each a load of cloth, beads, or brass wire as far as Kazé, as they do for the ivory merchants. They hoped to engage fresh relays on the march. The former caravan-captain, or cafila-bashi, Sheikh Said bin Salem, occupied that post again. Carbines were put into the hands of fifty of the Wanguana, who were drilled and formed into companies of ten each, under Baraka as general. The party, including but three or four women, when it started for the interior, was more than two hundred strong,

and might have seemed fit to go anywhere or do anything
in Africa, could the loyalty of the newly-levied guards
and the honesty of the porters have been relied upon.
But a great number of the freedmen and porters turned
out to be cowards and deserters, and this caused most of
the troubles of the march. Even while they were mus-
tering at Ugéni, a place resembling the richest parts of
Bengal, ten of the men given by the sultan ran away on
the first day after receiving their bounty, having been
told that the white men intended to eat them when once
in the interior; and one pagazi, a slave, more honest than
the freedmen, left his pay on the ground and bolted. To
prevent the desertion becoming infectious, Speke determined on an immediate start, and they left Ugéni on the
2d of October 1860. The procession was as follows: The
kirangozi, distinguished by ostrich plumes, led the way
with a load on his shoulder, flag in hand; then came the
pagazis, carrying in their hands spears or bows and arrows,
and bearing their share of the baggage in the shape either
of bolster-shaped loads covered with matting, each tied
into the fork of a three-pronged stick, or coils of wire tied
in even weights to the ends of sticks carried on their
shoulders; then came a mob of Wanguanas with carbines
in their hands, and miscellaneous utensils on their heads;
next the Hottentots, using gentle compulsion to get on
the mules with the ammunition; and, finally, Sheikh Said
and a Beluch escort, who went with them for the first
thirteen stages, followed by the goats, invalids, women,
and stragglers. Some of the Hottentots proved very delicate from first to last, and accordingly rode the hospital
donkeys.

They soon cleared the rich gardens, mango clumps, and
cocoa-nut trees, which characterise the fertile coast-line,
and, through well-wooded grass-fields, arrived at the little

settlement of Bomani, where camp was formed, and everybody put in his place. Sheikh Said, assisted by Bombay, issued the rations of cloth; the Hottentots cooked the dinners, or lay about overcome by fatigue; the Beluches, professing to guard the camp, gossiped or brightened their arms. Some men were told off to watch the grazing cattle; the rest had to pack, pitch tents, cut boughs for huts and fencing the camp—the last an often-neglected duty. Business over, the night was ushered in with an everlasting dance, attended with clapping of hands and jingling of small bells strapped to the legs, to an accompaniment of certain measured articulations, which did duty for a negro melody. As for the occupations of the rest, Rahan, a peppery little blackamoor who had served at the taking of Rangoon, was Speke's valet, and Baraka, who had seen service at Multan, was Grant's; the first of little experience, the latter a highly intelligent fellow, who had been invaluable to Colonel Rigby as a detector of slave-traders. The first duty of Speke himself was to map the country. This was done by timing with a watch the rate of march, taking compass-bearings, and noting the watershed and all other topographical phenomena. Every day he had to find the altitude above the sea-level by boiling a thermometer, the latitude by the meridian altitude of a star taken with a sextant, the compass variation by azimuth. Sometimes certain conical stations, at intervals of sixty miles or so, had to be fixed by lunar observations, or distances of the moon from the sun or given fixed stars, for the determination of the longitude, so that the course could be drawn out with certainty on the map. Moreover, he had to sketch and keep a diary, the most troublesome work of all, and make geological and zoological collections. Captain Grant's work was to make botanical collections, and look to the thermometrical registers and the rain-gauge. He was also to do the photography; but this was soon given up, as considered too severe work for the climate, and he took to sketching in water-colours instead. The march was usually made in the morning, followed by breakfast or early dinner, and between that time and sunset the neighbourhood of the camp was explored.

The 500 miles between the coast and Kazé were accomplished in seventy-one days of actual marching; but stoppages, resulting from the caprices of the men, the difficulties of the country, and the desertions of the porters, made the journey last from October 2, 1860, to the 25th of January 1861. There were all kinds of excuses for halts, the most common being that there was no water ahead; and whenever they arrived at the headquarters of a sultan, an officer would call, demanding perquisites for his master and himself. This business sometimes took days to settle, while the sultan was reported absent, or more often, drunk. They passed through three distinct countries—Uzaramo, Usagara, and Ugogo—before they came to Unyamuézi, or the Land of the Moon, in which Kazé lay. The four countries were divided into provinces, each from twenty to thirty miles across; and each had its despotic ruler, who enforced black-mail from travellers. For twenty marches after leaving the coast the path ran up a broad, flat, dry valley of grass and trees up the course of the river Kingani, which they did not altogether lose sight of till the thirteenth march. This was a white, muddy, sluggish stream about forty or fifty yards across, edged with tall reeds, and so winding that no steamer could have made its sharp turns. Except what they got from this river, their water-supply was somewhat short till they reached Unyamuézi, which was blessed with abundant springs. Notwithstanding the

fineness of the weather and the moderate temperature,
which Grant compares to that of the cold season in the
Punjab, the expedition suffered, as on the last journey,
from acclimatisation fever — the Hottentots to such a
degree that most of them were disabled; while the mules
and donkeys fell sick and died of some incomprehensible
ailment, whose symptoms were those of poisoning. The
terrible tsetse fly, familiar to Dr Livingstone, was not observed here; but it was rather remarkable that within
several marches of the coast the people seemed to keep
no cattle but a few goats. The land of Uzaramo—the
first passed through—stretches from the coast to the bifur-
cation of the Kingani with its upper branch, the Mgéta
river, westwards, and from the former north to the Lufiji
river south. The land in the central line (the route
pursued) consists of slightly elevated terraces, which
in the rainy season are drained by nullahs into the
rivers north and south. It is most agreeable to travel
over in the dry season, when the long luxuriant grass
has been burnt up. The villages are small and widely
spread, generally consisting of ten or twenty conical
grass huts, some few being gabled, as is the fashion on
the coast. The people are agricultural, of low stature,
and thick-set, of a somewhat boisterous disposition.
Being expert slave-hunters as well as farmers, they can
afford, as compared with the people of the interior, to
dress well, making up for the scantiness of their attire by
its quality. They take much care of their hair, and smear
the exposed part of their bodies with ochrish clay. They
are very particular about their bows and arrows, keeping
the latter well poisoned and in curiously-carved quivers.
The caravans shun their society as much as possible, and
generally camp in the jungles beyond the villages, as they
have the character of being desperate thieves. A kind of

albinos was sometimes noticed among them, with greyish-blue eyes and straw-coloured hair. They appeared to be in the habit of burning witches, if the explanation was true which was given of certain small heaps of white ashes, with calcined bones among them, seen at the side of the road. Grant, however, speaks highly of their gallantry towards younger ladies; so that, in the manner they behaved towards their women, they would be neither better nor worse than our own ancestors in the times of chivalry, which for a tribe of polygamists was as much as could reasonably be expected.

Only twelve miles from the coast they had a specimen of the rapacity of the petty chiefs in the large *hongo* or tribute demanded by a man appropriately called Lion's Claw. After a little experience of the natives, the traveller only thinks how he can best avoid dealings with them, and often finds that a roundabout road taken to avoid them is the shortest cut to his journey's end. When the caravan arrived at the ninth stage, where, from a high ridge of pebbles and sandstone, the coast-range was first sighted, eight of the sultan's men ran away, and, what was worse, carried off all the goats, which were sadly wanted as provision for the sick men. Speke tried the plan of putting all the well-behaved of the sultan's men, by emancipating them, on the same footing as the Wanguana, and joining their camps, but they would not readily club together. At the twelfth stage the diggings for gum-copal, common before, were no longer seen, the Dum palm was left behind, the large rich green-leaved trees of the plateau gave way to the mimosa; and now they passed up the gentle slope of the Kingani, no longer confined to its own bank, to an open park-land, a paradise of sport, where antelopes roamed at large, buffaloes and zebras were sometimes seen, and guinea-fowl abounded. The discordant noises of the caravan scared the animals, and it was not possible to follow them far without stopping the march. They next entered the richest part of Uzaramo, where the first expedition to this country came to a tragical end, through the murder of the French traveller, M. Maizan, by a sub-chief named Hembé, at the instigation of the ivory-traders. This miscreant had not been punished when Speke arrived; he talked over the matter in a friendly way, and exacted the usual tribute. They now came to a little hill near the frontier, which cropped out through pisolitic limestone, in which marine fossils were seen. This formation might possibly extend here from the Somali country, as Speke had seen the same shells there. He remarks that a vast band of limestone is known to stretch from the Tagus, through Egypt and the Somali country, as far as the Burrumputra.

The march now, swerving a little from the Kingani, led through rolling, jungly ground, full of game, to the tributary stream Mgéta. This branch rises in the Usagara hills, to the west of the hog-backed Mhambaku mountain. The source of the Kingani Speke was not able to ascertain, but heard that it rose in a gurgling spring on the eastern face of the same mountain, which, if true, would make the Mgéta the longer of the two branches. Usagara is a mountain district a hundred miles across, forming a link of the great East Coast Range, bounded on the north by the Mukondokua, or upper Wami river, and on the south by the Ruaha, or great northern branch of the Lufiji river. The ground they marched over had imperceptibly reached an elevation of 500 feet. From this level the range rose before them in some places to 5000 or 6000 feet, in two detached lines, separated one from the other by elevated valleys, table-lands, and crab-claw-

like spurs of hill inclining towards the flanking rivers.
The whole reposes on a strong foundation of granite and
other igneous rocks, exposed in many places in massive
blocks, otherwise the hill-range is overlaid in the upper
part with sandstone, and in the bottoms with alluvial
clay.   On the further or western flank of the hills the
elevation of the interior plateau is 2500 feet—about half
as high as the hills themselves from the seaward plains.
The tops and sides, when not cultivated, are covered with

Bugu, Calabash, or Gouty-limbed Trees.

bush and bamboos; whilst the loamy bottoms produce
large and beautiful fig-trees, the huge calabash, and various other trees, and are beautified by flowers, especially
the lilac convolvulus.

This country, so blessed by nature, is cursed by the

devastations of man. The wretched inhabitants, hunted down for slaves, only feel tolerably secure when living in villages perched like eyries on almost inaccessible steeps. In occupation they are partly herdsmen, partly farmers; but from the reign of terror that prevails, they are a half-starved, timid, and distrustful race, slow to make acquaintance with the passing caravan. This is an advantage to travellers, in so far that the road through the country is exempt from tolls, but a manifest disadvantage as regards the commissariat. Before entering on the hills, however, Speke made an excellent bag in the natural park at the fork of the rivers, killing two brindled gnu, four water-boc, one pallah-boc, and a pig, which gave the whole camp a feast of flesh. While in these parts, Captain Grant was seized with the same sort of intermittent fever that Speke caught on his former

Mhambaku Hill, viewed from Zungomero.

journey. Speke's had lasted a year, but Grant's kept recurring, at intervals of a fortnight, till the journey ended. They now followed the Mgazi branch of the Mgéta, tra-

versed large tree-jungles, in which the tall palm was conspicuous, and encamped under the end of the lumpy
Mhambaku; then crossing the Mgazi, got to Zungoméro,
which lies on flat ground bisected by the Mgéta, in the
midst of a beautiful amphitheatre of mountains. It is a
naturally fertile spot, which has been demoralised and
depopulated by the slave-trade. Whilst the expedition
were there, a large party of Wasuahili (coast men) marched
past, with a hundred head of cattle, fifty goats, and as
many slaves in chains.

Zungoméro is the point of junction of two roads which
again unite at Ugogi, the western terminus of the great
Unyamuézi travelling line. One goes over the Goma
Pass to the Mukondokua; the other takes the Mabruki
Pass, and passes by the Ruaha river. On the former expedition Speke had gone by the northern and returned
by the southern road, and did not find much to choose
between them. The routes in these countries, like those
over the surface of Swiss glaciers, are for ever changing
their directions. The seasons make differences as to the
supplies of water and provisions, and from wars and slave-
hunts the locations of the people are continually shifted.
As the whole country ahead, especially Ugogo, was said
to be oppressed by drought and famine, Speke decided on
the southern route, hoping to follow up the Ruaha river
to Usénga and Usanga, and strike across to Unyanyembé,
sweeping clear of Ugogo. After stopping to send home
a large collection of specimens, they now turned south,
penetrating the forests between the greater and the lesser
outlying line of hills. At the foot of this is a deeply-
seated hot spring, which bubbles up through many open-
ings in a large dome-shaped heap of soft lime, obviously
thrown up by the force of the spring itself. After sur-
mounting the first well-wooded spurs, they got to the outer

settlements of a place called Mbuiga, and saw there a
curious blue mountain, standing up like a giant overlooking all the rest of the hills.

Hill view from Eastern Mbuiga.

This was a more striking landscape than any they had
seen since they had left the coast. Some emigrant fugitives had disposed their conical villages so picturesquely
about the heights, that it was to be hoped that the poor
people might at length be suffered to remain here in
peace. Having had an opportunity of lightening the
expedition, by sending back some of the sick Hottentots,
they now breasted the steep ascent of the Mabruki Pass,
which they surmounted without much difficulty. The
first range of hills was now passed, and they dropped into
the elevated valley of Makata. In consequence of information as to the land in front having been laid waste,
they changed their route again to a middle and new

line. Here the first and only giraffe killed on the journey was shot by Grant. Though the abundance of game tempted delay, fearing to waste time, they crossed the flats of Makata, and ascended the higher lands beyond, where they met the last down trader from Unyamuézi, generally known to the men by the name of Mamba or the Crocodile. This man, dressed in a dirty Arab gown, with a coronet of lion's nails decorating a threadbare Cutch cap, greeted them with great dignity. Having been the last trader to leave Unyamuézi, he had bought his ivory cheap, but had suffered many hardships in consequence of staying so late. He and his large party had been obliged to live on the road on the products of the jungle, and by occasionally boiling down the skin aprons of the porters for soup. Fearing he should never get through by the route this man had travelled, Speke determined now to take a more northerly route to Ugogi.

After reaching the high ground, they marched over rolling tops, covered with small trees and pretty bulbous plants, to a village where, with great trouble and expense, they got some provisions from the shy inhabitants, and proceeded to the upper courses of the Myombo river, which flows northwards into the Mukondokua. The scenery was most interesting, wild, and well wooded, with every variety of hill, roll, plateau, and ravine; but as soon as the advance of the caravan was heard, all the people vanished into the jungles, running off with their grain like scared rats. A few arrow-shots were all that foraging parties got for their pains. They now came to a great lagoon swarming with snorting hippopotami, about which the tracks of all the other large game were seen. A halt of three days was made to buy corn at New Mbumi, a pretty spot lying at the foot of a cluster of steep hills, as this was said to be the last place

I

where they would be able to get any till they reached
Ugogo. The road next led over a height into the valley
of the Mdunhwi, another tributary of the Mukondokua,
and over a similar height into that of the Chongué, the
country reminding Speke of the middle heights of the
Himalayas. The table-land of Manyovi was next reached,
overhung with much higher hills, which the Hottentots
thought like the range of Kaffraria, and, from the herds
that covered the slopes, fancied themselves in the land of
promise. In this they were soon disappointed, for a kind
of desert of rolling plateaux as barren as the Somali country was next entered, a solitary village being seen, built in
flat-topped mud huts, which the natives call tembé. On
the right were the massive mountains overhanging the
Mukondokua, in front the western chain, and to the left
the high crab-claw-shaped ridge, which, running out from
the western chain, embraces the swelling knolls which lie
between the two main ridges. In this stony country
the plants which thrive best are twisted green thorn-trees,
" elephant-foot " stumps, and aloes.

They were now getting on fast by forced marches, much
to the satisfaction of Speke, as there were no chiefs to detain them, and loitering always demoralised the camp. At
last the party arrived at the foot of the western chain, but
not all together. Some of the porters lay scattered along the
road, knocked up with heat and thirst, while the corporal of
the Hottentots got lost in the bush, in a chase after a mule
that had strayed. Knowing that the hungry savages were
out living like monkeys on what they could pick from the
trees, Speke ordered twenty armed men to carry back water
to the straggling porters, and bring home the corporal. In
the evening they returned, firing their guns in triumph,
and highly satisfied with their performances. They had
not only rescued the corporal, but brought back two men

and two women prisoners, with a spear that had been thrown at them, as a trophy. Speke at first thought of keeping the prisoners as hostages for the missing mule; but as soon as it was ascertained that the beast had strayed quite away of itself, he released them, very much to their disgust, as the poor creatures had hardly ever known such good living, which was to be accounted for from the fact that Grant, in one pot-hunting excursion, bagged a striped eland, a Saltiana antelope, four guinea-fowl, four ring-doves, and a partridge, and that previous to their arrest they had been starving on calabash-seeds.

Speke now directed Grant to get on with the mules and heavy baggage over the Robého (or windy) Pass, while he remained to bring up the rear-guard of tired men. It was a stiff ascent, covered with trees and granite blocks, except where cleared for villages. He found the van of the party at one of these on the crest of the pass commanding the interior plateau, which was a fair sample of African scenery, and they all went together down the last slope of the hills of Usagara. They now marched over the plain, across fields diversified with fine calabash and fig trees, stopping only to bivouac at night, and carrying water through the thorny jungles. The ground they passed over was a rolling plateau, sloping southward to the Ruaha river, which runs from west to east, and carries to the sea its portion of the rainfall of the East Coast Range. To the northward could be seen some low hills, occupied by the Wahumba, a sub-tribe of the warlike Masai; and in their westward track lay the great forest-wilderness of Mgunda Mkhali. They finished all their Mbumi corn just before entering Ugogo. This was a comparatively barren land. Small outcrops of granite broke the surface here and there, which, like the rest of the rolling land, being covered with trees, principally acacias, look well enough in the rainy season, but have a brown and arid appearance for the rest of the year. In many places large grass-prairies were seen, as well as agricultural clearings. The people looked as wild as the land. More like the Wazaramo than the Wasagara, they carried arms for use as well as for show. The men are never seen without the spear, the shield, and the assagé, or at least a club. Wherever springs of water are found they build their flat-topped villages, and keep cattle enough to supply not only themselves, but passing caravans. Their costume principally consists of ornaments, the most striking of which is an uncouth plug of gourd thrust through the lobe of the ear. Their wool is bound by hanks of fibre into straight tresses, which fly in the air as they run. These are sometimes strung with beads, or decorated with an ostrich-feather. Their general disreputable appearance is increased by their being followed by bandy-legged curs, resembling the bull-terriers kept by London "roughs" for their Sunday amusements. The Ugogo dogs are probably more useful, as the natives appear to fatten them for the table. The colour of this people is a soft ruddy brown, with a dash of black, not unlike that of a ripe plum. They are greedy, impertinent, inquisitive, and intrusive, and, like the Wazaramo, avoided as much as possible by caravans, which prefer encamping under the " gouty-limbed " trees outside the villages, surrounding their bivouacs with a ring of thorns.

They found Ugogo little better off for supplies than Usagara, as the people were hoarding their corn. On one occasion the British officers' mess consisted of two grains of maize, with salt. As for water, the case was as bad as in Touraine in the dry summer of 1865, when water was purchased by its measure in wine, for it cost as much as the beer of the country; and the price of all kinds of meat and poultry would have astonished our own butchers during the cattle plague. On the night of the 27th of November Speke bagged his first rhinoceros. Taking advantage of the moonlight, he went after two more, attended by the sheikh's lads carrying a second rifle. The big beasts approached in a stealthy, fidgety manner, and while they were reconnoitring, he planted a bullet in the larger one, and brought him round with a roar and "whoof-whoof," with his broadside fairly exposed. On looking round for the extra rifle, however, the black boys, who ought to have had it at hand, were seen scrambling up a tree. The rhinoceros, fortunately for Speke, changed his mind, and shuffled away, leaving no traces of blood, as is usually the case when conical bullets are used. On coming back to the one he had killed, he found the men of the camp and the Wagogo engaged about it like so many vultures. It was a scene at once grotesque and disgusting. All were at work with swords, spears, knives, and hatchets, cutting and slashing, thumping and bawling, fighting and tearing, tumbling and wrestling, some of them up to their knees in filth and blood, in the midst of the carcass. Individuals might be seen secreting and scampering away with a piece of tripe, or liver, or lights, like the astuter hounds when the fox is thrown among them by the huntsman. It was fortunate that all this did not end in a battle royal. The flesh of the rhinoceros does not appear to be bad, but to require very strong teeth to chew it.

At Khoko, the last district in Ugogo, the inhabitants turned out in force to oppose them, thinking that they had come to avenge the plunder of the camp of an Arab named Mohinna, who had killed their chief, nicknamed "Short-legs." When matters were explained, however, no difficulty was made with regard to their further progress, and they entered on the outskirts of the wilderness of Mgunda Mkhali. Here Speke killed a two-horned rhinoceros at the distance of five paces only, and a vixen of the species *Otocyon lalandii*, whose cry is supposed by the natives as of evil omen, and indicative of danger. But better sport awaited him. Taking, as before, two of Sheikh Said's cowardly boys to carry his spare guns, he diverged into the wilderness to the westward. Hearing in the bush the grunt of a buffalo close on his left, he took his "Blissett" in hand, and soon came to a place where he saw a large herd quietly feeding. They seemed unconscious of his approach, so he first wounded a cow, and then, after reloading, a bull. The two accidents confused the herd greatly; but as they did not know their origin, they only shifted about in a perplexed and purposeless manner, so that he had time to kill the first cow and fire a fourth shot, which induced the bull to walk off, leaving the herd to their fate, who then followed their leader's example. Leaving the cow and the bull for future attentions, Speke called up the boys and followed, and found the herd again. They were in the same bewilderment as before when fired at, and received many wounds, which, as they were stern shots, and the jungle was too thick to afford a good view, were not likely to be fatal. Presently, however, a cow, with her hind leg broken, pulled up on a white-ant hill, and, tossing her horns, came down charging on Speke as he drew near. She was rolled over in an instant, and then the traces of blood soon allowed him to come up with a second lame bull. He got a second bullet in the flank, and after hobbling a little, threw himself into a thicket. As Speke followed him to the spot, he plunged headlong from his ambush, just giving him time to present his "Lancaster." An absurd scene followed. Suliman, one of the boys who was at Speke's side, with the instinct of a monkey, made a spring and swung himself up into a bough just overhanging the infuriated beast, while Faraj, the other, gave him leg-bail. At this crisis the bullet, grazing the edge of one of his horns, sunk into his spine, and rolled him over like a rabbit at Speke's feet. Having cut the throat, according to Mussulman usage, Speke was going back after the first wounded bull, when they came across Grant, who was highly amused by the narrative of the boys, who told of their own cowardice as a good joke. While he went back to get parties to carry home the game, Speke, following by the traces of blood, found the first bull standing in some bushes, looking as if he wished to be put out of his misery. A bough unluckily stopped the next bullet, and the big bull galloped off. The "spoor," however, being excellent, the sportsman followed him up, and in ten minutes more, as he came to a small clearance, the great brute came charging from the thicket on the opposite side, looking a very ugly customer, with his forehead all shielded with horn. Fortunately, a small mound stood in his way, and as he rounded it Speke jumped to one side and let fly at his flank, but without the effect of stopping him; for, as quick as thought, the monster was at his feet, battling with the impalpable smoke of his gun. It fortunately hung so thick on the ground that he could not see his man, though he was so near that Speke might have felled him with an axe. To his intense relief, as if the smoke was an apparition not to be explained, the bull turned tail and galloped off. In endeavouring to find him again Speke lost himself. Night came on, and he had to sleep on the ground as he best might, being only occasionally disturbed by wild beasts sniffing at his feet. The next morning he struck the right track, and walked into camp, having been thrice charged by buffaloes in one day, two of which he had despatched with the dexterity of a matador, while in the case of the third the smoke served the purpose of muffling his adversary quite as well as the Spaniard's cloak. The buffalo was regarded by Gordon Cumming as the most formidable of all his antagonists among the wild beasts.

In this part of the country there was infinite trouble with the Wanyamuézi porters, who, frightened by the bullyings of the Wagogo chiefs, kept deserting in squads till half of them had run away. More were lost in the confusion of the march through a country which, the rains having now set in, was in a state of flood; and at last they were all brought up by a wide nullah for five days, the men being reduced to live on wild herbs and white ants. The rain ceased on the 17th of December, in consequence, as the natives supposed, of Speke putting out the rain-gauge, and they managed to push on for eight marches through the wilderness in very loose order, Grant and Speke being hard at work shooting for the pot every day. On the 28th they arrived at a landmark called the "Boss," a huge granite block, from the top of which the green foliage of the forest-trees looked like a soft, waving, interminable cloud. Some more men here deserted, as they knew that they were only a day's march from food; but, on the other hand, some of the old deserters returned, saying that help, which had been sent for, was coming from Kazé. They rested at last from the desert march on New Year's Day 1861, at Jiwa la Mkoa, or the Round Rock, a village inhabited by Wakimbu emigrants, who had taken refuge from the pastoral Warori. There was a halt of a week at this place for want of porters. On the 7th an alarm was given that one Manua Séra (the Tippler), with whom the Arabs were at war, meant to attack the camp with thirty musketeers; and this was, in fact, the truth. When the "Tippler" came,

however, the sight of Speke's men, with their sword-
bayonets fixed, drawn up in battle array, made him re-
consider the case, and he came to pay a friendly visit
instead. Speke says he was as fine a young man as he
had ever seen, and the very beau-ideal of a captain of
banditti. He complained of having been shamefully
treated by the Arabs, who had deposed him in his brother's
favour only for being a protectionist, so that he was now
a vagabond against his will. He tried hard to bring over
Speke to his side, but only succeeded in obtaining his
promise to mediate with the Arabs on condition that he
would return to the free-trade principles of his father.
They got on at last by the return from Kazé of Bombay,
who had been sent forward with seventy slaves to act as
porters. He brought letters from Snay and Musa, begging
Speke, if he met Manua Séra, to put a bullet through his
head, or at least bring him on in chains, as the scoundrel
had spoiled all their trade.

On arrival at Mgongo Thembo, the "Elephant's Back,"
so called from a granite rock of that shape, Speke met an
old chief named Maula, a very honest fellow, who had be-
friended him on the former expedition. He was now a
fugitive and in a sad plight, the Arabs having deposed and
ruined him for harbouring Manua Séra, though, from the
power of that chief, he could not help it. Speke promised
him his protection to Kazé; but he declined it on account
of his age, and said he would send his son instead. He was
afterwards treacherously put to death by the Arabs. They
now held their course till they emerged from the wilderness
on the open district of Tura, or "put down," so called because it was the first place cleared some years ago. The
country here ought to have been prosperous from its fertility, but it had been reduced to waste and misery by those
human locusts, the slave-hunters. On arriving at Eastern

Unyanyembé, within five miles of Kazé, Speke took stock, and made out an account of his losses on the march up to January 23d. They consisted in one Hottentot dead and five returned; one freedman sent back with the Hottentots, and one flogged and expelled; twenty-five of Sultan Majid's gardeners, as well as ninety-eight of the original Wanyamuézi porters, deserted; twelve mules and three asses dead. Besides which, more than half the property had been stolen; and the famine which prevailed had enormously increased the expenses of the march.

To set off against these losses, the gains of the expedition up to this point consisted in a number of scientific observations, and, besides the game killed and consumed on the way, a variety of specimens of natural history sent off in batches at different times to Zanzibar, some of which, however, never reached their destination. The sporting was partly done for its own sake, partly with the object of collecting, and partly as a matter of necessity. The black rhinoceros would rarely charge, even though the sportsman was standing close; but the feints he made caused excitement, as well as his deep hoarse grunt. Grant tells a striking anecdote of the affection, not of the dam for its young, which is common enough with all animals, but of the young one for its mother. He wounded a large female one night, and next day, tracing her spoor for four miles, found her squatting like a hare in its form. He heard a great deal of whining or puling near the spot, which he took to be her dying cries. As he advanced cautiously, he saw the cocked ears of another, a young one, which, after receiving his fire, crashed away through the underwood. Coming to the first, he found her quite dead and cold, so that the plaintive cries must have proceeded from the young one wailing for its mother. The flesh of the beautiful zebra, which, curiously enough,

fraternised on the march with the donkeys and mules of
the camp, was found to taste too strong of stable to make
it pleasant eating. It lost this flavour by being cut
into long strips, sun-dried or jerked, and toasted in
ashes. The meat of the buffalo was as good as any
Christmas beef. The brindled gnu, a much more beautiful beast, was equally good. Only one specimen of the
giraffe, a bull, was shot. They are wary animals, and,
owing to their long necks, can see the sportsman over the
tops of the acacias. The long, stiff, black hairs of the
tail are much valued by the natives for stringing their
bead necklaces, and their thick skins for sandals, which
were much appreciated by the men among the acacia-
thorns. The wearers of them, however, left a strong
scent of menagerie to leeward. Lions were fired at once
during a moonlight march, and were heard day and night
making short coughing noises, but never roaring in proper style. Whenever they are trapped, they are the perquisite of the sultan. In Ugogo the tracks of the elephant
were frequent. They came across a party of elephant-
hunters there, Makua from the Lufiji, who were armed
with long "Tower" flint-muskets, looking as good as
new. Their system was to lie in wait for the elephant
at night by solitary pools, and fire a volley into him,
considering that the best place to hit him was in front of
the orifice of the ear. Eland, hartbeest, black antelope,
and several smaller species were shot or observed. The
saltatrix, with its startled bark and spring, reminded
them of the *goorul* or chamois of the Himalayas. They
cling to the rocks by the fore-feet, which are extremely
long in the heel. The hirax or coney, about three times
the size of a hare, was seen basking on the rocks; and
the hare of the country, seldom seen, more resembled the
English rabbit.

They seldom met with lungoor or monkeys; the latter are hunted for their skins with the pariah dog in Uzaramo, but the natives do not eat them. The squirrels were much like the European variety, and had a longitudinal white stripe running down either side. There were also weasels, brown ferrets, small foxes with black muzzles, and red foxes of the size of the jackal, white-chested, with elegant dark brush, and barking like dogs. The hyenas were as wretched-looking as usual. Only one, a specimen of the *Crocuta*, was shot, which the men, unlike Indian servants, had no objection to carry into the camp for dissection. The wild boar, with his long narrow head, with four warty protuberances, and face as broad between the tusks as between the eyes, is about the most ill-favoured of the beasts; but he has a fine mane, and a herd in full flight, with erect heads and tails, brings to mind a race of Arab horses. A tiger-coloured crocodile was seen near the Kingani, where the spoor of hippopotamus occurred. There were few chameleons or serpents; but they saw a puff-adder $2\frac{1}{2}$ feet long, with abrupt tail and four fangs. Amongst the many lizards was one 12 inches long, with vermilion head and shoulders and bright blue body. Grant had to pay twelve cloths for shooting two of these on some rocks, as he was told that the spot was holy. They were seldom troubled by rats, bugs, or mosquitoes, but during rain frogs and crickets made sleep difficult; and at night white ants and other insects were attracted in swarms to the candle. They observed small yellow butterflies, apple-green underneath, fluttering in suspense over the edge of little puddles. Excepting a lark on the coast, which had a short sweet note, there were few song-birds. Of game-birds, the guinea-fowl was the commonest. They killed one rare species, red round the eyes and on the throat, having a standing-up purple

collar of loose skin, a ridge of ostrich-like black feathers
from the occiput to the nostrils, of the weight of the
ordinary kind, about 3 lb., but of a more compressed body
in running. The best flavoured bird was the florikan;
it has a rough gritty call, and is very shy. The green
pigeons were handsome in their feathers, as well as on
the table after they had grown plump on wild figs. They
sometimes shot rock-pigeons, snipe, quail, plover, and
several kinds of partridge, also a very pretty pin-tailed
dove in Ugogo, where pigeons, frequently white like those
in Europe, were often kept by the villagers. Only one
gang of ostriches was seen in Ugogo, where their plumes
are made into showy wreaths. Other birds observed
were crested cranes, hawks, a raven or two, a few parrots,
and possibly a crow. All such beasts and birds are taken
with pitfalls or nooses by the natives. The former are
cut like a wedge, eight feet deep, and but one across the
top, which is daintily covered over. The nooses are hung
from an elastic bough, and neatly concealed in a frequented track. Small birds are caught in traps, and
soaring birds with horizontal nooses. Fish and fishing
seem to be rare in this country. By the sea, women
were seen standing in a circle using cloths as nets, and
some stake-nets were also seen; and in the interior they
came on a party who had caught with hand-nets some
slimy-looking fish, probably makumbara, and slung them
by their heads to a cord round their waists, after the
fashion of a kilt.

CHAPTER II.

FROM KAZÉ TO KARAGUÉ.

UNYAMUÉZI AND ITS PEOPLE—THE MARCH TO UKUNI—DIFFICULTIES
AND DELAYS—THE SULTAN UKULIMA—SPEKE IN ADVANCE—GRANT'S
CAMP PLUNDERED BY MYONGA—ROBBER CHIEFS—ARRIVAL IN USUI
—SUWARORA'S PALACE—NATURAL HISTORY AND TOPOGRAPHY—
THE WATUTA—INTERVIEW WITH A WATUSI QUEEN—THEY LEAVE
UZINZA.

THEY were now in Unyanyembé, a central province of
Unyamuézi, or the Country of the Moon. Little inferior
in size to England, and something resembling it in shape,
this country was once a kingdom, but is now cut up into
a number of little states. It is divided into Usukuma
and Utakama—that is to say, the north and south country. The first accounts of this land came from Hindu
traders, who may have had dealings with it even before
the birth of Christ; and at that early date the Mountains
of the Moon sprang into existence in connection with the
name of this people, who have always been an active and
commercial race, travelling to the coast with the same
zest with which our country-folk go to a fair. The whole
of their land ranges from 3000 to 4000 feet above the
sea-level, being a high plateau studded with outcropping
hills of granite, between which, in the valleys, are numerous fertilising springs of fresh water, while the sandstones

are rich in iron ore, to the possession of which the industrial habits of the people are doubtless to be ascribed. Besides being cunning workers in iron, they are also weavers, agriculturists, and herdsmen. In appearance they are darker than the Wazaramo or Wagogo, though many of the men are handsome, and the women pretty. The former, though they walk about with bows and arrows, to judge from the porters who went with the expedition, seem to be more deficient in spirit than the tribes about them. They were found cheerful and amusing by the British officers; but familiarity with them soon bred contempt, and it was necessary to keep them at a proper distance. In sporting they were invaluable as trackers, and never at a loss for expedients. For instance, they would make a pipe by putting a grit of clay an inch or two into the end of a tube of bark; but they generally preferred using "Duncan's smoking mixture" as snuff. Their practical knowledge of botany was a safeguard against their starving under any circumstances. Their dress, or rather undress, consisted in a goat-skin hung in front from the right shoulder, and many of them had marks of caste above their cheek-bones. They wore massive copper or brass rings on their wrists, extracted their lower incisors, and cut an open wedge between their two upper ones. They were all much given to drinking and smoking. The women wore long cloths fastened under their arms, with necklaces of beads, large brass or copper wire armlets, and a number of thin circles, called "sambo," made of the hairs of giraffe-tails bound with fine wire. They were indefatigable smokers as well as the men, and appeared to be quite as manly, plying the flail lustily, and busying themselves with field operations generally. The head wool, dressed with an oily preparation, looked as if they wore a scalp of shining beetles, amongst which were scattered red beads or rings of brass. They cut three lines on each temple, and sometimes one down the forehead to the bridge of the nose; but some of the Watusi females (a superior foreign race) had their shoulders and breast tattooed to resemble point-lace in front, with a cross like a pair of braces behind. Notwithstanding their manliness, they fully appreciated a looking-glass that Grant had brought with him; and they appeared to be affectionate mothers, never selling their children, as is the practice elsewhere, even when starving. The boys were very ingenious little fellows, and played all sorts of games. They could shoot small birds with crossbows, and teach birds to sing—make guns out of cane, going off with a trigger, with a cloud of sand for smoke—copy in mud the double guns of the officers, representing their smoke with cotton; in fact, they seemed capable of being taught anything.

Having arrived at Kazé, in 5° S. lat. and 33° E. long., Speke and Grant were welcomed by the Arabs, and took up their quarters in the house of Musa, one of the merchants. He had round him an establishment of 300 natives, the most esteemed of his servants being of the Wahuma tribe from Karagué. His abode was surrounded by a circular wall, which enclosed the houses, gardens, and stock. All was presided over by a portly duenna, whose word was law. Musa was a man of regular habits; at three in the morning he would call for his little pill of opium, which he had not missed for forty years. This would brighten him up till noon. He then transacted business, and gossiped with any one who would sit with him on his carpet, not even stopping while the Koran was being read to him. The reason perhaps of this was that his domestic chaplain was the same man who made his shirts. After a siesta he would take a larger pill of opium, transact business again, and so end the day. In the harem department there was great activity. At dawn, women in coloured chintz, with neatly plaited hair, gave fresh milk to the swarm of black cats, or churned butter in gourds by rocking it. At noon the whole place was swept clean. Some fed the game-fowls or looked after the ducks and pigeons; two women chained by the neck fetched firewood, or ground corn at a stone; the children ate together, kept in order by a matron. Whenever any of the wives had a child there was convivial rejoicing, and great lamenting when one died. The presence of the white men was utilised to overawe the naughty children. The head-keeper was a great functionary, very civil to the Europeans, and very entertaining with his stories of extraordinary sport. The Watusi cowherds were a very important part of the establishment. There were ten men and women. The men were distinguished by leaving a crescent of their wool unshaven. Their gums were blackened with a preparation of the tamarind-seed. The women had fine oval features, and erect figures clad in well-dressed robes of cow-skin down to their small feet. Their huts were of a novel kind, shaped like the half of an orange, only five feet high, made of boughs, and neatly covered with grass. They have many peculiar customs about the management of cattle; amongst others, if a cow is difficult to control, she is not led by the horn, but driven by a man holding a rope tied to the hock; and in leading a goat the fore-leg is held up, the man trotting along by its side.

The expedition was delayed no less than fifty-one days at Kazé on account of rains and difficulties about porters. The country was surrounded with small bare hills, which every morning were hidden in mist. After a few days' stay many of the party were laid up, and Grant was

severely ill with intermittent fever. The prevalent winds
during their residence were easterly, but after rain the
westerly were the coldest. The days were dark and hazy.
They had no sunsets like the equatorial at sea; but on
certain evenings there was a very fine effect of the setting
sunlight on the flowering grasses, such evenings being
followed by a few dry days, with temperature at 82°.
Two-fifths of the time, on an average, was rainy, the
greatest fall being two inches in twenty-four hours; but
when the rain had cleared off the air was cool and fresh,
not muggy and steaming as in India. This province of
Unyanyembé has four months of rain, from the end of
November to February, when the greatest fall takes place.
When the soil of sand or black spongy mould is softened,
the seed is dropped, and by the 1st of February all is as
green as an emerald. Still for fifteen days the rice has
to struggle against a small black caterpillar, green underneath. Unless rain falls then this insect will eat the
plants to the root. The women work the fields with
hand-picks, and drop the seed in holes made by their
toes. All the cereals of Zanzibar grow here: the cotton,
which is very fine, seems only to be used for making
wicks. Near the village no song-birds were heard, but
many of the birds seen had very brilliant plumage.
Flocks of beautiful little birds, with black bodies, golden-
tinted scarlet heads and backs, pecked at the ears of corn,
and the locust-bird of the Cape walked familiarly about
the rice-fields. Crows with white bands round the neck
were seen in twos or threes. The wars were going on
between Manua Séra and the Arabs during their visit,
and in one of these Sheikh Snay, Speke's friend, was unfortunately defeated and killed.

They had great difficulties in getting off on the journey
to the north, and when they did, were, from lack of porters,

obliged to leave the greatest part of the kit behind in charge of Bombay. In fact, the *impedimenta* of a march never so thoroughly deserve this name as on an African journey; for besides all the ordinary luggage for the use of the travellers, money to pay the way must be carried in the shape of bulky articles and presents for the native kings, always the most expensive mode of repayment for hospitality. Sheikh Said, being quite disabled by illness, was now left behind, Bombay taking his place, and directed to carry letters and specimens to the coast, while the British officers, with Baraka, set off for the northern frontier of Unyanyembé, now in a very disturbed state in consequence of the war, on the 17th of March 1861. After marching for five days they came to the boma of the chief of Unyambéwa, Singinya, whose wife was the former maid-of-honour of Speke's old friend the Sultana Ungugu. On the death of her old mistress, the people of the country, fearing disputes about the succession, had desired her to marry Singinya as the readiest way of settling matters. She received them very graciously, and regretted much that her husband lost the pleasure of seeing them by his unavoidable absence on the war-path. In the district of Ukumbi the people all turned out under arms, but finally let them pass without molestation. Now, alternately crossing strips of forest and cultivation, studded here and there with small hills of granite, like the country on the way to the lake, they entered the rich flat district of Mininga, where the gingerbread-palm grows abundantly. The great man here was one Sirboko, who, having failed in the ivory trade, and lost all his property, had acquired some land in return for the assistance he gave a native chief against the plundering Watuta. Speke, hearing that these Watuta had lately wasted the country ahead, and wishing to refresh his men, was inclined to make a halt of some duration with Sirboko, who gave the party good entertainment. He begged from Sirboko, as a special favour, the liberty of one of his slaves, who was then attached to his suite under the name of Farhan (Joy). This man had had a hard life of it. He had been captured by the Watuta, who had cut off several of his toes. It was his good fortune ultimately to reach Cairo, having proved himself an excellent servant to the expedition.

It was fortunate that the quarters they were in were so good, and that the chief with whom they were staying, though a hard taskmaster, seems to have been on the whole an honest fellow, for they were actually obliged to remain in Mininga till the 20th of May. It seems surprising that there should have been so much more trouble on this route than on that parallel to it a few leagues to the eastward, by which Speke reached his great lake in the summer of 1858. But then the circumstances were different. There was no general war raging, only the usual feudal disputes between the petty chiefs; and then Speke took with him only a flying column unimpeded by much luggage, and his Beluch guard were thoroughly trustworthy, and, on the whole, suffered little from the climate, whereas the Hottentots' constitutions had all broken down on this march. Jaundice had turned the poor fellows all yellow, except one who was too black to be affected in that way; and, in short, Speke decided that it would be cruel to take them any farther, and they were all sent back to the coast.

Leaving Grant at Mininga, Speke now walked back the forty miles to Kazé to try if anything could be done to get guards and porters, and to bring on Musa, who had promised to accompany him for a certain distance. He took infinite trouble to try to patch up a treaty of peace between Manua Séra and the Arabs, but found that the latter had put themselves so completely in the wrong by allying themselves with the robber tribes, and by a flagrant breach of hospitality in the murder of old Maula, that nothing was to be done. Manua Séra's envoy, a one-eyed man, whom Speke nicknamed Cyclops, left in disgust, throwing down the arrow of defiance as a farewell. Speke then left the Arabs in mutual despair, they imploring him to stay and protect them, and went back to Mininga with as many men as he could collect. On arriving there, he found Grant much better, and heard, as the news of the place, that three villagers had been attacked by lions; two had escaped, but the third was caught as he was rushing into his hut, and carried off and devoured. At last a move was made, Grant going on first, and Speke joining him at Mbisu, a village in Ukuni, held by a chieftain called Mchiméka, who had just finished a two years' war with Ukulima (the Digger), a powerful sultan who lived at Nunda (the Hump). This war, probably owing to the respect which each side had for the other, had only cost six men altogether. A characteristic incident was reported here. The chief of Unyambéwa, after concluding the war, had returned to his wife, and was accidentally wounded by an arrow that fell from her hand. The injury having taken a serious turn, the chief sent for his magicians, who said it was not the wife's fault, but that some one must have charmed the arrow to cause such a result. They then took the magic horn, primed with the usual powder, and let it lead them to where the culprits dwelt. On this kind of circumstantial evidence four unfortunate men suffered death, and then the chief began to amend.

There were now many difficulties in finding a kirangozi, or leader of the caravan. At last Speke succeeded in engaging one called Ungurué, or the Pig who had been

often to Karagué, and was a good linguist, but afterwards
proved that his name was justified by his nature. While
Speke was being worried at Kazé, Grant had been resting
to recover his strength, and notwithstanding his weakness,
had employed his time profitably in making observations
on the people and the country. He describes the route
from Kazé to Ukuni as very fine. They never lost sight
of trees, wooded hills, or valleys, and water was everywhere
abundant. The forest was what might be called " Donkey
or Zebra forest," bare-poled trees and no underwood. The
hills, now close, now distant, were richly clothed and very
graceful, reminding him of the Trosachs. Grey rocks of
fantastic shape looked out from among the trees. Huge
blocks lay one over the other, or abruptly ended a range
of hill. The valleys had been cleared by the axe, the
wild grasses were most luxuriant, and palisaded villages
frequent. The way led from one valley to another, or
threaded the woodland, which rang with the songs of the
train. The road was generally of fine sand, which was
loose and yellow when washed by recent rains. Once it
crossed a quicksand—a rarity in Africa—very shaky and
watery, along which a patch of rice grew. Two streams
running west were forded—the Gombé, a sluggish stream,
at a place where it was twenty yards across and four and
a half feet deep; the other about breast deep, the current
of which was nearly too much for Grant in his weak state.
The general elevation of the country was 3400 feet, rising
gently up to the low ranges of hills everywhere around.
It was more open than Unyanyembé. Mists rarely lay
on the plains. The greatest rainfall measured was three-
fourths of an inch in half an hour, after a violent thunder-
storm, which wound up the rainy season, on the 13th of
April. The morning dews were heavy, and a S.E. wind
then blew; but the coldest breeze was from S.W. The

daily temperature inside a hut was 78° to 80° at 1 P.M.
The drinking water was always good, and at Mininga a
copious spring gushed out of the shell of a tree lying level
with the earth in the centre of a rice-field. As this well
afforded cool water the whole year round, it was with some
reason considered sacred. The flora was new and interesting, and grasses with pendant panicles grew to the height
of ten feet, otherwise the crops were not heavy, a fact which
was probably to be attributed to the lightness of the soil.
The palms were found here for the first time in groups:
their stems served for fencing, thatching, firewood, and
building-poles, and their fruit for toddy. The fruit hung
in large rich clusters, tempting the passing traveller. Several of these palms, with leaf-stalks still remaining, were
observed to support a species of parasitical ficus, the roots
of which were not near the ground, but formed a complete
network round the palm. There were numerous tamarind-trees, umbrageous, and beautiful in outline. There
was the rumex, from ten to twelve feet high; and the
bark fig-tree, from which the Waganda make their clothing, was seen here for the first time. The bark is taken
off in strips, then damped and beaten into pliancy with
heavy mallets, and afterwards sewn into a sheet the colour
of chamois-leather, but much thicker, the outer skin being
thrown away. Near the villages a few scrubby bushes of
cotton were grown on the white-ant mounds. The rude
looms converted its produce into a hard, stout, heavy
cloth, about four or five feet broad, with one-fourth a
black border, and worn by women only. Sesamum grew
in ridges with the sorghum, its oil and that of the ground-
nut being used by the natives, mixed with red clay, for
anointing themselves. It gives the skin a fine colour, and
a gloss like that on polished marble. The people's staff
of life is Indian corn, ulezi, and sorghum, rubbed into

meal between stones in the same way as colours are ground. The vegetables are sweet potato, and the leaves, flowers, and fruit of pumpkins. They brought for sale daily ground-nuts, tobacco, and fowls. On the 3d of April the rice-harvest was being gathered in, the crop having been seemingly produced without irrigation. The thrashing was a novel process. The ears were placed on a cow's hide, and there worked by the feet of chained slaves, then winnowed in the wind; and after being sun-dried on a plot of cow-dunged ground, the grain was fit for the process of shelling with a large pestle and mortar. The stubble was afterwards turned over by powerful long-handled hoes, and the sweet potato planted. All these processes were accompanied with a merry song. The yams, which were not large, were grown on mounds about the fields, the branches trained to a stick, or allowed to crawl on the ground. The grain is housed under the eaves of stack-shaped huts; but sometimes a cluster of Indian corn may be seen suspended from a bough. Provisions were found to be cheap on this route, the men usually managing to live luxuriously on the daily allowance of a necklace of beads per man. The beads were the small change of the country, and the natives were very whimsical about taking them; for one colour was current in one place, and another in another: silver was represented by ells of cloth, and gold by armlets or anklets of metal wire. When the cattle were brought in at night they were thoroughly fumigated, as a protection against insects, and seemed to enjoy this operation. The sheep were small and rather scraggy, either white, white and black, or bay-brown, with no wool, but crisp hair, and tails that tapered from a broad fatty base. The head was the only handsome part, and two pieces of skin hung from the throat, as is seen in the long-eared breed of Indian goats.

They shot no wild animals on this route, though tracks of the larger game were seen, away from the cultivations. Lions were about during harvest-time, and concealed themselves in the crops; hence the accident at Mininga. When travelling at night, the natives moved quickly in bodies, blowing horns to scare them. A load of fine black geese, with curious horns to their shoulders, was shot by Speke. Grant had seen the same variety farther south flapping their wings and pluming themselves between showers on rocks in the bed of a stream, and then took them for cormorants. Their wings were white outside and black under, and the wing-feathers were converted by the natives into head-dresses. About the palms flocks of pigeons and varieties of small hawks were found. The former, though plump, were not very good to eat, but had fine plumage. A large red wattle surrounded the eyes. The wings and rumps were blue, with one white bar across the black tails; the shoulders and elbows chocolate; the feathers of the crop forked, and the legs grey. The crested crane is a bird of the size of a heron, with shorter hackles, of a slaty blue or black colour, but with a head adorned with beautiful contrasts of colour. He has a black bill, a topknot of rich black feathers, behind it a straw-coloured bunch of fibres, with black featherlets at their roots; a chalky white bare skin on the cheeks, and a scarlet wattle hanging underneath, and quantities of beautiful blue down about the rump: his call at night, when roosting, is harsh and grating. Large fish were caught in the muddy pools, but the natives had a prejudice against them. Eaten with eggs, however, these makumbara tasted very good.

The villages in this country were fortified with high palisades, like the wolf-fences round farmhouses in Sweden; many of these of great strength, besides having a broad dry ditch, a quickset hedge of euphorbia, and a covered way in front of them. Sometimes a bastion of mud is added, to give a flanking fire of arrows. On the tops of the palisades, over and near the gate of the village, were often seen the skulls and finger-skeletons of enemies, put there as a warning to intending burglars, just as game-keepers nail vermin on a barn-door. These were also seen in trees and on poles stuck in a mound. Outside and opposite the only entry of the village, an old hoe, protected by an awning, was planted on a hillock; this was said to be a charm against the evil eye. There was gene-rally a club-room in the village, where the caravan rested till the men could be billeted about. This was where the young men usually gathered to hear the news. They passed the time in smoking, pulling out each other's eye-lashes and eyebrows, filing their teeth, and cutting marks of caste on their faces. Dances either by day or night were held in front of this building. The regular dance of the country consists in laying on the ground a strip of bark or cow-skin, on which a line of men, the tallest in the centre, stand; the drums begin, and a howling song accompanies, while, with hands on their haunches and heads bent down, they beat time with their feet. A shout of laughter or applause winds up the performance. The huts themselves were shaped like corn-stacks, 15 to 18 feet in diameter, supported by bare poles 15 feet high; sometimes the grass roofs were protected from sparks by Indian corn stalks. All of them were unswept, and dark inside as the hold of a ship. The furniture was composed of a few earthen jars like Indian "gurrahs," tattered skins, an old bow and arrow, some cups of grass, some gourds, and perhaps a stool. Goats and calves were free of the house, so it was necessary to secure the grain in band-boxes of bark.

The officers were daily visited by parties of women,

copper-coloured and flat-featured, and attired much as those about Kazé. They would sit silently for hours, smoking and playing with their infants. Some handsome Nyambo girls were seen on this route; their men confine themselves to herding, while they stay at home, cooking, coquetting, and showing off their beautiful feet and ankles. Two of these sat with their arms round each other's necks, till asked to sit apart that they might be sketched. They were quite models for a "Greek slave." The woolly hair was combed out and raised up from the forehead and over the ears by a broad band of the skin of a milk-white cow, which contrasted well with their light copper skins. The Waha women are much like them, with tall graceful figures and intelligent features. Though they wear their hair like the Watusi, and have similar fashions, they are considered as an inferior tribe; and their robe is of a different colour, being of a yellow ochre. A good opportunity presented itself of studying the different races in the settlement of a trader named Sungoro, who travelled with sixty wives in a double-poled tent. An Abyssinian, from whom much might have been expected in the way of beauty, was but a poor specimen, though she was fair for a negress, and had a distinctly bridged nose. Another was a beautiful Watusi, with large dark eyes and all the fine points of that aristocratic caste. Speke said she strongly resembled a Somal. Her race prefer death to slavery, and reckon fowls and goats as unclean. The slaves at Mininga appeared to Grant as very hardly used. They were fastened to each other by a chain which was never unfastened day or night, so that if one moved the whole gang must go with him. They were watched and kept in severe order by a small boy who had lost his ears, probably from Uganda. Their work, however, appeared to be light, it being the owner's sole object to keep them alive, and prevent them from running away, till they could be sent to the coast and sold. One of them came of a cannibal race from the N.W. of the Tanganyika, and the rest made a butt of him for his supposed propensities.

The Wanyamuézi were found to be, on the whole, honest, notwithstanding their inquisitiveness and acquisitiveness. No actual theft occurred till they came to Sirboko's, who was robbed one night, as well as his guests; but the missing articles were mostly recovered by the fear of the magic horn, which was believed to be an infallible detective. The great difficulty, as has been seen, on this march were the Wezee (short for Wanyamuézi) porters. It was not hard to get them, as there were plenty of idle fellows about; but to get them in any number together, or to keep them for any length of time, was the difficulty. On the least caprice of fear or offence they were off again. This accounted for a large part of the journey being performed by Grant and Speke separately. One went on, while the other had to remain behind to beat up for men. They were like two planets connected with each other, and going in the same general direction in different orbits. First, Grant had to push on to Ukulima's at Nunda, where he was detained a hundred and nine days. This jolly old gentleman was a kind of African "King Cole," and was generally found towards evening in a state of pombé. As the god Odin is said to have lived by perpetual quaffing of wine, throwing his rations of meat to his tame ravens, so did this sultan breakfast, dine, and sup on pombé, leaving contemptuously the more solid food to his seven wives and his courtiers. His example was demoralising. The people kept no regular hours, and fed on pot-luck when and where they could. The infection spread to Grant's men, and they were generally either tipsy or sorry. The hardy old fellow himself, who was about seventy, did not seem the worse for it, and was extremely active; and his people also seemed to thrive on their irregularities, which was perhaps owing to their early habits, as they were all in the fields before sunrise. The sultan was very good-natured to Grant, and condescended to play the fool in his company, helping himself to quinine from his medicine-chest, by way of adding "bitters" to his beer, and putting on Grant's thick shoes and trailing them about the village. It seems, notwithstanding, that he was highly respected in the neighbourhood, and when, as often happened, any of the other sultans called, he used to borrow Grant's guns to fire salutes. The old sultana seems to have been an admirable housewife, and a very motherly person altogether.

The country on the way to Ukuni was found to lie at a general elevation of 3260 feet. The lands all ran southwards, cleared for cultivation; and the low hills were well wooded, their ridges capped with huge masses of rounded rock, some single blocks forty and fifty feet in height, balanced on each other, or forming gorges and passes. Some of the peaked forms of the granite brought to mind baronial castles, while the dense foliage about them suggested European parks. Great water cavities are sometimes found in these boulders. One basin, worn by the crumbling of ages, measured fifty feet round, and was from six to eight feet deep. From June (inclusive) to September 12th they had but one or two slight showers (in July), preceded by dull cloudy weather, which prevented a comet in Ursa Major from being seen. The sun rose and set in a haze, obscuring the sky for 40°. During the day a veil of mist lay about, unless the S.S.E. wind blew hard. This wind was unhealthy, and gave coughs and colds, generally beginning at eight in the morning. By the 12th of September it had more easting

in it, and brought beautiful clear weather.   The mornings
in June were piercingly cold, and by the end of that
month the trees had shed their leaves.   The evergreens
alone looked well in the forest, all else had been burnt
up; the fields were in powder, and yet looked decidedly
wintry.   This country, it must be recollected, was to the
south of the equator.   Spring began again in August.
Speke and Grant were both affected by the climate, the
former getting a hard painful cough from walking about
the country to recruit men, joined with anxiety.   Grant
had fever at intervals of two days, between which he used
to manage to go shooting for the pot.   Half of the Seedis
or Wanguana were generally unfit for duty.

At this dry season the flora did not offer much interest,
being in its dormant state.   Some jasmine-scented shrubs
were found in the stream-beds, and the little seeds of the
abrus peeping out of their open curled-up pods, while the
plant, twined delicately round small trees, had a beautiful
effect.   Some thorny bushes of a vermilion flowering-
shrub, and large umbrageous ficus-trees, from which the
natives extracted birdlime, and several sweet plums, now
ripe, but nearly all stone, were also remarked.   The mi-
ombo-tree was the most useful to the natives.   Its wood
makes a brilliant fire, which lasts all night.   Most of the
trees were bare-poled, just adapted for palisades, and
might be carried by two men.   The miombo is a kind of
banyan, which affords the fibre that the natives attach to
their wool.   In spite of the sultan possessing three hundred cows, milk was difficult to get, as the calves drank
most of it.   It had to be boiled without the knowledge
of the natives.   Butter was not to be got, except when
rancid, and not always then, as it was all wanted for
pomade.   The animals were all killed with bludgeons,
after a hunt through the lanes and amongst houses.   The

neck of the goat was twisted, to avoid injury to the skin.

The natives used to trap game with nooses and pitfalls, occasionally getting up battues. Grant followed some rhinoceros near Nunda, and killed a light bay hornless female antelope which was new to him. It had four white cuts across the saddle, the spinal ridge and inside of the legs white, spotted sides, and the tail a tuft of white hair. The natives considered it so unclean that they would not even admit it into the village. The Seedis said it was called "bavala" in their country. Among smaller mammalia was a pig called the Ngeeree, highly esteemed for food, which dug wells in the forest, and another animal, considered uneatable, called the Ngrooweh, described as having no tusks, but teeth like a goat and hair like a buffalo, so probably an antelope. There were also fierce wild-cats of a deep brown colour, barred across. They saw troops of the beautiful little mongoose, which is easily tamed, searching for water. Their dark bodies are barred to the tip of the tail. On one of them being wounded by a bullet, he began tearing at it with the greatest viciousness. Lions and lynxes are the perquisite of the sultan, and when killed are brought to his door on a stretcher, with great jubilation. Grant was sentenced to a fine of two fathoms of calico for measuring a lion, but refused to pay, on the ground that he had only walked round, not stepped over it. The putrid flesh is cut up and boiled by the sultan in person. The grease is preserved as a valuable magic medicine. The tail and paws are hung over the royal doorway, and the skin, carefully pegged out in the sun to dry, is prepared for the sultan's exclusive wear. The lynx is even more prized than the lion, though not much heavier than an English fox. He has immensely powerful arms and great length of body, and

is believed by the natives to kill both the lion and the
buffalo, watching his prey from a tree. Considering his
courage, Grant did not think this unlikely to be true.   On
the arrival of a lion or lynx, the sultan and his two head-
wives sit in solemn conclave before the body, the crowd
squatting or standing round. A small lump of serpent's
dung is made into a paste with water on a stone. Spots
of this white ointment are put by the sultan on the forehead, chest, shoulder, tips, instep, and palms of himself
and the two wives, as a charm to bring plenty to the
house, because the serpent is very prolific. None but
kings are allowed to use this charm. Notwithstanding
the scavenger habits of the vulture and adjutant, the feathers of these birds are valued as head-dresses. Another
bird of prey was a slate-coloured hawk, strong and fine-
looking, and able to knock over a guinea-fowl. Of eatable
birds there were three kinds of partridge, quail, florikan,
blue pigeon, guinea-fowl, and knob-nosed duck. The tree-
partridge (kengo), resembling the painted one in India,
has yellow legs, fine plumage, and weighs about a pound.
It is trapped in nooses of hair. The "kewtee," or "nœnœ,"
is a plump little partridge of about half that weight, found
scraping in open places, and in colour resembles a quail.
It has reddish legs, with a button-like pearly spur. A
third and commoner kind is the "quake." It has handsome blue plumage and red legs, with sometimes an
appearance of a double spur. Other birds remarked during a morning or evening walk were a few parrots, a long-
tailed bird of paradise, with most graceful flight, some
handsome yellow birds about the size of a blackbird, and
others with black bodies and white primaries, taking short
and languid flights. The Seedis kill great numbers of
fish by raking the pools in the streams with hurdles.
Besides the makumbara already mentioned, which occa-

sionally run to an enormous weight, there was another called the "gogo," resembling a large stickleback, which weighed up to three-quarters of a pound. The night's rest was often disturbed by rats, fleas, or ants. The last were the worst, though no larger than the English kind. When they came the calves broke through their pens, and a general alarm followed. They fixed in the skin in a moment, biting viciously, and clinging like leeches till crushed. A line of burning charcoal was efficacious in keeping them off; but the sultan, who dreaded fire, preferred bringing in a large flock of goats and polluting the place, so as to make it obnoxious to the insects.

On the 27th of June there was an alarm of war, but the warriors being mustered, returned, after a parade, to pombé. On the 4th of July, however, the people of a Msalala village having lifted some cattle, all the available troops were sent out under a red-robed leader; in ten days they all came back safe, reporting the death of six of the enemy, and bringing one head, which was duly stuck on the palisading over the eastern gate. On another occasion, after a dance in the morning, the sultan held a kind of durbar for consultation about the war. The tusk of an elephant lay in the central space. For an hour the sultan addressed the crowd, sometimes stopping to find words, and then pulling out hairs from his beard with an iron tongs. Other speakers followed. With the exception of the beard-plucking, the rest of the ceremony was most orderly and impressive. The tusk had been sent by the sultan of Msalala to denote that he submitted the matter to arbitration, and its remaining in its place signified that the decision of the court was against him.

Ukulima had about twenty guards, who dressed very jauntily, and declined all menial work; they were chiefly used for enforcing the conscription. Their usual occupation, however, was playing at pitch-and-toss. In default of coins, they played this game with circles of bark or leaden discs. The stakes were bows, arrows, or ankle-wires, and pieces of stick served for counters.

All Africans are great drummers, and every country has its own style of drumming. Here the conductor had always the largest drum, which the band watched for the time, while a little youth rattled incessantly a wooden trough at his feet, producing a peculiar jumble. The drums were of wood, three to four feet high, slung on a beam. All events of any importance were marked by different kinds of drumming. The only religion of these people seems to consist of certain superstitious fancies. On one occasion when Speke arrived at a village, he was refused admittance, because it was believed that the boxes he brought were either the much-dreaded Watuta themselves transformed, or contained them packed in them like the Greeks in the wooden horse at the siege of Troy. Three stones in a triangular form surrounded the house of the sultan. Within the area of these he might even, it was thought, be fired at with impunity. Grant witnessed the driving-out of a devil from the sultan's daughter. This was an elaborate ceremony, chiefly consisting in the sacrifice of a cow, with the blood of which the possessed was anointed, who thus anointed her friends in turn. Then she walked in procession about the village, hooded and attended by guards and followers, shaking gourds and uttering strange cries. An old woman was appointed to wrestle with her for a broomstick, finally leaving it in her hand. She sat in the ring with her face and those of her friends curiously painted, and received offerings, some of which she put on the broomstick. She was then pronounced cured, but paraded the village for two days afterwards with the decorated broomstick. Trials for witch-craft, as in medieval Europe, generally ended in conviction and execution. The custom of making brothers, the pro-cess of which was mentioned in a former chapter, was very common here. Rahan made brotherhood with an Uganda lad, the sultan's magician, whose bamboo tube was supposed to possess two wonderful but seemingly inconsistent powers. With one blast he could blow away into space all the enemies of the sultan; with a second, if he deigned to accompany a sportsman, he could collect all the beasts of the forest, and make them stand to be shot at.

Speke passed Grant at Ukulima's, after staying a couple of days, and passed on into Phunzé. On arriv-ing at a chief's, called, like his guide, Unguruè, or the Pig, all the belles of the place came crowding round him offering themselves for wives. He was relieved from his delicate position by a fortunate attack on the cattle of the village by an angry father-in-law, who could not get a dowry paid, which drew off the crowd to the scene of action. At Takina, in the district of Msalala, he and his men had to run the gauntlet of a shower of arrows, which, however, did no harm; but in the confusion two cows were stolen. He now made for the village of a chief named Myonga, whose extortions almost amounted to stopping the way. However, after some preliminary menacing demonstrations, Myonga sent a message that he should be glad to see the white man; and Speke sent him his tribute, with the remark that it must frank Grant also when he passed that way. This potentate, however, de-clined a personal visit from Speke, on the pretext that he did not know the court language. Such messages, which were not uncommon, probably arose from fear of the evil eye of strangers, acting on a bad conscience. Speke then marched on through a jungly tract to a nullah, which forms the boundary between Unyamuézi and the kingdom of Uzinza.

Uzinza is ruled by two chieftains of the Wahuma race, an Abyssinian stock, specimens of which are seen all over Unyamuézi, some being found as far south as Fipa. Travellers see little of these people, because they are of pastoral and roving habits. Their dress is chiefly composed of cow-hides tanned black, with a few charms, brass or copper bracelets, and immense numbers of sambo instead of stockings on their long legs. They smear themselves with rancid butter, which makes their presence undesirable to any but negro noses. They carry for arms both bow and spear. The southern Wazinza are much like the Wanyamuézi, but in the hilly north country they are more active and energetic. Their grass-hut villages are fenced in the south, and open in the north. Their country, rising in high rolls, increases in altitude as it approaches the Mountains of the Moon, and is well cultivated, being more subject to periodical rains than Unyamuézi, though the springs are not so abundant. Speke was now obliged to pay tribute to a princess named Ruhé, a relation of his guide the Pig, who seemed to take delight in taking the caravan wherever toll was to be exacted, instead of making quick marches past the turnpike-keeping chiefs. After getting to the station of one of the harpies, called Makaka, Speke's men all struck, being frightened by the accounts they heard of the plundering Watuta, and of the impossibility of getting through to Usui. Speke, in despair at their obstinacy, marched back, and joined Grant for consultation. It seemed impossible to get to Karagué by the road they were going, and a scheme was discussed of proceeding to the Great Lake, and building a raft there to communicate with the Nile.

Though suffering from a painful cough, Speke at last determined to march back to Kazé to try if he could not get assistance from the Arabs. Musa had died, and he found his son Abdallah installed in his place. The Arabs by their alliances had driven Manua Séra to great straits, but Speke was told he could get no men till the war was over. He succeeded, however, in bringing away two guides, named Bui and Nasib, who knew all the languages as far as Uganda. He reached Grant again on the 11th of July, having in going and returning accomplished a journey of 180 miles. He then went back to his own camp at Mihambo, and adjourned to the village of a chief named Lumerezi, where he was laid up with severe illness. All this time his men were more discontented and mutinous than ever, and the expedition seemed at a dead-lock: however, on the 21st of August hope dawned again. A large caravan of Arabs and coast-men arrived from Karagué, saying that both Suwarora the dreaded sultan of Usui, and Rumanika the sultan of Karagué, were most anxious to receive the expedition, and on the morrow the first four envoys from Suwarora arrived, begging him to come on. They carried a sort of sceptre as Suwarora's warrant. He now prevailed on his men to proceed, and only waited for Grant. On the 17th of September he received a letter from Grant stating that on passing Myonga's the caravan had been attacked and plundered of all the property. Grant wished to pass Myonga's, and to the demand for "hongo" had answered that all had been paid by Speke. He ordered his men to go on, but after they had proceeded about seven miles, a sudden rush was made on their Indian file from the woods. All the parties and guards vanished as if by magic, only three remaining with Grant. Little Rahan alone stood up bravely with his cocked gun defending his

load.   In the afternoon, however, a message came from
the sultan to apologise for the mistake, and to say that
all the stolen property would be restored.   A letter afterwards came to say that Myonga had restored the bulk of
the goods, but that a great many things were missing, as the
packages had all been broken open in the scuffle.   After
a detention of seven days with this ruffian, Grant managed
to get away by the payment of an enormous hongo; and
as Speke was just writing to him to resist further pay-
ments, as he had secured the help of Lumerezi, walked
into the camp.

With at last a sufficiency of porters they all set out
together, walking over a new style of country.   Instead of the everlasting granite outcrops of Unyamuézi,
with valleys between, there were two lines of little hills
visible to the right and left, whilst the ground rose in
long swells of sandstone covered with forest trees, among
which were often seen flowers like primroses, only much
larger, and generally of a pink colour.   On the 11th of
October they marched out of Bogué into the district of
Ugombé, where they crossed the Ukongo nullah, draining westward to the Malagarazi.   They continued their
course through some more villages of native chiefs, who
fleeced them like the rest, and had the drums beat after
the process, which was the signal that they were graciously
allowed to depart, till at the north end of the Wanga
country they came to a wilderness separating the posses-
sions of Rohinda from those of Suwarora.   At one place
the villagers attacked the men of the camp, but the
show of guns dismayed them, and they fled helter-skelter
into the fields, leaving the village at the mercy of the
caravan.   They, however, returned in the evening peace-
ably.   After this they crossed the border of Usui,
Suwarora's territory, guided by the bedells, who made

them pay their footing at the frontier, and whose previously civil bearing underwent a decided change when they found themselves on their own king's land. All Suwarora's officers at the different stations exacted large tolls, most of which went into the king's coffers, and it became evident to Speke that he had only been invited into the country to be fleeced. On the 31st of October they came to Suwarora's palace, lying in the Uthungu valley, behind which rose a hill of sandstone, faced on the top with a dike of white quartz. The palace enclosures, of great extent, were well laid out for effect. Three circles of milk-huts, one within the other, formed the ring-fence. The chief's hut was three times as large as the others, standing at the farther end, whilst the officers' huts stood in little groups within the circle. They were conducted by the direction of the mace-bearer to the huts of the commander-in-chief, two miles from the palace, where they found a caravan of Arabs under one Masudi already encamped. These started the next morning for Karagué. They had been more than a year accomplishing the distance between Kazé and this place, owing to the detentions. Plenty of provisions were brought here by the people, of whom Speke remarked that he never saw so many with hazel eyes, though their general features indicated a considerable mixture of races.

On the evening of their arrival they were visited by a man of Uganda, named Nyamgundu. He was dressed in a wrapper made of many small antelope-skins, as soft as kid, and as well sewn as a kid glove. His manners were as superior as his dress to what they had been accustomed to. It was, however, impossible to communicate with him except through Nasib, who had known him before. He was the brother of the queen-dowager of Uganda, and with a body of officers had been sent by King Mtésa to

demand the hand of a beautiful daughter of Suwarora.
During their residence here the maiden had died, and now
Suwarora, to atone for the disappointment caused by his
procrastination, was endeavouring to make up a handsome
tribute in wires.   This would account for the fleecing
which Suwarora's guests were doomed to undergo.

The next day a man named Sirhid called, who said he
was the first officer of state.   He was a comely young
man, who seemed to have a good deal of the Wahuma
blood in him.   Flashily dressed in coloured clothes and
a turban, he sat down in one of the chairs quite at his
ease, and spoke with great suavity.   Speke represented
their difficulties as those of great men in trouble, and
hoped that Suwarora would be moderate in his demands,
as so much had been taken from them on the road.   He
told him he had brought some presents for Suwarora fit
for so great a chief,—a five-barrelled pistol, a tin box, and
so forth,—and asked if he could not go and pay his respects at once.   Sirhid said he was afraid that if the presents were shown immediately they would frighten the
Mkama, who would think them magic, and he himself
might lose his head, and that Speke must let him pave
the way before he could pay a personal visit, as his chief
was very superstitious, and not a man of the world, like
himself and Speke.   He then took his leave, after begging for the iron chair he had sat upon, which was refused him, on the plea that Europeans did not know how to
sit on the ground.   Two days afterwards another man
of Uganda, named Irungu, came to pay his respects,
opening his commission with a humble request for beads.
He said that Mtésa, the king of Uganda, had heard of their
approach and was most anxious to see them, and regretted
that he himself could not wait to go with them.   With
many compliments to his majesty of Uganda, Speke

begged him to take him a present of a revolving rifle and some other things ; but he declined, on the same grounds that Sirhid had declined similar presents for Suwarora, and would only consent to take as Speke's card to Mtésa a red cotton pocket-handkerchief. Irungu told him that the line by the Masai was now open, and that Mtésa, desiring to keep it so, would give him as many men as he liked, if he wished to go back that way. This was agreeable news, as Speke had written to the Geographical Society that in case he found the Nile question solved on arriving in Uganda, he should wish to return by that route.

Suwarora still declined on various pretexts to see the British officers, and during the time of their stay the camp got excessively drunk and disorderly, and they were pestered by the intrusions of the Usui people, who were indefatigable beggars, though their simplicity was amusing. If water was thrown at them to drive them away, they would come back again to the charge, thinking it was done in fun. On the evening of the 13th, to Speke's great relief, some officers of Suwarora's came to settle the hongo, with many excuses from Suwarora that his business still prevented his seeing them. The hotel bill was very heavy, but as their expectations had been raised to the utmost, it appeared almost moderate. And what was better, they were free to march away on the 15th of November, under an escort of officers appointed to see them over the border. This was apparently a great honour, but was really due to Suwarora having convinced himself, from reports that had reached him, that they were " no canny," and to his anxiety to get rid of such formidable wizards. Rising out of the Uthungu valley, they passed over undulating ground drained by many rush rivulets. On the roads they passed some cairns, to which every passer-by contributed a stone. As Speke had seen the same in the Somali country, he thought that the cognate Wahuma must have introduced the custom here.

After passing a fine forest they came to the head of a deep valley called Lohugati, which was so beautiful that they instinctively pulled up to admire it. A stream of most attractive appearance to a trout-fisher flowed down its well-wooded side towards the Nyanza. Just beyond it the valley was clothed with fine trees and all kinds of luxuriant vegetation, amongst which the pretty pandana palm was conspicuous, besides rich gardens of plantains, the common weeds being enormous thistles and wild indigo. Beyond that there were high undulations, over which in the far distance they could see a line of cones, something like the extinct volcanoes of Auvergne ; and in the far background, higher than all, were the rich grassy mountains of Karagué and Kishakka. When the march was resumed, a bird called *khongota* flew across their path, on which old Nasib, beaming with joy, called out, "Look at that good omen! Now our journey will be sure to be prosperous!" After fording the trout-stream, they sat down to rest, and were visited by all the people, who were very naked, and apparently very innocent. From this they rose over a stony hill to the settlement of Vihembé, where, as it was the last place on the Usui frontier, they dismissed their uncomplimentary guard of honour with the usual fees ; and bade adieu for ever, as they hoped, to the country of the churlish Suwarora.

As the Watuta race had given some trouble on this march, more by the terror of their name acting on the porters and villagers than by actual hostilities, a notice of them will not be out of place here. Two men among the camp-followers had been their prisoners, and consequently knew something about them. Their sultan had his headquarters at Malavie, a province bordering on the north-west shore of the lake Nyassa. A brother of his had wandered north and fixed his royal residence at Utambara. Such grandees seldom went in person in search of cattle or slaves, but sent their officers and followers in thousands to roam about the country, leaving nothing but desolation behind them. If a village had no cattle, they demanded slaves, besieging it until their demand was complied with. Cases were known of their doing this for months, and drawing so complete a cordon round the place that those who escaped through it were supposed to bear a charmed life. The only race in the south that could master them were the Wabisa, living to their west. They had large boats, with which they navigated the Nyassa, making piratical descents on the people of Nyassa and Uhiao. The pure race adopted the Kafir costume, with all its quaintness. Their arms were two or three short spears, which they did not throw, but used to stab the foe at close quarters, covering their bodies with a leathern shield. The British officers once heard the alarm beaten, but the Watuta never came to that village till they had left it, and thus the people managed to escape. They saw, however, their line of circumvallation at 200 yards from the village. Forked sticks were stuck in the ground to support the cow-skins which their women carry to shade them from the sun. Most comfortable beds of grass lay about the position. If long in one place, they built huts of a half-orange shape, very low, and surrounded by an euphorbia fence, which is considered poisonous, and only fit for the use of such people.

Grant's friend, Myonga, who plundered the caravan, and eight or ten petty chiefs they had to pass afterwards, were no better than these Watuta. It did not appear to be the guard that prevented them from taking everything they had, for those poltroons could not be relied upon in any real danger, but they owed the preservation of some of their property partly to their reputation as wizards, partly to the fact that every chief who was known to have made a very successful haul of plunder was sure to be attacked by others equally greedy. The porters began to desert as soon as the war-drum was heard, and as soon as the same drum beat a "receipt" for all demands, the porters who remained would strike, and often run away when they had got what they wanted, just when all was ready for a start. Nothing would do with them but to take their bows and arrows, which succeeded only because they were afraid to pass through the country unarmed. Then the Zanzibar Seedis would stand out for higher pay, and sometimes desert. The only good result from their continued losses was the lightening of the baggage. Their goods had melted so fast in Usui that they found themselves in Karagué with a supply of beads insufficient for six months' consumption.

The first sixteen marches from Ukuni had been through very pleasant undulations of tall soft grass and umbrageous forest-trees, with cultivated clearings capable of yielding grain for two or three thousand travellers through the season. In Usui the watershed had changed, and all the streams went to the Victoria Nyanza. The path crossed three or four escarped hills, tailing off gently to lower ground in the north. About Lohugati the wild rocks and crags, interspersed with trees overhanging the valleys, brought to mind the echoing cliffs above the lakes of Killarney. A waterfall, too, added a rare charm to the scenery. The water fell on hard, black, volcanic-looking conglomerate boulders in a cascade of two cubic feet from the top of an escarpment seventy feet high.

Beautiful ferns and mosses grew abundantly within reach of the spray, but no land-shells were found, though crabs were about the water. The natives were afraid that the Europeans visited the fall with the intention of stopping the water or drinking it all up, as their own chief went through a magic ceremony at this place to bring rain when it was wanted. This year rain had been abundant. The rain-doctor had put out his instruments under a tree by the 20th of October, and expected it fifteen days after at the new moon, the end of his year. He wanted paper to assist him, and on half a sheet of foolscap being given him, said he should prefer it written over! From the 26th of September, and during October, they had very pleasant showers and slight thunderstorms. At new moon, as the doctor predicted, they had a heavy downpour; but by the 5th of November the rain had stopped, owing, as the natives thought, to the rain-gauge having been put out. When they were in low ground, or where water was near the surface, the mornings were so cold that gloves would have been a comfort. During the day the sun was oppressive, but with a north-east wind it was agreeably cool in the shade. Water abounded for the first part of the journey, in wells dug outside the villages; and in the latter half in the boggy dips which drained the country to the north. For the first time in Africa they got clear crystal water bursting from under the hard stratified rocks of the parallel ridges of Usui; and the men suffered less in health in these parts, while the leaders of the expedition were rapidly recovering.

The country of Uzinza, from the variety of forms, appears to possess much geological interest. One day, from the path of splintered rock, the face of a long, bare, sloping hill may be seen, the surface of which is half rock, half bog, like a Highland moor, except that the landscape is

diversified by plantain gardens. At another time, wal-
nut-sized nodules of iron covered with rusty dust might
be picked up, which the natives know how to convert
into glistening spear-heads. Then the lofty escarpments,
raised into their position by some great convulsion of
nature, are well worthy of notice, as well as the volcanic
mounds in Kishakka, as seen from the space above Vihembé, some bare and red, and strewn with white quartz;
others covered with pale-green grass to the summit, and
dotted with trees sweeping down to and shading the
valleys below. Their forms were saddle-shaped, horse-
shoes, and frustums of cones; many were crowned with
rock, and nearly all had stratified splinters bursting from
their sides.

The eastern slopes below the escarpments, where the
debris lay, were better cultivated than the western
rocky parts. The fields were hoed up by the 8th of
October for the expected rain, the weeds being collected in a heap and burnt. The plantain trees stood
at intervals of six feet, yielding food and wine in due
season. The decayed leaves and stems were allowed to
remain to preserve the roots and soil from the heat,
and afford nourishment to the "maharageh" beans, which
thrive in the shade. The other crops seen ripening in
November were Indian-corn and manioc. The sweet
potato was ripe and abundant, but sorghum was scarce
and dear; and tobacco, fowls, goats, and cows were dearer
than in Unyamuézi. The cattle were here the large-
horned heavy variety of Karagué, without humps, hornless like the Teeswater breed, but, unlike them, bony and
gaunt from bad grazing. They are allowed to remain in the
field all night, without fence, round the smouldering fires.

In the southern forests of Uzinza much the same sort
of game were seen as in the countries noticed before,

but the greatest number and variety of animals he had seen in Africa were noticed by Grant in the valley of Urigi, between Uzinza and Karagué. This valley is covered with four-feet-high grasses, is from three to four miles broad, and probably twenty miles long, having evidently once formed a part of the Nyanza. In one place they counted fourteen rhinoceros at once. No elephants, however, were seen, as the country was too open, and hyenas were rarely heard. The quills of porcupines were picked up in the woods. Serpents were rarely if ever seen. Beeswax was never met with, though hives of logs were seen. Amongst the commoner game-birds, which were the same as those which occurred before, Grant noticed a new kind of partridge. It had a curious way of running with the body thrown back, and a strange cry like the note of the Himalayan cheer-pheasant. It had orange-red on its throat and round the eyes. One specimen was double-spurred, and weighed $1\frac{1}{2}$ lb. Many pretty varieties of birds were observed during the detention in Usui. Three species of swallows were noticed; also small birds resembling black robins, water-wagtails, creepers, &c., and a peculiar bird with plain brown plumage and long tail was shot among the rushes. This unpretentious fellow was considered by the Seedis the king of birds, and called Mlinda, and he was said to move with a train of little birds, whose duty it is to tear to pieces every feather that drops from his wing, to prevent it being put upon an arrow. The skin of this Mlinda is as thick as that of a mouse, the feathers might be called hairy, the bill is stronger than a linnet's, and the feet are soft and red.

Among the people of this country, often called Wanyambo, whose general characteristics and costume resembled the Wezees, except that they were more active and had more air about them, there were a curious class called the Walinga, who worked in iron, and dressed like the Watusi. Their furnaces were in the heart of the forest, the spots being usually marked by charcoal and clinkers. To reduce the metal, four lads, squatting under a grass roof each with a double-handed bellows, blew away at a mass of live charcoal with nodules of metal mixed with it, the melted matter running into a recess.

Having met with a surprisingly courteous reception at the entrance of one " bomah " in an out-of-the-way place, Grant followed into it the two men who had welcomed him, and found a most lady-like and beautiful Watusi woman sitting under a tree. She received him with gentle dignity, and invited him to partake of her hospitality. She wore the usual Watusi costume of a reversed cowskin, teased into a frieze with a needle, coloured brown, and wrapped round the body from the chest to the ankles. Lappels, showing zebra-like stripes of colours, formed a "turnover" round the waist; and, excepting that one arm was ornamented with a highly polished coil of thick brass wire, and the right wrist with two equally bright and massive rings, and the neck with a pendant of brass wire, the upper part of her person was bare. Her peculiarly formed head and graceful long neck, her fine eyes, mouth, and nose, her little hands and feet, were all faultless—the only exception being her large ears,—here, however, considered a beauty. With arms and elbows rounded like an egg, sloping shoulders, and the small breasts of the crouching Venus, she was perfectly beautiful, though darker than a brunette. Her hut was formed of grass, flat-roofed, and too low to stand up in; three stones formed the fireplace; milk-vessels of wood, bright from scouring, were ranged on one side of the dwelling. A good-looking woman sat churning butter in a gourd. Buttermilk and butter on a clean leaf were offered to the guest, who went away highly gratified with his visit to the Watusi queen, who seemed to have communicated her grace and gentleness more or less to all the women of the district.

The language of the country, as spoken by the Watusi, the dominant race, was quite unintelligible to the men of the expedition, but .they picked up words and phrases, and pronounced it less difficult than the dialect of Unyamuézi. Notwithstanding Grant's trouble at Myonga's, he was enabled to observe a kind of dance which seemed peculiar to the country. A circle being formed, singing and clapping of hands commenced, and either a woman came out and made her best curtsy to a favourite in the crowd, retiring skilfully backwards to her place, or a "cavalier seul" bounded to the centre, threw himself into attitudes, performed some gymnastic feat, bowed to the belle, and then made way for the next performer.

After Grant had joined Speke at Bogué, on the 7th of September 1861, a letter was received by him from Colonel Rigby at Zanzibar, dated 31st October 1860, advising the despatch of a number of delicacies, with a packet of letters. They were much disappointed that these never came to hand, and consequently for twenty-seven months they had no news from the civilised world, till, in February 1863, they arrived at Gondokoro on the Nile.

CHAPTER III.

KARAGUÉ.

SCENERY ON THE WAY TO KARAGUÉ—BEAUTIFUL SITE OF RUMANIKA'S
PALACE—THE LITTLE WINDERMERE LAKE—HOSPITABLE RECEPTION
—RUMANIKA AND HIS BROTHER NNANAJI—HIS FAT WIVES, HIS SONS,
AND COURT—THE WANYAMBO—THE ROYAL MUSICIANS—SPORTING
ADVENTURES—SPEKE'S CONVERSATIONS WITH RUMANIKA—HE IS
SENT FOR BY THE KING OF UGANDA—GRANT DETAINED BY ILL-
NESS—GENERAL REMARKS ON THE COUNTRY AND ITS PRODUCTIONS
—GRANT'S DEPARTURE.

THE accounts of Karagué and Uganda read so like stories
of strange kingdoms in the Arabian Nights or Gulliver's
Travels, that they would appear scarcely credible did we
not receive them on the unimpeachable testimony of two
such eyewitnesses as Captains Speke and Grant. What
a wide field these countries appear to open for commercial
and missionary enterprise, if they could be only reached
with any degree of comfort! But unfortunately they appear, as far as we can see as yet, to be surrounded by a
cordon of the most implacable savages, who fancy rightly
that the slave-trade would disappear before the influx of
legitimate traffic, and are difficult to convince that such a
loss would be a gain to them in the end, even in a material
point of view. Of their respective kings, Rumanika and
Mtésa, the former appears, for a savage, so perfect a character, that he seems to realise the definition of "all the

cardinal virtues bound in black morocco," and it is almost
a relief to find that Grant had some slight complaint to
make of him before the end of his visit; while Mtésa,
though a most horrible barbarian, and fit to be held up as
a frightful example of man as he is by nature—not to say
without Christianity, but without any sort of decent religion—appears to be capable of management through his
intelligence, and still more through the childlike vanity
and desire to stand well in the eyes of all men, which
seems to be his ruling passion. But we must not antici-
pate the narrative. Our travellers felt that they could at
last breathe freely when they saw the Usui escort depart-
ing in the distance. They had got beyond the regions of
a direct taxation, which amounted to gradual confiscation
of their effects. For some time at least hospitalities would
only have to be acknowledged by presents, and this seemed
pleasant at first, though in the end the system of "leaving
it to your honour" was found nearly, if not quite, as costly
as the other.

Gradually descending from the spur which separates
the Lohugati valley from the bed of the lake of Urigi,
the track led first through a pleasing prairie, and then
through a pass between the domes they had seen from
above Lohugati. Here they were struck by a new geological formation. From the green slopes of the hills, set
up at a slant, as if the central line of pressure on the
dome top had weighed on the inside plates, protruded soft
slabs of argillaceous sandstone, whose laminæ presented
a beef-sandwich appearance, puce or purple alternating
with creamy white. Quartz and other igneous rocks were
also scattered about, lying like superficial accumulations
in the dips at the foot of the hills, and red sandstone con-
glomerates clearly indicated the presence of iron. The
soil itself looked rich and red, like that of Hereford or

Devon. While encamping under some trees, they were
greeted by an officer sent by Rumanika to help them out
of Usui. This was Kachuchu, an old friend of Nasib's,
who no sooner saw him than he joyfully exclaimed, "Now,
was I not right when I said the birds flying about on Lohugati hill were a good omen? Look, hear what this
man says: Rumanika has ordered him to bring you on to
his palace at once, and wherever you stop a day the village officers are instructed to supply you with food at the
king's expense, for there are no taxes gathered from strangers in the kingdom of Karagué. Presents may be exchanged, but the name of tax is ignored."

Having seen from the top of a hill the broad waters of
the lake of Urigi, they imagined that, according to the
account of the Arabs at Kazé, they were within sight of a
creek of the Victoria Nyanza; but when they arrived in
camp they were informed that it was a detached lake, but
connected with the Great Lake by a passage in the hills
and the river Kitangulé. Formerly, said the village officer, the Urigi valley was covered with water, extending
up to Uhha, when all the low lands they had crossed from
Usui had to be ferried, and the saddle-backed hills were
a mere chain of islands. But the country had dried up,
and the lake of Urigi became a small lagoon. It had
shrunk, he added, to its present dimensions by a miracle,
exactly as the breath left the body of the late King Dagara! The day's march of the 19th of November had been
novel and entertaining. The hilly country around, with
the valley, brought to Speke's memory many happy days
he had spent with the Tartars in the Tibetian valley of
the Indus—only this was a more picturesque country, for
though equally wild and sparsely populated with the other,
this was covered with verdure, and dotted here and there
on the higher slopes with thick bush of acacias, the haunts

of white and black rhinoceros; whilst in the flat of the
valley herds of hartebeests and fine cattle roamed about
like the kiyang and tame yāk of Tibet. To add to these
pleasant impressions, they enjoyed the first-fruits of Rumanika's hospitality in the attentions of his officer, who
was quite grateful for a few yards of red blanketing in return for his handsome entertainment. The farther they
proceeded in the country the better they liked it, as the
people were all kept in good order, and the village chiefs
were so civil that they could do as they liked. On a stroll
near the second village in Urigi, Speke shot his first white
rhinoceros, but felt rather sorry afterwards, since no one
would eat the flesh. When, some days afterwards, they
went down into the old bed of the Urigi, they were constantly excited with the variety of game seen. Often the
rhinoceros were so numerous and impudent as to contest
the right of road, and it was a ludicrous sight to see the
Wanguana going at them in parties of three or four, and,
firing their carbines at discreet distances, run one way
as the rhinoceros ran another.

Rising out of the bed of the Urigi, they now passed
over a low spur of beef-sandwich clay sandstones, and
descended into the close rich valley of Uthenga, enclosed by steep hills more than a thousand feet high,
overhanging the way, as prettily clothed as the mountains of Scotland, while in the valley there were not
only magnificent trees of extraordinary height, but a great
amount of cultivation, the banana being the commonest
crop. After arriving in a village they were surprised at
meeting the Uganda officer, Irungu. Instead of going on
to Uganda as he ought to have done with Speke's present
to Mtésa, this worthy had stopt here to live at the expense
of the poor Wanyambo, and get drunk on their *marwa*,
or plantain-wine. For the rest of the march, the drum-

mers and fifers that he had with him served to enliven the
way.   They heard afterwards that it was the peculiar privilege of Uganda grandees to be accompanied by this sort
of music, which otherwise, except at dances or festivals,
is supposed to convey a declaration of war.   Leaving the
valley of Uthenga, they then rose over the spur of Nyam-
wara, attaining the delightful altitude of 5000 feet, and,
thus tripping down the greensward, worked their way into
the Rozoka valley.   Kachuchu here told them that he
had orders to go before and prepare Rumanika for their
arrival, as the king wished to know whether they would
prefer to reside at the Arab depôt at Kufro, on the direct
line to Uganda, in the palace with himself, or outside his
enclosures.   Overwhelmed by the delicate consideration
implied in this message, the officers answered that their
great object was to see the king himself, and whatever
honours he chose to confer they would take with a good
grace, but that he must understand they were not traders,
and therefore had no relations with the Arabs.   `

The geological formation of the hills here was much
the same as before; the bases were streaky clay sandstones, with the addition of pure blue shales, and above
these were sections of quartzose sandstone lying in flags,
as well as other metamorphic and igneous rocks lying
about.   Over hill and dale they next came to the junction of two roads, where Irungu with his band, and
the men with Suwarora's hongo, who were going the
same way, took the way to Kufro, and the expedition
took the other, which led to the royal residence.   The
hill-tops in many places were breasted with dikes of
pure white quartz, as they had seen in Usui, only that
they took here a more northerly direction.   The appearance was striking, as the chief substance of the hills was
a pure blue or otherwise streaky clay sandstone, which

must have been formed when the land was low, before the
elevation which made these hills the axis of the centre of
the continent.   Within a few miles of the palace they
were ordered to stop and wait for Kachuchu's return ; but
they no sooner arrived in a plantain grove where pombé
was brewing, than that officer arrived saying that the king
was most anxious to see them.   As, however, fatigue and
beer together chained the men to the place, Bombay and
Nasib were sent to make excuses, and in the evening they
returned with a huge pot of pombé and some royal tobacco, which Rumanika had sent, with a message that it
was for the exclusive use of the officers, that the royal tobacco was strong and sweet as honey-dew, and the royal
beer required a strong man to drink it.   Next morning
they crossed the hill-spur of Weranhanjé, the grassy tops
of which were 5500 feet above the sea.   Descending a
little, they came suddenly in view of what seemed to be a
rich clump of trees, and beyond it, 1500 feet below them,
and two miles distant, they saw a beautiful sheet of water.
This was what Bombay, after his visit of the day before,
had profanely described as a great pond.   The clump of
trees was the palace enclosure.   The lake was of oval
form, lying snugly among gently-swelling grassy hills,
and so thoroughly shut in that it seemed a puzzle where
the waters could come from, or whither they went.   On
its western shore trees hung over its clear sweet waters ;
wooded islands dotted its glassy surface, and a deep fringe
of the papyrus bordered its southern side.   From the summit also in a westerly direction there was a most interesting view ; here they saw four distinct parallel ranges of
hill, with water showing here and there between them ;
and occasionally, about sunset (for they had other opportunities of seeing this view), appeared in the distance
a sugar-loaf mountain, called by the natives Mfumbiro, or

"Cook." This was the highest mountain in the country, estimated at 10,000 feet. Two brother cones of less altitude lay to its left, and all were so steep that the natives said they could only be ascended on hands and knees. Their distance from the spot where they stood was about fifty miles. Unfortunately they were never reached, as they were off the direct route, in a different kingdom, and many obstacles intervened. The nearer country reminded them of the lake district of England, and induced Speke to call the Karagué lake "The Little Windermere."

The capital of Karagué is 1° 40′ south of the equator, within a complete zone of vapour all the year round. Fruitful showers seemed to be continually falling. On the same day, in the absence of marked seasons, sowing, ingathering, and reaping might be seen; and from November to April the rainfall increased or diminished as the sun became more or less vertical. The rain reached its climax about the 10th of April, when it again began to decline. In December, till 7th January, the usual maximum temperature in a hut open to the south was 81°, and the minimum 56°, at an elevation of 5000 feet above the sea-level. They had a great number of English grey days, very few bright ones, and never a perfectly Italian sky. Brushwood was used instead of firewood, which was scarce and dear, otherwise a fire would have been welcome in the mornings and evenings. The hilly nature of the country caused the rains to run off very fast, so that the ground was agreeable to walk on immediately after a shower.

To do honour to the king of this pleasant land, in approaching his palace Speke ordered the men to put down their loads and fire a volley. It immediately produced an invitation to come in. So, leaving the traps outside, Speke and Grant, attended by Bombay and a few of the seniors of the Wanguana, entered the vestibule, and, walking

through exterior enclosures studded with huts of royal
dimensions, were escorted to a pent-roofed *baraza*, which
the Arabs had built as a sort of government office, where
the king might conduct his state affairs.   Here, as they
entered, they saw, sitting cross-legged on the ground,
Rumanika and his brother Nnanaji, both men of imposing appearance.   The king was plainly dressed in an
Arab's black choga, and wore dress stockings of rich-
coloured beads and neatly-worked wristlets of copper.
His brother, as being a great doctor, which included the
pretensions of priest and magician, in addition to the
check cloth wrapt round him, was covered with charms.
At their sides lay huge pipes of black clay.   In their
rear, squatting as quiet as mice, were the king's sons,
some six or seven lads, who wore leathern coverings about
their middles, and little dream-charms tied under their
chins.   The first greetings of Rumanika, delivered in good
Kisuahili, the language of the coast, were warm and affect-
ing; and he heartily shook hands with them in a style
common to England and Karagué, so as to make them
feel at once they were in the company of men of a far
superior order to those of the adjoining districts.   They
had fine oval faces, large eyes, and high noses, denoting
the best blood of Abyssinia.   Rumanika was six feet two
inches in height; and his towering stature, combined with
the simple dignity which stamped him as the shepherd
of his people, as well as the pastoral staff, might have
suggested a negro Agamemnon.   After first asking their
opinion of Karagué, which he thought the most beautiful
country in the world, he inquired with a sly smile their
opinion of Suwarora, and Usui hospitality in general; on
which Speke took the opportunity of suggesting to him
that it would be in his interest to call Suwarora to order,
as his extortions acted as a dam in stopping the stream

of traffic which would otherwise flow into Karagué. His curiosity had been excited by a letter which had come for Musa when he was staying with him during Speke's former expedition, and he inquired of Speke how information could be conveyed in that way, and asked, in fact, about all the wonders of the outer world, so that time flew with magic speed till it was time to retire; and the officers went to the spot they had chosen outside the palace for their encampment, with a fine view to the lake. Speke had, however, to return once to show Rumanika how white chiefs sat on their thrones, as one of the young princes had caught a glimpse of him sitting on his iron chair. When he had thoroughly enjoyed the sight, Speke took the opportunity of telling him that they had tasted no milk in Karagué in consequence of the prejudices of the people about their eating forbidden food; so the king gave them a cow for their especial use, and they found on their return that he had thoughtfully sent them another pot of his excellent beer. The Wanguana were in high good-humour now, and goats and fowls were continually brought in from all sides by orders of the king, though beads had still to be expended on the humbler articles of grain and plantains. But the coast-men found the wind very cold, and suspected they must be drawing near to England, which was the only cold place they had ever heard of.

The next day after the introduction, after astonishing Rumanika with the present of a revolving pistol, they were shown into his private hut, which surprised them by its neatness. The roof was supported with numerous clean poles, to which were fastened a large assortment of spears, brass-headed with iron handles, and iron-headed with wooden ones, of excellent workmanship. A large standing-screen of fine straw-plait work in elegant devices partitioned off one part of the room; and on the opposite side, as mere ornaments, were placed a number of brass grapnels, and small models of cows, made in iron for the king's amusement by the Arabs at Kufro. A return visit was paid by Rumanika and his brother the same evening, which was partly prompted by their eagerness to enter with the British officers on some rather delicate business. As they had heard they could find their way all over the world, they thought they would not have much difficulty in prescribing a magic medicine which would kill their brother Rogero, who lived as an outlaw on a hill overlooking the Kitangulé, and was a very sharp thorn in Rumanika's side. As a preliminary to the negotiations, the king' had to tell how the case stood. Before their old father Dagara died, he had unwittingly said to the mother of Rogero, although he was the youngest born, what a fine king he would make; and the mother in consequence tutored him to expect to succeed, although primogeniture is the law of the land, subject to the proviso, which was also the rule with the ancient Persians, that the heir must have been born after his father's accession, which condition was here fulfilled in the case of all three brothers. Accordingly, as soon as Dagara had given up the ghost, the three princes fell out, Nnanaji siding with his elder brother, but half of the people siding with Rogero; and a war began, which was of doubtful issue, until Rumanika succeeded in obtaining from the Arabs the assistance of their slaves armed with muskets, and thus forced Rogero into exile, swearing he would have his revenge as soon as the Arabs were gone. Rumanika maintained that Rogero was entirely in the wrong, not only because the law was against him, but the judgment of Heaven also. On the death of the father, the three sons, who only could pretend to the crown, had a small mystic drum placed before them by the officers of state. It was only feather-weight in reality, but being loaded with charms, became too heavy for those not entitled to the crown to move. Neither of the other brothers could move it an inch, while Rumanika easily lifted it with his little finger.

It was of no use for Speke and Grant to deny that they possessed any such charm as Rumanika wanted; so, thinking they were only deterred by scruples, he then promised that, if they would only get his brother into his power, he would not kill him; in fact, he would not touch a hair of his head, but only gouge out his eyes to prevent him seeing to do any more harm. Speke's only alternative, under these circumstances, was to turn the conversation. He told Rumanika that if he would only bridle Suwarora, he would get so powerful through the visits of civilised men, joined with increased trade, that he need not be afraid of anybody; and offered to take one or two of his sons to be instructed in England, since he admired his race, and believed them to have sprung from the Abyssinians, whose king, Sahéla Salassie, had received rich presents from the Queen of England. The Abyssinians, he added, were Christians, and Rumanika would be so now, but that unfortunate accidents had caused his ancestors to forget their traditional faith. A long theological and historical discussion followed, which so pleased the king that he said he should be delighted if two of his sons could be taken to England. To the disappointment of the officers he subsequently drew back, some meddler having told him that there was no milk in England, and milk the young princes must have; and having also hinted that when they got there they might be sold as slaves. Speke finally explained the object of his visit, which was, besides seeing great kings like himself and strange countries, to open a road for commerce to the north, and hoped that Rumanika would assist him. The conference left the king in the best possible humour; he offered to do anything that would please his guests; admired their pictures, beads, boxes, and general outfit, and then took his leave.

As Speke had heard strange stories about the merry wives of Karagué, he now paid his respects to Waze-zuru, the king's eldest brother, but who was in an inferior position, as born before the accession of his father. He found this worthy sitting with his wife in his hut, with a number of milk-pots ranged before him. The lady was of pleasing countenance, but so fat that she could not rise, and the flesh of her arms between the joints hung down like puddings. After the pretty children had been duly admired, Speke inquired the meaning of the milk-pots, on which his host pointed to his wife with pride, and observed: " Look at the product of those pots; we keep them to their mouths from early youth upwards, as it is the fashion at court to have fat wives." The king's five wives were of the same portentous proportions. They could not walk without resting every two or three paces, or without supporters on each side, like a nobleman's coat of arms; and sometimes they were seen crawling on all-fours from inability to stand upright. One of these that Grant observed when seated, had her head uncovered, the wool being allowed to grow into a mop, neatly tied off the face with a thong, and surmounted by a bouquet of feathers. The face was a handsome oval, with intelligent eyes; and the flesh of her arms, bare from the shoulder, depended like loose sleeves. Of course this artificial obesity, which insured complete idleness even more than the Chinese ladies' stunted feet, was confined to persons of distinction. It was worthy of note here, as a custom peculiar to the country, that when the ladies came to call on the strangers, their heads were muffled in a shawl, so that only one eye could be seen.   The milk diet did not seem to have had a similar effect on the princes, probably because they kept down their fat by exercise.   The royal caste was denoted by slight marks cut below the eyes, but the teeth were not tampered with.

There were four grown-up princes—Chundira, Kienj, Kananga, and Kukoko.   The first was a slim young spark of twenty-five, about five feet eight inches in height, with a sentimental countenance.   He affected the dandy, and was always on the look-out to see life.   He endeavoured to make up for deficiency in the quantity of his personal decorations by their quality.   He was particular about the cut of his waist-cloth, and *recherché* in his ornaments. He was bare from the tuft on his crown to his waist, excepting the decorations that covered his upper arm and neck.   From below the calf to the ankle he wore a mass of iron wire, and always carried, according to the custom of his country, a long knotted staff in his hand. The second son was by a different mother—the sister, probably, of the king of Unyoro; he was six feet high, very black, and so long and heavy about the head that he was nicknamed "The Camel."   In comparison with his brothers, he was a mere bumpkin; like them he was married, and had one child, but lived in the palace enclosure. The third son was so shy that he was seldom seen, but came once to have his likeness taken.   The fourth, Kukoko, was his father's favourite and inseparable companion.   He was very good-looking, and would call on the British officers every day, putting out his left hand when wishing good-morning, and remaining to chat for an hour at a time. Although none of these lads had more covering than a sheet of leather round the loins, longer behind than before, it was so jauntily put on, their ornaments were so becoming, their persons so finely bronzed, their gait was so polite and distinguished, that their nudity was forgotten; and when Kukoko put on a pair of white kid gloves, he had quite the air of a civilised "swell." Their food chiefly consisted of milk in the morning and some boiled beef or goat at night; they were allowed no grain, or mutton, or fish, or fowls. They acted as their father's head graziers, and had agents who travelled for them "*in cattle*," but they themselves were never known to sleep out of their own country.

The Wanyambo were the ryots or peasantry of the land. In the low swampy grounds near Urigi they were black and lanky. All greased their bodies to prevent the skin being dried by the sun, and fumigated themselves with sweet fuel having a heavy odour. The district governors, or Wakungu, were distinguished from the herd by a sheet of calico or a scarlet blanket. These Wanyambo were generally very civil in the camp, though from their excitable natures and uproarious habits it was considered unsafe for the Seedis to wander out amongst them. When near the palace they never carried arms; the only weapons allowed being the universal knobbed staff, which was used in salutations by presenting the end to be touched. This people, however, were mighty archers, and possessed bows more than six feet high, and very strong; the arrows were the cloth-yard shafts of our own ancestors, such as decided the day at Azincour. Of course, those who could use such did not condescend to poison them. Speke records with admiration the archery-practice at long distances of the young princes. The spears had no particular character, the handle being from six to twelve feet long, and the iron head indifferently made. The bow was evidently the favourite arm. The Wanyambo were fond enough of drinking and carousing, chanting wild airs till early morning, and yet their self-respect taught them when to stop, and they were seldom, if ever, found in an incapable state. Those who could not afford milk lived on grain, sweet potato or pulse, and meat when they could get it ; but fowls and fish were forbidden food to all. Their marriage ceremonies appear to have been of the simplest kind. One day some men were seen carrying in their hands a bride to the hut of her betrothed, in the shape of a bundle wrapped up in a large sheet. It reminded Speke of the well-known Welsh custom of " bundling."

As Speke was anxious to push on with his journey, he instructed Bombay to take Rumanika a present consisting of samples of European produce, apologising for its humble character, on the ground that the robberies on the road had nearly cleared him out. He also sent one to Nnanaji. Amongst the articles was a Raglan coat for the king, and a déolé, or gold-embroidered silk shawl, for the brother. Although the presents were not so handsome as Speke would have wished to give, they pleased Rumanika as much as if he had come in to a fortune. He said, however, he could not let them go under a month, for he must let the king of Uganda know that they were coming, and get his answer, as without his own recommendation they would be stopped at the frontier of Uganda. Ever attentive to his guests, the king one day sent the royal musicians to give them a concert. The Wanyambo excelled as musicians, and invented pretty plaintive airs which could be easily recollected. They had drums, and wind and stringed instruments. The most perfect of these was the " nanga," a sort of lute which had seven or eight strings. In one of these, six of the seven notes were a perfect scale, the seventh being the only faulty string. In another, three strings were a full harmonious chord. The instrument was formed of heavy dark wood, the shape of a tray, with three open crosses in the bottom, and laced with one string seven or eight times over bridges at either end; sometimes a gourd as sounding-board being tied on to the back. The fife, which is more common in Uganda, consisted of a hollowed reed, about as thick as a German flute, and was held like a flageolet, having a slit at the top, and six finger-holes. With this they often whiled away the time on a march. Their bugle was shaped like a telescope, and was made of several pieces of gourd fitting into each other and covered with cow-skin. An expert performer could produce a whole chord, varied by the thumb acting on the key. The drums differed in shape according as they were intended to be played by the hand or a stick. The hand-drum was a log four feet long, hollowed like an inverted dice-box, open at the lower end, and covered at the top with the skin of an ichneumon. It was slung from the left shoulder, and played by tapping and stopping with the fingers. The drums seen in the ceremony after new moon were of every possible shape except round, which they all tried to be. They were made of hollowed trunks, and covered with skin. Two copper kettle-drums had found their way into the collection. The royal band was composed of sixteen men—fourteen buglers and two hand-drummers. When they performed before the king's guests they formed three ranks, the drummers in the rear, and played, like the regimental bands of the Turks, bugle music in march and waltz time, with great spirit and precision. At first they marched up and down, and then commenced dancing a species of hornpipe, blowing furiously all the time.

The largest orchestra was exhibited at the new moon

levee, which the king held every month by way of ascertaining how many of his subjects were loyal. In the first court was a horn of the magic powder stuck in the ground, with its mouth pointing in the direction of Rogéro. In the second were thirty-five drummers ranged behind thirty-five drums, and then the guests were ushered into the third enclosure by a knot of princes and officers, where they found Rumanika sitting on the ground in the principal hut. He wore a tiara of beads on his head, from the centre of which rose a plume of red feathers, and on his lower face was a large white artificial beard, set in a stock or band of beads. This was supposed to give dignity to the countenance, like the wigs worn by our judges. They were beckoned to squat by Nnanaji, the master of the ceremonies, and a large group of high officials outside the porch of the king's hut. Then the thirty-five drummers all struck up together in harmony, but with a deafening noise; and when this was over, a smaller band of hand-drums and reed instruments was ordered in to play. When this second performance ended, through the performers being out of breath, district officers advanced one by one, with strange gesticulations, and holding drumsticks or twigs in their hands; frantically swore loyalty and devotion to the king, adding the hope that he would cut off their heads if they ever turned from his enemies; and then, kneeling before him, held out their wands that he might touch them. This scene was constantly repeated, the salutations alternating with music, interrupted only once by a *divertissement* in which a number of girls danced a sort of Highland fling, and the day's ceremonies ended.

Nnanaji, the king's brother, was a sportsman, and one day invited Speke to go out shooting with him on the slopes of the hills overlooking the lake. The king's sons came with three or four dogs and a posse of beaters. They drove the covers as if they were well used to the sport ; perhaps, indeed, they had driven them too well before, for that day nothing was seen but some "montana" and other small antelopes, all so shy that no bag was made. Speke was more fortunate on another occasion with the white rhinoceros. Accompanied by the young princes, he started at sunrise to the bottom of the hills overlooking the head of the Little Windermere lake. On arriving at a thicket of acacia shrubs, he found all the men of the neighbourhood assembled to beat. Having been assigned his position, in a very short time a fine male was discovered making towards him, but looking perplexed as to the direction in which he should bolt. To help him in making up his mind, Speke stole along between the bushes, and sighting him seemingly anchored by the side of a tree, gave him a shot on the broadside with Blisset; which, being too much for his constitution, sent him trotting off, till he lay down exhausted with bleeding, and received a settler. The young princes congratulated Speke most heartily on his success, and wondered at his calmness in going up to such dangerous beasts, pointing out a bystander who showed fearful scars where he had been gored by one of them. Just then a halloo was heard in the distance, signifying that another rhinoceros was hid in a thicket, and off they started in pursuit. Arriving at the place, Speke settled on going in with only two men carrying spare guns, for the acacia thorns were so close that the only tracks into the thicket were runs made by these animals. He stole in first, bending cautiously down till half-way through the run, when straight before him, like a pig from a hole, a large female with her calf behind her came straight down, "whoof-whoofing" upon him. Advance or flight was not

to be thought of, so Speke jammed himself back into the
thorns as well as he could, and gave her such an effec-
tual box on the ear with a bullet, that she swerved out
of his way and took refuge in the open, where he followed her down and repeated the attention. She then
took to the hills and crossed over a spur, Speke following
still, till in another thicket at the head of a glen he saw
three more, who, apparently taking courage from the odds
in their favour, came all at once charging down on him.
Fortunately his gun-bearers were more stanch than those
he had when after the buffaloes in Ugogo ; so, stepping
out of the way, he managed to hit them all three in turn.
One dropped dead a little way on, but the others did not
pull up till they got to the bottom. As one of them
appeared to have his fore-leg broken, Speke went at the
sounder one and administered another pill, which only
caused him to walk away over the lower end of the slope.
Then turning to the disabled one, he desired the Wanyambo to polish him off with their spears and arrows,
that he might see their mode of sport. As they moved
up to him, however, he made such furious lunges that he
kept the whole party at a discreet distance, and Speke
was obliged to bring him to his bearings with another ball.
At last their turn was come, and every man sent his
spear, assagai, or arrow into him with a will, till he sank
at last like a porcupine covered with quills. The three
heads were ordered to be cut off and sent, like those of
state traitors, as a trophy to the king. The meat, which
the Wanyambo would not eat, was given to the Wezees
belonging to the Kufro Arabs, and they trudged away
highly delighted, borne down by enormous flitches ; but
their Mussulman masters would not allow them to eat
them, because the throats had not been duly cut. When
the spoils were brought before Rumanika the next day,

he remarked that something stronger than powder must have effected the result, as neither the Arabs nor Nnanaji, though they talked much about shooting, had ever been able to accomplish anything like it.

In return for all the information that Speke gave Rumanika about the wonderful things in Europe and the world in general, the latter amused him with a variety of local stories, some of which might have had a foundation of truth. He said, for instance, that in Ruanda, a country to the west behind Kishakka, there were pigmies who lived in trees, but occasionally came down at night, and, listening at the hut doors, would wait until they heard the name of one of the inmates, when they would call him out, shoot an arrow into his heart, and disappear as they came. But more formidable than these little men were certain monsters, who kept out of the way of men, but lay in wait for women, and when they saw one pass by, would attack her and squeeze her to death. Rumanika added that the villages in Ruanda were of enormous extent, and the people great sportsmen; for they turned out in multitudes, with small dogs on whose necks were tied bells, and blowing horns themselves, to hunt leopards. These people, however, were extremely inhospitable; for some years ago when some Arabs came there, a great drought and famine set in, which they attributed to their agency, and, expelling them the country, said they would never again admit their like. It was from a Ruanda man that Speke heard of the Wilyanwantu or men-eaters, who despised all other food, and he was disposed to connect them with Petherick's Nyam Nyams.

On another occasion, Rumanika introduced a very ugly old woman who came from the island of Gasi, in the Luta Nzigé lake. Her incisor teeth had been extracted, and her upper lip bored with small holes, extending in an arch from

one corner to the other.   She had been sent as a curiosity
by Kamrasi, king of Unyoro, to Rumanika.   This Luta
Nzigé Speke had often heard of as a salt lake, because
salt was found on its banks, and he was induced to think
that it was of no great size, and a mere backwater to the
Nile.   It has since been explored by Sir Samuel Baker
to a great extent, and its importance has induced its discoverer to place it by the side of Speke's lake under the
name of the Albert Nyanza.*

When discoursing on the history of Karagué with
Rumanika, the king informed Speke that his father
Dagara's body, according to immemorial custom, was
sewn up in a cow-skin and placed in a boat floating
on the lake, where it remained for three days, until
decomposition set in and maggots were engendered, of
which three were taken to the palace and given in
charge to the heir-elect; and then one worm was transformed into a lion, the other into a leopard, and the other
into a stick.   After this the body was deposited on the
hill Moga-Namirinzi, where a hut was erected over it, and
five maidens and fifty cows having been thrust in, the
door was closed in such a manner that the whole of
them died of starvation.   Rohinda the Sixth, said Rumanika, who was his grandfather, was so old that it was
thought he would never die, and he himself was so concerned about his standing so long in the way of his son

* Another of Kamrasi's servants was a man of Amara, a people living
near the Nyanza, where it is connected by a strait with a salt lake and
drained by a river to the north.   A Mr Leon fancied these people might
be Christians, but his only grounds seemed to be that they raised both
their hands in prayer, and uttered the word Zu when sacrificing.   He
said that a white tribe called Wakuavi used to cross the lake and make
raids on their cattle, which led the Wamara far in pursuit into the enemy's country, and at a place called Kisiguisi they found men robed in
red clothes.   He had also heard of a great mountain somewhere about
the country of the Masai.

Presenting Spoils to Rumanika. Heads of three White Rhinoceros shot in Karague.—PAGE 198.

Dágara, that he took some magic powders and charmed away his own life. He was put to lie in state on the same hill as his son was afterwards; but, as an improvement on the maggot story, a young lion came out of the heart of the corpse and kept guard over the hill, and from him sprang a race of lions whom Dagara used to assemble instead of an army for making war on neighbouring nations.

Alluding to his own accession, he moreover said that a new test had been invented in his case besides the ordeal of lifting the drum. The supposed rightful heir had to plant himself on a certain spot, when the land on which he stood would rise up like a telescope drawn out till it reached the skies. If he was entitled to the throne, it would then let him down again without harm; but if otherwise, collapse and dash him to pieces. Of course, as he survived the trial, it was successful. On another occasion a piece of iron was found in the ground, about the shape and size of a carrot. This iron could not be extracted by any one but Rumanika himself, who pulled it up with the greatest ease. His father Dagara had picked up a thunderbolt in a storm, which he kept in the palace during his lifetime, but it vanished after his death as soon as the contention with Rogéro began. It is difficult to suppose, from Rumanika's character, that he was perfectly in earnest in telling these stories. Perhaps he only wished to be even with Speke, who had been telling him about the electric telegraph, steam-navigation, and railways. In many little matters Rumanika showed that he was above the superstitious fancies of his country; but habit was strong upon him, and when Speke asked him what he expected to get by sacrificing bullocks at his father's grave, he said he hoped to produce a good harvest. His mind, however, appeared to be quite open to conviction on these matters, and in a ripe state to receive the elements of Christianity, which Speke endeavoured to recommend by dwelling on his Abyssinian extraction and supposed descent from King Solomon.

Amongst other pleasures which Rumanika invented for his guests was a canoe-party on the Little Windermere. He was desirous of combining with this a pilgrimage to his father's tomb on that Moga-Namirinzi hill, which is a spur of an eminence behind the lake overlooking the Ingézi Kagéra river, which separates Karagué from Kishakka, and commanding the small lakes and marshes that feed the Kitangulé river. He was himself to go by land, and his guests in canoes. At the further end of the lake they came to a small strait which led into another lake, drained at its northern end into a vast swampy plain, quite covered with tall rushes, excepting patches of open water and the passages cut by the main streams from the Ingézi and Luchuro valleys. The whole scenery was beautiful. The slopes were all covered with fresh green grass, with small clumps of soft cloudy-looking acacias growing at a few feet above the water, and above them, facing over the hills, fine detached trees, and here and there the gigantic medicinal aloe. On the shore of the second lake they were received by a concourse of officers, and led to Rumanika's frontier palace, where he sat waiting to receive them, clad in a robe made of skins of the curious marsh antelope called nzoé. After a picnic collation he led them over the spur to the Ingézi Kagéra side, where, to their surprise, they found their canoes waiting. These had gone out of the lake at its northern end, then into and up the Kagéra to where they stood, showing the connection of these highland lakes with the rivers which drain the various spurs of the Mountains of the Moon. The stream itself was deep and dark, and as it was only one of the many affluents of the

Kitangulé, Speke saw that the latter river must be a very powerful tributary to the Victoria Nyanza.

When Speke was thinking about departure, Rumanika said that he wished to make him a large present of ivories in return for the honour of his visit, since, though his father Dagara had often entertained Arabs, he was the first king who had entertained a white man. This offer was gratefully declined; but Speke said he should be much obliged if Rumanika would enable him to recruit his exhausted treasury by selling ivories to the Arabs at Kufro, and getting beads, &c., in exchange, for which he would give him orders on Zanzibar. The exorbitant demands of the Arabs made him anxious to avoid direct dealings with them. Rumanika's unselfish kindness extorted many presents from Speke which he did not intend to have given at first, including a revolving rifle which he had meant for Mtésa; but the king gave him to understand that what would please him most, if other Europeans came, were gold and silver embroideries, and American clocks with the face in a man's stomach, whose eyes rolled with the pendulum, &c.—in fact, any curious toys. When Christmas came, their thoughtful host sent the British officers an ox, having heard that in England this great religious festival is chiefly celebrated by a great sacrifice of beef. He did all in his power to prevent their feeling home-sick, though by this time they were getting anxious about the possibility of returning by the north.

The New Year, 1862, however, brought good news. An officer of Rumanika's, who had been sent four years before on a mission to Kamrasi, came back in the train of a trading party, with a vaunting message from the king of Unyoro, that he had foreign visitors as well as Rumanika. They were not actually with him, but in his dependency, the country of Gani, coming up the Nile in vessels. The

Gani people had attacked them, but Kamrasi had promised to protect their farther progress. Speke at once concluded that this report must allude to Petherick, and despatched Baraka with Ulédi, one of Rumanika's officers, to ascertain the truth of it, and, if possible, communicate with Petherick from the court of Kamrasi. This joyful intelligence was followed by news that the king of Uganda had despatched messengers to fetch them; and, in fact, on the 8th of January they heard the sound of the Uganda drum.

Maula, a royal officer, with a large escort of men, women, and boys, handsomely dressed, leading dogs and playing on reeds, had arrived with the king's invitation, desiring them to come at once, and informing them that he had orders to frank them on the road. There was but one difficulty, and that a distressing one. Grant was laid up with a most troublesome complaint in his leg, as a result, probably, of the intermittent fever he had had. It was contrary to the laws of Uganda for any sick person to enter that country, and yet this was an opportunity which might never occur again of seeing it; so Speke, with great reluctance, was obliged to leave his companion to be nursed by the family of his friend Rumanika, knowing that he could not leave him in better hands. Half-a-dozen of the escort were left to attend him. Rumanika would not let Speke depart without putting him in charge of an officer named Rozaro, who was to accompany him everywhere in Uganda, and then bring him safely back; for he felt quite sure that he would never be able to get north from Uganda, in consequence of the disturbed state of the relations between that country and Unyoro. Rumanika himself seems to have been on good terms with both of the kings.

Grant's residence at Karagué lasted for four months

more, during most of which time he was kept a
prisoner by his complaint, and though convalescent
he was not quite well when he finally left. That he
recovered at all is marvellous, as he felt obliged to try
the prescriptions of all the amateur doctors that surrounded him, including magic charms of various kinds,
which, at all events, were the most innocent of the reme-
dies. But the world at large derives an advantage from
his distressing detention, as, while Speke was making observations in Uganda, Grant was doing the same as well
as he could in Karagué, so that no time was lost. In
other parts of their respective *memoires* the same incidents
are often repeated in different words and aspects, but at
this period this is less the case than at others. During
Grant's illness the family at the palace were very kind in
coming to sit with him. The sons brought plants and
flowers, birds' nests, eggs, or other things which they
thought would interest him; while he sketched for them
or their father, and sent a servant to get the news and
inquire for the king every morning. The supplies, however, did not come quite so regularly as before, and one of
the men lost his life while foraging in consequence, the
natives having set upon him. Grant's loneliness was enlivened by daily calls from all sorts of people—officers,
barbers, ivory-traders, musicians; and in the evening his
few men would gather round the fire and sing a sort of
song in reference to his health. His couch, the height of
a table, was made of the trunks of plantains, and covered
with grass and blankets. This was roofed over with a
low grass hut, with its gable-end open to the south, where
no wind blew at that season. Much to the surprise of
the natives, there was no fence round the encampment,
and dogs walked into the hut by day and hyenas by
night, and carried off the fowls. One night Grant was

awakened by one these brutes sniffing close to his couch, but he ran away when he shouted at him. After this a trap was set.

The country of Karagué rarely affords space enough for a single tent to be pitched, but there are thousands of acres in grass which would profitably repay cultivation. Tea, as well as coffee, might probably be grown with advantage, as frosts do not prevail. Wild grapes were sometimes found in the lower ground, but there seemed to be no soil exactly suitable for vines. A few clumps of wild dates grew in the valley, but the natives had no fruit, from their ignorance of the sex of the trees. Sugar-cane is scarcely known. There are two heavy crops in the year, sorghum and plantain; while English garden-pease, and a kind of bean called "maharageh," and Indian corn, can grow at all seasons. In February great care is bestowed on the plantain; acres of it cover the hillsides, a rivulet sometimes dividing the field. The trunks are trimmed of the leaves, fresh shoots are planted, and the whole orchard is carefully tended. The produce of the country was found to be generally very dear, six pipefuls of the tobacco, for instance—which was, however, very fine—costing the daily allowance of one porter.

The plantain wine, here called "marwa," was made by every family that possessed an orchard. It appears to be a sweet wine, with a raisin flavour, somewhat resembling hock. A quart could be drunk with impunity, but after the third day it became dead, sour, and intoxicating. The effects on the men of the camp were such that the king was requested to diminish the daily allowance of one gourdful. The process of making it in Karagué generally lasted two or three days. To make a large quantity, a large log, scooped like a canoe, was tilted at one end, and dammed up with grass in the centre. The ripe fruit was mixed with clean grass, then a woman mashed the mass at the upper end with her hands or feet. The liquor strained through the dam, and was strained again till fine. It was then placed to ferment in the canoe freshly cleansed. Some burnt bruised sorghum was put into it; all was covered up from the air, and allowed to remain in the sun or near a fire for two or three days, when it was skimmed and fit for use. It was never exported or bottled, and generally all consumed at once. The natives, even the youngest children, carried gourdfuls of it about with them everywhere like pilgrim's water-bottles. Karagué is more a depot for trade than a producing country. It was no wonder that the slave trade flourished, if, during the war in Unyanyembé in 1861, a slave could be bought on the spot for less than the value of a shilling, and, if transported beyond the equator, sold for the value of £12. But the rapacity of the local sultans threw many obstacles in the way of traffic.

Between Karagué and the Nyanza there is a country called Uhia or Mohia, whose people trade to the north. They bring coffee to Karagué in bundles covered with plantain-leaf, containing two handfuls, which they sell dear for one necklace of beads. It took a handful to make a pint of weak coffee, as the bean when taken out of the husk is no larger than a grain of rice. It is more often chewed than infused. These Uhia traders were sturdy, very black, middle-sized men, with bare unshaven heads and beards. Their dress was a cow-skin, with the leg parts neatly rounded off, of a saffron yellow, friezed inside, knotted over the right shoulder, and hanging to the middle of the thigh. Above this dress they generally wore a brick-coloured bark-cloth, well greased. Their ornaments were a sheep or goat's horn tied with a strip of leather round their bare heads, and a few rings worn round the ankles. Their arms were as peculiar as their dress. The spear-shaft was six feet long, and the head was heart-shaped, or like the ace of spades. Grant obtained much information about these and other tribes from one Jumah, a coast-trader, whom he found an amusing companion, as he had been everywhere, and told him most extraordinary stories, especially about the Kilimandjaro Mountain, which, being guarded by demons, no mortal could ever ascend.

The cattle of Karagué resembled those of Cape Town, having immense horns and staring ribs. The king had 400 of them at his residence on the high grounds; and on the banks of the Kitangulé, where they appeared to thrive better, he may have had 10,000 more. They seemed to be inferior milkers, only giving half the quantity given by the plump shorthorns of Unyanyembé. The sheep were a small species, with hair for wool, generally white, and not common. Sometimes the white rhinoceros was observed grazing near them, looking like a stack in a field of haycocks. The goats, on account of their skins, are more valued than the sheep. The breed of dogs was like the pariah dog of India, long-legged, with smooth red hair, but much more amusing and familiar. One called by the musical name of Keeromba was a special favourite in the camp, furnishing a subject for songs. Mention has been made of the *nzoe* antelope, a robe of whose skins Rumanika wore on grand occasions. One of them was captured alive in the papyrus of the lake by orders of Rumanika. He was a male, very timid, and, as he seemed to pine and would not take food, was killed. His coat was of long, dirty brown, rather soft, hair; but instead of being striped like the water-boc found by Livingstone on the Ngami lake, he was faintly spotted, and his toes were so long that he could hardly walk on dry ground. His horns were from five to six inches long, hinting at a spiral form, and his height was more than three feet. The habitat of this animal is entirely on the borders of lakes, where it feeds on the leaves of the papyrus. In honour of its discoverer, it has since received the name of *Tragelaphus Spekii* from Dr Sclater.

The hartebeest and white rhinoceros were the common beasts of chase. The former is very combative in the rutting season. There were several varieties of antelope. The mountain gazelle bounded very prettily over the bare hills, and did not seem very wild. Pigs were found in the low grounds, and hippopotami swam in the lake. In spite of the stories about lions, none were ever seen. Otters were said by the natives to live in the lake, ruled over by a snow-white king, about whom there was some strange superstition. Great numbers of moles, larger than the English variety, were caught in the camp. Their fur was black or brown, and some few were white. They found nearly the same game-birds as in Uzinza and Unyamuézi. Small red sparrows were seen, and many kinds of ducks. The king was highly delighted with the present of an Egyptian goose, which Speke shot by the lake. The rhinoceros-bird was observed here sitting as calmly on the back of the beast as a man on the top of a coach. He is the size of a blackbird, and has black wings, with a grey or white rump, and is about as gregarious as the magpie with us, three having been seen together. They appear to feed on the ticks which infest the hide of the rhinoceros. A new kind of swallow was observed, skimming the grasses of the hillsides; it has black or dark-brown wings with a slaty tinge, white belly, a black ring at the neck and round the rump, the tail-feathers not forked but slightly convex, the body of the size of a sparrow, and not so fish-shaped as swallows commonly are. The gold-headed and crimson-backed finch of Unyanyembé was found here perching on the maize-stalks near dwellings. Another bird, which, according to Speke's description, had a black coat and plush waistcoat, contrasted beautifully with the tree on which it sat, a thorny jessamine, blooming in pink and white in December. In the absence of songsters there was one " bugler " who had a very rich note. The crows were handsome, with a white ring round the neck, never seen in greater numbers than from two to four together. The natives had a great spite against them, as they would eat even the red little sorghum, while they prevented the white from being sown at all. Curiously enough, this bird, as with the classic ancients, was supposed useful in divinations. Against the mischief of the barn-door fowl, the crops were protected by cutting off the toe-nails of the birds, which made them all cripples. Among the few snakes was one of a bluish-black colour, said to be poisonous, but no fangs were visible. Rats were a great source of annoyance, especially in secreting the beads and cowries of the traders. In the low flats near the water, there were large grey-legged mosquitoes, who could bite through socks and trousers, but in high windy places they were not found. There was a bee resembling that common in Europe, but no hives were seen, though fine granulated honey was brought for sale. The absence of flowers on the hills would account for their rarity. Fish were not sought after by the natives, but a specimen of the " makambara " was brought alive in a jar, and a half-pound " macquareh " was caught in the Kishak-ka lake. This fish grows very large, has large scales, no feelers, and a ridge of sharp-pointed fins along its arched back, and is a sweet feeder.

The comparative civilisation of Karagué might be estimated by its penal code, which was not so severe as that at Muscat and Zanzibar. For murder, all the property was confiscated to the relations of the victim, and the murderer's eyes were put out, or he was thrown over the precipice below the palace. For adultery, though death might be inflicted *in flagrante delicto*, an ear was cut off; though, if it was aggravated by the respective rank of the culprits, the principal offender was tortured in a peculiar manner, and his throat cut. Larceny was punished by two to ten months in the stocks, while at Zanzibar the thief is buried up to his neck on the shore till the tide drowns him. An assault with a stick was punished by a fine of ten goats, so that, as elsewhere, it was comparatively cheap to those who could afford to pay. But for assault with a deadly weapon, half the property was confiscated to the king and half to the victim. In default of payment, the stocks were put in requisition. One of Grant's men was once asked to arbitrate in a case which brought to mind the judgment of Solomon, the difference being that it was a dispute between two men as to which had the best claim to a child. It was decided by an appeal to the likeness in baby's black face, by which it would seem that infants in Karagué have a more distinctly marked individuality than with us. The only religion these people seemed to have consisted in a reverence for magic horns, which were filled with powder, and used in divining the future. Possession was believed in, both in the cases of men and animals, but the devils were supposed to be amenable to incantations. This kind of negative religion, as Speke seemed to have been convinced, would not present the slightest obstacle to missionary enterprise. The people were also utterly ignorant of reading, writing, or arithmetic, properly so

o

called. They treated books as children do pictures. This would account for Mohammedanism, which depends entirely on the Koran, having made no progress with them, though they have been in contact with it for twenty years.

By the end of March 1852, Grant was sent for by the king of Uganda to join Speke. An Unyamuézi doctor or priest, named Kyengo, was to join the party, and the march had to be deferred till his arrangements were complete. The Waganda would not carry luggage, so three-fourths of the goods were obliged to be left behind. At last, on April 14, 1862, Grant was placed on a wicker stretcher, under which four sturdy Waganda put their heads together, and then trotted away with him.

CHAPTER IV.

UGANDA.

THOSE well-meaning people in England and America who are eager to admit the emancipated negro at once to the fullest franchise of a man and a brother, would do well to suspend a judgment, formed perhaps after one tearful perusal of ' Uncle Tom's Cabin,' until they have read Captain Speke's unvarnished tale of his experiences in the kingdom of Uganda. If there is one quality that distinguishes Speke from other writers, it is his extreme honesty in recording facts, and reluctance in drawing hasty inferences. His record is not without its lesson for other theorists —for instance, the admirers of irresponsible government and centralisation. In Uganda we have a picture of a race of joyous children, never apparently knowing a care, yet governed by a system of terror which does not allow them to feel their lives their own, even for a minute. They are ruled over by a young man, whose vanity approaches to madness, and is allied with the usual good-nature of vain people; yet so cruel, without consciousness or conscience, that he condemns people to death daily for small breaches of etiquette, orders off his wives to execution with as

much nonchalance as if he were ordering his dinner, and
tries his new guns by shooting down the first convenient
subject within range; while his people are so thoroughly
impressed with the divine right of kings, that for every
punishment short of death, and even death itself, they
thank him by prostration, esteeming it rather a privilege
than otherwise to be slain by his sacred hand. "Order
reigns" in Uganda to such an extent that every whis-
per of the subject reaches the court, and great Roman
roads cover the country for the use of the king's messengers, and transmission of his presents; repression of
opinion is carried to a perfection never dreamt of by
French or Prussian police—every mention of foreign or
domestic politics, and even of men or things beyond the
frontier, being severely discountenanced; while manners
are so brutal, that the very body-guards of the palace
fight for their meat like famished dogs. Yet that meat is
artistically cooked, and a system of court etiquette prevails which has never been approached in any of those
little German courts which Count Bismark has so coolly
superseded, and is not even surpassed by Japanese punc-
tilio; and there is a decency exacted from the million,
combined with an exception in the king's particular case,
which can only be accounted for by the monarch being
considered as raised far above all rules and opinions.
While no article whatever can be presented to the king
in its naked state, but must always be covered by a
wrapper, realising the myths of American delicacy—while
it is as much as a courtier's life is worth, in prostrating
himself, to expose an inch too much of his natural black
stockings under his robe, and even Grant had to change
his costume to appear at court because a bit of his leg
was seen between the knickerbockers and the hose—the
king himself is attended at his toilette by sable Graces

as little draped as Canova's, and waited upon in his cups
by Hebes in the same condition. But to look on these,
or even to be caught glancing at the draped beauties of
the harem, involves capital punishment without judge or
jury, so that "peeping Tom of Coventry" would have
stood an extremely poor chance in Uganda. Speke found
it in the end his best policy to quietly break all the customs of the country, and the more he did so the more
respect he seems to have won from the eccentric monarch,
who at last came to reverence him as a strange being of
superior order; and by the time Grant arrived, every
difficulty of intercourse, founded on traditions as rigid
as the laws of the Medes and Persians, rather than the
temper of the king himself, had completely disappeared.
It would have been idle to argue with King Mtésa, but
no man could bow with a better grace to the logic of
accomplished facts.

Uganda is the most
powerful state in the
great ancient kingdom
of Kittara, and its mon-
arch, like those of Kara-
gué and Unyoro, belongs
to the race of the Wa-
huma, who are closely
connected with the
Abyssinians and the
Gallas, the distinction
between these two races
probably consisting
chiefly in the former
being agricultural and
the latter pastoral, not
excluding, however, a

One of the Wahuma.

relation of dominion and dependence, just as the Wahuma, being likewise a pastoral race, have managed to get the upper hand of the agricultural populations in Uzinza, Karagué, Uganda, and Unyoro. The most probable supposition is, that a race of shepherds originally came over from Asia, and subjugated the tillers of the ground, receiving in course of time, by intermarriage with the aborigines, a darker skin and more crisp hair, but still maintaining a high stamp of Asiatic feature, of which a bridged instead of a bridgeless nose is the most prominent characteristic. This effect would have been increased by the distant migrations of the junior or weaker members of the original conquering stock, so that the discoverers of the pasture lands of Unyoro, and founders of the great kingdom of Kittara, lost their religion, forgot their language, changed their name to Wahuma, no longer remembering that of Hubshi or Galla, and extracted their lower incisors like the natives, though, oddly enough, the kings who are their present descendants maintain a tradition that their ancestors were once piebald, having hair on the white side straight, and on the black side frizzly. And the strength of this tradition was shown by the fact that when Grant and Speke attempted to enter Unyoro in two directions, the Wahuma chief was immediately afraid that the original white rulers were come to take back the country, from which they were supposed to have once been driven by the negroes, in alliance with the Wahuma.

The old kingdom of Kittara was bounded by the Victoria Nyanza and the Kitangulé on the south, by the Nile on the east, the Luta Nzigé or "Dead Locust" Lake on the north, and the kingdoms of Utumbi and Nkolé on the west. The general name is now seldom applied except to the western portions, whilst the north-eastern part is called Unyoro, and the other Uddu, which is connected with Uganda. No one can tell how old the reigning family in Unyoro is, but some division in the royal family drove a weaker branch to settle in Nkolé, where an independent government was established. Since then, it is said, that twenty generations ago the Wahuma dynasty of Karagué was established in the same manner. A conspirator named Rohinda fled from Kittara to Karagué with many followers, and sought the protection of Nono, a native Wanyambo king, whom he afterwards invited to a feast, and treacherously killed in his cups, setting himself on the throne.

Rohinda was succeeded by Ntaré, and princes of these two names alternated, varied with a few others, like the Batti and Arcesilai of Cyrene in Herodotus, till Rumanika came to the throne. During this time another split had taken place, and a Wahuma dynasty was established in Uzinza, and remained till the last generation under one king, till Ruma died, and his two sons, Rohinda and Suwarora, divided the country between them, Rohinda taking the eastern half and Suwarora the western, at the arbitration of Dagara, the late king of Karagué. This is the most northerly kingdom of the Wahuma, but not the most southerly settlement of their race, for under the name of Watusi they overlook the Tanganyika Lake from Uhha, are scattered as herdsmen over Unyamuézi, and appear as the Wapoka in Fipa, south of the Rukwa Lake. The princes are called Wahinda in Karagué, but Wawitu in Unyoro; and these appellations are also, to the confusion of the traveller, often falsely claimed by the aboriginal chiefs, and this confusion is increased by the Wahuma willingly adopting the habits of the countries they inhabit.

The most remarkable of all the separations from the

original stock was that which gave rise to the kingdom
of Uganda. In the earliest times the Wahuma of Unyoro looked upon all the lands by the Victoria Lake as
their garden, and imposed the name of Wiru, or slaves, on
the aborigines. Wiru in the northern district becomes
Waddu in the southern, hence the country was called
Uddu or slave-land, and stretched in one line from the
Nile to the Kitangulé until eight generations back.
Then, according to tradition, a sportsman from Unyoro
named Uganda came with a pack of dogs, a woman, a
spear, and a shield, hunting on the left bank of the
Katonga valley, not far from the lake. He was but a
poor man, but so great a hunter that all the Wiru flocked
to him for flesh, and invited him to be their king, saying
that it was of no use to have a king who lived so far off
that when a cow was sent as tribute, the cow had a calf
on the journey, and the calf became a cow and had
another calf, and so on *ad libitum*, without the present
ever reaching its destination. Uganda at first hesitated
to commit high treason, but the people insisted, and it
was settled that he should give his name to the country,
and take the name of Kiméra the First. The same
night Kiméra stood upon a stone with a spear in his
hand, and a woman and dog sitting by his side; and to
this day it is said that his footprints and the mark of
his spear-butt, as well as the place where the woman and
dog sat, may be seen by the curious. When the great
king of Unyoro heard of this important slice being taken
from his dominions, he is reported to have quietly
observed, "The poor creature must be starving; allow
him to feed there if he likes." So Kiméra became a
legitimate monarch, and the eighth in succession from
him is Mtésa, who had not yet been crowned at the time
of Speke's visit.

This Kiméra, so despised by the king of Unyoro, proved a most troublesome rival, for he turned out a great warrior and lawgiver, and all the peculiar institutions of the country were invented by him, some of them presenting a strong contrast to the habits of neighbouring nations. Having been enthroned by the will of the people, he was determined not to be dethroned by a caprice of the same power, and established an enlightened centralised despotism, whose organisation is in many respects quite equal to that of the great military monarchies of Europe. Kiméra was a far-sighted man, and when his life was closing was determined that his system should not die with him. He had created a clan of officers out of slaves, called Wakungu, and by giving them importance made his interests theirs. The honours paid to him in life were to be continued, under their superintendence, after his death. They buried him with great state, putting the body in charge of the late king's favourite wife; and it was her duty to reduce the corpse to a mummy, by scientifically baking it. After this the lower jaw was cut off and worked with beads, and put aside, together with the umbilical cord, which had been preserved from birth. The body itself was consigned to a tomb, and guarded ever after by this favourite, assisted by a sisterhood of those who came next to her in order of favour, all of whom had gardens assigned them for their maintenance, but were not allowed to see the succeeding king, and in fact were to be considered as dead to the world. Amongst the numerous family of the king a successor was chosen, the son by preference of an obscure mother, lest in his pride he should put the nobles to death. The rest of the brothers were placed under the charge of keepers, and allowed to enjoy life until the coronation of the heir-apparent, when all were

to be burnt to death but two, who were to be kept as the
king's companions as long as he wanted them, and when
he had no longer need of them were to be banished, one
to Unyoro, and the other to an outlying estate in Uganda.
The mother of the king, or Nyamasoré, was to enjoy
peculiar privileges. She was to take as maids of honour
all the wives of the late king not condemned to a
conventual life at his grave, she was to keep up a state
only inferior to her son's, and to guide him in all affairs
of importance until his majority. The princesses became
the wives of the king, and were forbidden to intermarry
with any one else. Both mother and son had their
Kamraviona, or commander-in-chief, and a complete set
of court officials, down to the musicians. Amongst these
was a spirit, a kind of Neptune, supposed to live in the
depths of the Nyanza, who communicated his will through
his appointed minister, and guided the king in all matters
relating to his navy, being a kind of spiritual First Lord
of the Admiralty. Under pain of attainder in goods and
chattels, it was the duty of all officers to be constantly
in attendance at court, any prolonged absence being
supposed to imply disaffection; and neglect of dress on
such occasions might be punished with death, though the
punishment was often commuted by a fine, which went
into the royal stores. Every act of the king, whether for
good or evil, was to be received with the same thankful-
ness, and the ceremony consisted in a course of prostra-
tions and whinings, after which they suddenly took up
sticks to imitate spears, pretended to charge the king, and
swore life-long devotion. A milder form of homage was
to kneel in an attitude of prayer, throw open the hands,
and repeat several times the word "nyanzig."

All this ceremonial did not tend to the despatch of court
business, but the king made up for lost time by finding

trifling faults, which led to confiscations, and so kept his civil list up to the mark. When the king was standing still or sitting, none dared approach him, except with downcast eyes and bended knees. To touch his throne or clothes, or look upon his women, was certain death. His attendants in court were certain sorcerers called Wabandwa or Wichwézi, fantastically dressed and decorated with charms, their chief duties being to avert the evil eye from the king, and keep his cup constantly supplied with plantain wine. Besides these there were the royal pages, a set of small boys always ready to run with messages, or execute any command of the king. This running is to be taken literally, for if they presumed to walk, it would be supposed to imply deficiency of zeal, and be punished with death. The arms of Uganda are a necessary accompaniment of court pageantry, consisting in a dog, two spears, and a shield. When a court was held, the company squatted in a half circle or three sides of a square before the king, while the musicians occupied the central space, and the king, sitting on his throne in a dignified manner, issued the orders of the day, the most important of which referred to military matters. The commander-in-chief, after receiving his commands, communicated them to his subordinates, and so on, until they were carried out. After this culprits were brought up to receive sentence. If any expostulation was attempted, the voice of the condemned person was instantly drowned by the drummers, and he was dragged away with studied brutality. Then young virgins, the daughters of the Wakungu, were brought to be presented for the king's harem, and seizing-officers were sent off on their errands of confiscation, while, as an interlude, some offenders against etiquette were summarily punished. Then fines in kind were brought in and presented; they were first smoothed down by the offender's hand, and applied to his face, to show there was no evil spirit lurking in them, and then they were presented, with thanks for the king's leniency in not punishing the offence more severely. The spoils of a plundering excursion perhaps followed, thousands of cattle and strings of women and children being brought in, or it may have been as the result of some wholesale confiscation. The best propitiatory sacrifice an offending officer could offer were a few young beauties, who might afterwards be bestowed on other officers as a reward for signal services. After this the royal magicians displayed their charms, and the chief huntsman his spoils of the chase. The fishermen and gardeners followed with their offerings, and then the different royal artificers presented their manufactures. When the king had had enough of business, he rose, spear in hand, and walked off without word or comment, leaving his company to take care of themselves. Every new moon it was the custom of the king to seclude himself, that for two or three days he might arrange and contemplate his magic horns. These periods would answer to his Sundays or holidays.

On other days he would take his women by hundreds at a time to bathe or disport themselves in ponds, or lead them long walks into the country, the procession on such occasions being led by the musicians, the Wakungu and pages, who were crowned with cords of aloe fibre, coming next, followed by the king in the centre, with the train of women behind him. If any one dared to stop and look at the royal procession on these occasions, he was hunted down by the pages, and might think himself lucky if he escaped with the loss of all his goods. Sometimes these walks took the shape of a pilgrimage, or resolved themselves into a yachting excursion, but on all occasions the same order was observed.

The ceremonies of the coronation, which Mtésa was looking forward to, were so important as to account for its delay in his case. All the neighbouring princes had to be
solicited to give one of their daughters in marriage to the
king, or her value in presents. The suit of Suwarora's
daughter was doubtless connected with this custom. Then
the Ilmas (the monthly nurse who had attended at the
king's birth) had to make a pilgrimage to the tomb of the
late king, and prognosticate from signs, derived from the
growth of trees and plants, the destinies of the future reign.
The voice of the Mgussu, or Nyanza Neptune, was also
heard in some mysterious manner. When the coronation
itself took place, the king was to cease to communicate
any longer with the queen-dowager, the brothers were to be
burnt, and the king, if the omens were in favour of war,
was to take the field at the head of his army, and march
either into Kittara or Usoga. As a result of such coronation forays, one half of Usoga and the remaining half of
Uddu had been annexed to Uganda.

On the next day after leaving Rumanika, having crossed
some hill-spurs to the first encampment, Speke was overtaken by Rozaro, who had remained behind to collect a
number of Wanyambo, whom he called his " children,"
for the purpose of sharing the benefits of the march. As
far as Karagué the British officers had had to pay black-
mail at all the stations; in Karagué itself they had free
quarters found them by the king; and it was now their
turn to be revenged by proxy on their former persecutors,
by taking black-mail from the unfortunate subjects of the
king of Uganda. This arrangement was naturally very
unwelcome to them, but they had no voice in the matter.
All the people disappeared from the villages before the
progress of the king's guests, and then the escort helped
themselves in the empty houses. Sometimes in the most

remote regions their exactions were resisted, and broken
heads were the result, which the English very much regretted, on more than one account. Grant was especially
helpless to exercise any control, being generally laid on
his back in his rude palankin, and quite at the mercy of
his conductors.

On entering the plantain-gardens of Kisaho, Speke
was informed that he must wait a day for Maula, who
had been detained that he might receive a present from
Rumanika, in the shape of the sister of Rozaro. She had
been married to another man, but as he had committed
some fault, had been confiscated with the rest of her husband's property. As soon as Maula had joined, they
marched down to near the end of the fork overlooking the
plain of Kitangulé, and then descending from the Mountains of the Moon, came across the plain to a settlement
named after the river. The dense forests which grew in
swampy places about this plain were said to have been
stocked by herds of elephants, before the ivory-trade drove
them to remoter regions. On the 16th of January Speke
crossed the river Kitangulé in pouring rain. It was only
after a long contest with the boatmen that he was able to
cross with his shoes on, as they thought that either the
canoe would upset, or the river dry up, in consequence of
the river-spirit taking offence. It was some eighty yards
broad, sunk to some depth below the surface of the land,
like a huge canal, and was so deep that it could not be
poled, while it ran at a speed of from three to four knots
an hour. They next came to Ndongo, a perfect garden of
plantains, the whole country being surprisingly rich, and
quite a paradise for negroes, who are not fond of too much
exertion. The same streaky sandstones prevailed as in
Karagué.

After this a low spur of hill was crossed, extending from the mountainous kingdom of Nkolé on the left towards the Nyanza. Here Nasib pointed out a village which was the last depôt in this direction of the Arab ivory-merchants. It was on some land of Rumanika's; for Sunna, the last king of Uganda, when he annexed Udda, gave Rumanika, with Machiavellian astuteness, certain strips of territory, that it might be his interest to prevent the property from being taken out of his hands again by the kings of Unyoro. The Arabs were so much complained of, on account of their oppressions of the Waganda, that Rumanika was ultimately obliged to withdraw their licence, and change their location to Kufro. To the right, at the end of the spur stretching out towards the Nyanza, was a rich, well-wooded, swampy plain, containing large open patches of water, which formerly, as Speke was assured, were navigable for miles, but now, like the Urigi lake, was gradually drying up. Indeed it seemed as if the Nyanza must once have washed the foot of the hills. Ngambezi was next reached, a place of extraordinary beauty and fertility, with a view on a rich marshy plain, covered with ant-mounds, on each of which grew the umbrella cactus, or some such evergreen. One of King Mtésa's uncles, who had escaped the fiery ordeal of royal brothers on Sunna's accession, was the proprietor of the place, and though not at home, the most liberal hospitality was administered in his name.

Over the same sort of ground, between other spurs of the sandstone hills, they came to the residence of a district officer of Rumanika's, who had three small huts in front of his residence set apart for devotional purposes. Many of the mendicant Wichwézi women, a sort of authorised witches, whose appearance resembled that of Ophelia in her madness, were here seen and heard. They imposed a tax on the superstition of the people, as the fakirs do in India. After another swampy flat, they reached a much larger group of hill-spurs pointing to the Nyanza, where lived Rumanika's frontier officer. Maula's house being one march distant, he first went home himself, then returned and brought Speke to his own clean hut, where, providing ample cheer, he kept him waiting for the return of a messenger to Uganda. Here Speke was joined by Nyamgundu, his Usui friend, who described Mtésa's ecstasies at receiving the message from him, and said that he had sent Speke four cows, which had indeed gone another way; but he (Nyamgundu) would fetch them, and then go to Karagué for Grant, for the notion of his not being able to come to Uganda while unwell was all a fiction of Rumanika's. Speke was out of patience at the different pretexts under which he was detained, and determined to march on, but his own men, finding themselves in clover, were intractable ; and it was here that Bombay, for the first and last time on the march, made a display of insubordination, so that Speke had to take the law into his own hands, and bring him to reason by punching his head. Nothing appears to be more useful to an African traveller than an adequate knowledge of the science of self-defence ; and Sir Samuel Baker, on his journey, as well as Speke, had reason to be glad that he had brought his fists with him. The natives were highly amused with the incident, and rehearsed the white man's action by digging at each other's heads for some miles afterwards.

With hills on the left, and a large low plain to the right, they had now to cross the first of a series of most disagreeable rush-drains, apparently some of the remains of the waters in the old bed of the Nyanza. This one was 150 yards wide, and sunk 14 feet below the plain. On the other side of it, from a small hill above the village where they encamped, Speke saw the Victoria Nyanza for the first time on this march. The way continued over the same sort of ground, the rush-drains occurring unpleasantly often, and the Wanyambo escort plundering the villagers everywhere, being highly indignant at Speke's trying to interfere with what they considered as their right.

On the 30th of January a letter was brought to Speke from Grant by a young man, who had on the skin of a leopard-cat (*Felis Serval*). The skin of the beast who figures in our own royal arms, is considered in Uganda as set apart for royal wear, and the young man immediately found himself under the eye of Nyamgundu in a very unpleasant position. A sort of court of inquiry was held, his genealogy was gone into, and when it was found that he had no claim to royal descent, he was adjudged to pay a hundred cows, and lose his skin, and was told that he might consider himself fortunate if he was not reported to Mtésa, in which case he would lose his head also.

After another course of rush-drains, they came to the ascent of some beautiful hills, covered with all kinds of verdure. Meruka—where, besides some other grandees, resided the aunt of the queen—was a delightful place, and the temperature was perfect. The roads were no longer the wretched tracks they had been accustomed to, but as broad as coach-roads, cut through the long grasses straight over the hills, and down through the woods in the dells. The huts and gardens were models of neatness, and there were signs of wealth everywhere. The whole foreground was a picture of peaceful beauty, with a boundless sea beyond. As Speke looked over the hills, it struck him that at one time the whole land must have been at a level with their present tops, and that it had been cut out into its present dells and hills by the denudation of constant rains, for none of the quartz dykes were observed which

P

protruded through the same aqueous formation in Usui
and Karagué, nor were there any other signs of volcanic
disturbance.

They passed now over hill and dale, and yet more rush-
drains, to Masaka, where was stationed the governor of
the district, one Pokino, before whom Nyamgundu had
to answer for some depredations of "Rozaro's children." Speke was welcomed by this officer with a cow,
sundry pots of pombé, enormous sticks of sugar-cane,
and a large bundle of indigenous coffee. It grew profusely here in large bushes, the berries sticking on the
branches like clusters of holly berries. Pokino gave the
case against the poor villagers, on the ground that the
king's guests were inviolable, and might do what they
liked in passing through the country. The same sort of
march continued to Kituntu, the last place in Uddu. Although decision was difficult, Speke pronounced this the
finest spot he had yet seen in the country, both from the
charms of its own site and the view it afforded of Uganda
proper, the lake, and the large group of islands called
Sésé, where the king keeps one of his fleets of boats.

When he came to the Katonga valley, instead of finding a broad sheet of water, as he had been led to expect
by the Arabs' accounts, Speke saw nothing but a succession of rush-drains, divided from one another by islands.
It took him two hours, with his clothes tucked under his
arm, to get through them all, and many were so matted
with weeds that the feet sank as if in a bog. The Waganda said that at certain times of the year, when these
drains were flooded, they could not be forded, but strangely
enough they were always lowest when most rain fell in
Uganda. No one knew where the water came from; but
from observation of the slow current in places, Speke
was convinced they all went into the lake. On crossing

some hills, however, he found other rush-drains going to
the northward. There were magnificent trees in the dells
of this equatorial region. They towered up clean-trunked
like enormous pillars, and then spread out their branches
like a canopy overhead. Speke thought that they were
on a larger scale than the blue gums of Australia, which
they resembled. They went on up and down through
this wonderful country, rich in grass, cultivation, and
trees, and new watercourses occurred, which were not so
unpleasant as those they had passed, as they were frequently bridged with poles or palm-tree trunks. Further
on a party of the king's gamekeepers were met, staking
their nets along the side of a hill, to catch antelopes by
driving the covers; and also a convoy of a hundred cows,
going as a present from Mtésa to Rumanika, in acknow-
ledgment of his goodness in forwarding Speke. It was a
truly royal method of sending compliments.

On inspection of the Mwérango river, a rush-drain three
hundred yards across, two-thirds of which were bridged,
Speke was convinced that the waters here came out of the
lake, and went to the north. He found the water out of
his depth, and was delighted at having apparently found
one of the branches by which the Nile makes its exit from
the Nyanza. It was said by the men to go to Kamrasi's
palace in Unyoro, where it joined the Nyanza, by which
they meant the Nile. At Nyama Goma, Speke found
Irungu, the ambassador he had met in Usui, with his
suite, and his old enemy Makinga, accompanied by the
deputation bearing Suwarora's present, in all a hundred
souls. The deputation was detained here until such time
as it should be Mtésa's pleasure to receive it, and in the
meanwhile had eaten up all the provisions of the country.
Speke was determined that he would not be kept kicking
his heels in an antechamber in the same style, and sent

Nyamgundu off at once with a message to the king to announce his arrival. Each of the men of the expedition then received a fez cap, and a piece of red blanket to make a military jacket. They were then instructed how to form a guard of honour, and Bombay was taught how Nazirs were presented at Indian courts. When this was done, Speke ascended a hill with Nasib, from which the lake could be seen on one side, and on the other a large range of huts said to belong to the king's uncle, the other unburnt brother of the late king Sunna.

Speke had received several messages on this journey, all of which testified the king's extreme impatience to see him, and Nyamgundu returned soon in a great state of excitement, saying that not finding the king at home he had followed him to a place on the lake, where he had gone yachting, that he was in an ecstasy of delight, and would return immediately to the palace to receive his visitor. He sent Speke four milch-cows by him, and gave him three for himself for bringing such pleasant intelligence. He was followed the next day by some of the king's pages, little rascals with their heads shaven, save two round tufts on each side, whose acquaintance Speke had made before, who said that the king would be starved unless he came quickly, as he had sworn not to taste food till he had seen Speke. So Speke made the best of his way through another rush-drain, called the Moga Myanza, which flowed into the Mwérango, and appeared to rise from some hills to the southward, and not in the lake. They had to pass the late king's mausoleum in the dark, as no profane eyes were allowed to look upon it, and in another march came in sight of the royal palace of Uganda, in the province of Bandawarogo, N. lat. 0° 21' 19", and E. long. 32° 44' 30", on the 19th of February 1862. It was a most imposing scene. A whole hill was covered with huts of gigantic proportions for Africa, each within its own fenced enclosure, with trees scattered amongst them. It was a sort of equatorial Kremlin in extent and grandeur, for it resembled that wonder of Moscow by being like a little city rather than a palace, though from the difference of climate it was not necessary to roof in large spaces, and the huts were rather bowers of privacy for the king, ladies, and courtiers, than state-rooms, which last were represented in fact by the open courts.

Notwithstanding the king's great impatience to see Speke, it was necessary that he should receive him in proper state; and as the rain prevented this on the evening of his arrival, the audience was deferred till the following morning. In the mean time he had to take possession of some huts outside, which had previously to be cleared of fleas, but was led to expect a better residence within the palace enclosure itself, after his introduction at court. As he was dressing the next day for the reception in the best clothes he could muster, it struck Speke that he would cut but a poor figure by the side of the Waganda. They wore neat bark cloths resembling the best yellow corduroy cloth, called "mbugus," crimp and well set, as if starched, and over that, as upper cloaks or togas, a patchwork of small antelope skins, which no European glovers could have sewn better; whilst their head-dresses, generally, were abrus turbans, set off with polished boar-tusks, stick-charms, seeds, beads, or shells; and on their necks, arms, and ankles, they wore other charms of wood, or small horns stuffed with magic powder, and fastened on by strings generally covered with snake-skin. The present was now got ready to be carried to the palace by a procession. It consisted of a block-tin box, four rich silk cloths, a gold chronometer, a revolving pistol, a Whitworth rifle, three rifled carbines with sword-bayonets, one

box of ammunition, bullets and caps, a telescope, an iron
chair, ten bundles of the best beads, and a set of knives,
spoons, and forks. Of course, during his long stay, a
variety of other articles were coaxed out of the king's
guest. Mtésa, as a beggar, stood midway between Rumanika, who did not beg at all, and Kamrasi, who begged
like a highwayman.

On advancing towards the palace, Speke observed that
the men with Suwarora's offering, consisting of more than
a hundred coils of wire, were ordered to take precedence
of his train; and he was especially annoyed at this, because these very brass wires had been his own, and intended by him for the king of Uganda, before they were
intercepted by Suwarora. His protests, however, had no
effect on the escorting Wakungu, so he walked along in
dudgeon, real or assumed, up the broad highroad into a
cleared square which divided Mtésa's domain from that of
the commander-in-chief, and then turned into the court.
He was surprised by the dimensions of the entrance
court, and its extreme neatness. The grass huts which
covered the hill were thatched like heads dressed by a barber, and fenced all round with the tall yellow reeds of the
tiger-grass; whilst walls of the same grass within the enclosure joined together the lines of huts, or partitioned
them off with their courts. It was here that Mtésa's
harem was domiciled, the rest of the ladies being with
the queen-dowager. They stood in little groups at the
doors, tittering among themselves at the triumphal procession. Each gate which they passed was hung with
jingling bells, like the gates in shop-doors in England,
and opened and shut by a proper officer. In the second
court, officials of high dignity stepped forward to meet
Speke, most fashionably and neatly attired. Men, women, bulls, dogs, and goats were led about by strings;

cocks and hens were carried in men's arms; and the
little imps of pages flitted about as if on errands of life
and death, each holding his skin cloak tightly about him
to prevent his naked legs from being seen.

Speke was now requested by the officers to sit in the sun
with his servants until the king could see him, this being
the custom when the Arabs came; but he was determined
not to submit to this, and in spite of the terrified remon-
strances of his men, walked straight away home, giving
Bombay orders to leave the present on the ground and
follow. Although the king is in theory inapproachable
except when he pleases, intelligence of Speke's wrath instantly reached him. His first impulse was to leave his
toilette and run after him himself, but on second thoughts
he sent the Wakungu instead, who overtook Speke in hot
haste, and, falling on their knees, begged him to turn back,
as the king had not tasted food, and would not till he saw
him. But the more vehemently they appealed the faster
Speke walked, until he arrived at his hut. Then Bombay and others entered in a profuse perspiration, saying
the king had heard of his grievances, that Suwarora's
hongo had been turned out of court, and that Speke, if
he wished, might bring his own chair with him—though
an artificial seat was an especial attribute of kings in
Uganda.

Having gained his point, and cooled himself with coffee
and a pipe, Speke returned to the charge. When he came
to the second tier of huts, everybody appeared to be in a
flutter of excitement, not knowing what would happen
after such a barefaced violation of court precedents; and
with extreme politeness the officers requested him to be
seated in his iron chair. He was not kept waiting many
minutes when a band passed, the musicians wearing on
their backs long-haired goat-skins, dancing like bears at

a fair, and playing on reed instruments decorated with
beads, from which hung leopard-cat skins, the time being
kept by hand-drums.   The king was now reported to be
sitting on his throne, in the state-hut of the third tier.
Speke advanced, hat in hand, the guard following in
" open ranks," and followed in their turn by the procession bearing the present.   Speke did not walk straight
up to him, but went outside the ranks of a three-sided
square of squatting Wakungu, mostly dressed in cow-
skins, some few of whom were also girt with the princely
leopard-cat skin.   Here he was desired to halt and sit in
the sun ; so he donned his hat again, spread his umbrella, a phenomenon which excited the utmost astonishment, ordered the guard to close ranks, and sat admiring
the novel scene, and the "admired of all admirers"
himself.

The king, a good-looking, well-grown, tall young man
of twenty-five, was sitting on a red blanket spread upon
a square platform of royal grass encased in tiger-grass
reeds, scrupulously well-dressed in a new mbugu.   The
hair of his head was cut short, excepting at the top,
where it was combed up into a high ridge, running
from forehead to poll like a cock's-comb.   No doubt
Speke smiled inwardly at the suggestion this arrangement of the wool conveyed.   On his neck was a large
ring of beautifully-worked minute beads, forming elegant patterns by their various colours.   On one arm
was another pretty bead ornament, and on the other a
wooden charm tied by a string covered with snake-skin.
On every finger and toe he had alternate brass and copper
rings ; and above the ankles, half-way up to the calf, a
stocking of very pretty beads.   For a handkerchief he
held a well-folded piece of bark, and a piece of gold-embroidered silk, which he constantly used to hide his large

mouth when laughing, or to wipe it after a drink of marwa, of which he took constant draughts from gourd-cups administered by ladies-in-waiting, his sisters and wives. A white dog, a spear, a shield, and a woman—the Uganda arms—were by him, as also a knot of staff-officers, with whom he kept up a brisk conversation, on one side; while on the other stood a group of witches, the pillars of his church establishment. Speke was now asked to draw nearer within the hollow square, where leopard-skins were strewn on the ground, and a large copper kettle-drum, surmounted by brass bells on arching wires, was placed, along with two other smaller drums, covered with cowries, and coloured beads worked into patterns. He longed to begin a conversation, but he did not know the language, and no one near dared speak, or even lift his eyes, for fear of seeing the fatal women, so the king and Speke sat staring at each other for full an hour, the latter silent, but the former making remarks to those about him on the strangeness of his guest's appearance, and desiring him by messages to lift his hat, open and shut his umbrella, and make the guards face about and show their red cloaks, for such wonders had never before been seen in Uganda.

At last, as the day was waning, he sent Maula as his envoy to ask if Speke had seen him, to which he replied, " Yes, for full an hour," and then, to the great relief of at least one of the parties, the king rose up, spear in hand, led his dog, and walked unceremoniously away into the fourth tier of huts, for this being a pure levee day, no business was transacted. His gait in retiring was evidently intended to be very majestic. It was the traditional walk of his race, founded on the step of the lion, but the outward sweep of the legs gave the impression of a ludicrous sort of waddle. It was only an act of humanity for Speke to wait a certain time now, for the state-

secret transpired that the purpose for which the king had
gone was to break his fast, having religiously kept his
vow of abstinence since he had heard of Speke's arrival.

King of Uganda retiring.

After this, Speke and his men were invited to Act the
Second, all native officers but the two guides having been
excluded.   The king was found standing on a red blanket,
leaning against a portal of the hut, talking and laughing
with a hundred or more of his wives, who, dressed in new
mbugus, squatted in two groups on the ground outside.
The men came crawling along the ground, afraid to look

upon the scene; but Speke rebuked them for their timidity in a loud voice, and stood gazing on the dark fair ones with hat in hand, till directed to sit and be covered. Mtésa then inquired what messages had come from Rumanika, to which Maula replied, overwhelmed by the honour of speaking to royalty, that Englishmen had been heard of up the Nile in Gani and Kidi. The king said he had heard the same, after which both the Wakungu thanked him enthusiastically, "nyanzigged," grovelled on the ground like flat fish thrown ashore, rose and fell, and fell and rose, with their faces covered with earth, presenting a specimen of the most abject form of "kotooing" to be found in any land. For the next scene he moved with his train to another hut, and, seating himself on his throne, with his women round him, invited Speke to approach within the nearest limits that propriety allowed. Again he asked Speke if he had seen him; and so his guest was at last able to get in a word, and open a conversation on the objects of his coming. The king never at any time paid very much attention to any remarks addressed to him, but seemed to be thinking more of the impression he himself was producing on the stranger, as if his chief motive in liking to have distinguished visitors was that he might show off before them. In Speke's case there was also the special difficulty that everything he said must first be told to Bombay, who told it to Nasib, who told it to Maula or Nyamgundu, it being contrary to etiquette to give a message except through an officer. Thus before Speke had time to answer a question the king had put him, the impatient monarch had forgotten it, and stopped the reply on its way to him with another query, so that the whole intercourse was something like our familiar Christmas game called "Cross Questions and Crooked Answers."

Finding it was difficult to do any business on these terms, to change the subject Speke gave the king a gold ring like a dog-collar; and the women having been sent away, the presents were brought in, and placed one by one on a red blanket, Nasib first smoothing them with his dirty hands, and rubbing his not over-clean face against them, before he presented them to the king. Mtésa appeared overwhelmed with wonder, and played with the things like a baby, till it was dark. Torches were then lit, and the whole collection—firearms, powder, &c., mixed with boxes, tools, and beads—were tumbled topsy-turvy into mbugus, and carried off by the pages. Mtésa then broke up the audience, promising to supply Speke with any provisions he wanted; and the next morning twenty cows and ten goats were driven in with the "king's compliments, and he had sent a few of his chickens!"

This abundant supply of provisions would have been very pleasant had it continued regularly, but the thoughtlessness of the king, rather than his niggardliness, caused his guests in after time to undergo many a compulsory fast. They had a general order to help themselves from the gardens of the inhabitants, and this he thought sufficient, as all the people being his property, of course their property was his; but it nevertheless led to many extremely disagreeable collisions, to avoid which much occasional privation was undergone. The next day after this interview, Speke heard that the king was occupied in receiving Suwarora's hongo of wire, sitting behind a screen himself, while the officer who brought it was made to sit in an empty court. Nor was the reception in other respects gracious; and it was told the officer that the king highly disapproved of the manner in which the things had been obtained, and of Suwarora's treatment of the white men in general. The officer tried to excuse his chief, on the plea that Suwarora could feel no respect for wizards who did not sleep in houses at night, and flew up to the tops of hills, and practised all sorts of sorcery. On which Mtésa gave him the lie direct, telling him that Rumanika would not have sent them to him had he not thought them perfectly respectable. He borrowed three muskets of Speke (which he faithfully returned the next night) that he might make up six with those he had already, to accompany him on a state visit to his relations to show the presents. His honesty was rewarded by the three muskets being given him. At the next interview the king wore the gold ring that Speke had given him, and miscellaneous business was transacted; but a shower of rain suddenly adjourned the court, while Speke was left walking about under his umbrella. When the rain ceased the king came out again, and sat in state as before, but now with a black bull's head, of which one horn was knocked off, placed before him. Four living cows were introduced, and he desired Speke to shoot them, which he did with a revolving pistol, to the king's great satisfaction, and they were given to the men.

The king now loaded one of the carbines with his own hands, and, giving it cocked to a page, told him to go out and shoot a man in the outer court. The page came back as delighted as a boy of his age would be at having robbed a bird's nest, and told the king he had done it capitally. Speke was sadly afraid that he had spoken the truth, but as the affair excited no attention, he could never ascertain whether any one was really shot or not.

These interviews were repeated without Speke being able to get in a word for a long time about Petherick or Grant. The only way to get at the king's attention was through what amused him for the moment, and Speke was very glad to find him bitten with a mania for shooting, which would place him in contact with him without ceremony, so he declined to shoot anything unless the king went with him. The medicine-chest proved another means of improving acquaintance, and the king fancied himself affected with all kinds of ailments, in order that Speke might prescribe for him, which he did as well as he could; and at last he was able to prevail on him to send an officer by water to Kitangulé, and another with two of Speke's men to Gani, *via* Usoga and Kidi. That these might go disguised, Speke asked for four mbugus and two spears, and the king characteristically sent twenty sheets of the bark cloth, four spears, and a load of sun-dried fish strung on a stick in the shape of a shield. Mabruki, the "fat boy" of Speke's party, and Bilal, were detached for the mission to the north, and then Speke called on the king to make arrangements for Grant, and to complain of his present beggarly residence, which he wished to change for a better one at the "west-end." Instead of attending to this request, the king desired him to call on his mother, telling him that she also required medicine. He was also told that etiquette required that he should attend on the king two days in succession, and every third day on the queen-mother.

As yet Speke had not been able to communicate with any of the Uganda court, the king's permission being necessary to allow him to do so; and he was not displeased to increase his acquaintance with the royal family. He found the queen-dowager's establishment very much like the king's, but on a smaller scale, and the same sort of etiquette prevailing, although the queen evidently cared less about it than her son, as she lived less for effect, and seemed chiefly concerned about creature comforts. Her majesty, fair, fat, and forty-five, was sitting on a carpet spread upon the ground within a curtain of mbugu, her elbow resting on a cushion of the same material. The only ornaments she wore were an abrus necklace and fillet of mbugu round her hand, whilst an old folding looking-glass stood open by her side. Before the entrance was placed an iron spit, with a cup on the top charged with magic powder, together with other wands used in divination; and within the room were a mixed company of ladies-in-waiting, with a sprinkling of sorceresses. Having secured privacy and pombé, she invited Speke to drink and smoke with her, and then ordered in the musicians and gave him a concert. Then she left him to go into her dressing-room, and returned, having changed her mbugu for a déolé or silk cloak, and entered into a conversation about her complaints, which appeared to be chiefly nervous. After examining the patient, Speke gave her two pills, the power of which was tasted by the Wakungu to prove that there was no devilry in them, and ordered her food and pombé to be restricted. Her majesty was pleased to express her entire satisfaction with everything except the stopping of the grog, which seemed to her a great hardship. In return for the presents which Speke had brought him, she gave him a beautifully-worked pipe for sucking pombé, in the manner that straws are used for imbibing American drinks; and she added to this sundry pots of pombé itself, a number of "sambo" or anklets, which, however, were useless to Speke, a cow, and a bundle of dried fish, of the kind called Kambari. Speke's picture-books were next inspected, and his clothes, rings, and the contents of his pockets, his watch exciting most attention, being supposed to be some magic instrument. She told Speke that he must come again in two days, and that she liked him indescribably, and then walked away.

Speke continued to ply the king on the subject of the inconvenience of his present residence, and Bombay, who was his go-between, told him that the only difficulty was that all the king's huts in the palace grounds were full of women, but that the king promised he would get him a suitable house, built in the fashionable quarter, if he would only give him time. He was certainly making his way in the royal good graces, for one day Nyamgundu and Maula came in great glee to say they had both been made captains, as a reward for their agency in bringing him. To acknowledge the compliment to himself, Speke gave them a wire each, which they immediately got drunk upon. The favour of the commander-in-chief was also shown one day by the present of an elderly woman "to carry water," with the addition that if she was not approved of, Speke might have the pick of ten others. It was not polite to refuse a present, and Speke would have been puzzled what to do in the case, had not the subject of his embarrassment relieved him of it by running away in the night.

The king's favourite recreation, since he had received the Whitworth rifle, was shooting cows in the palace-yard. An ugly report arrived one day that, having put two charges of powder in it, the bullet had gone not only through a cow, but through the court-fence, then through the middle of a woman, and then no one knew where. As to the queen-dowager, she could never see enough of Speke, and now received him, sitting on an Indian carpet, in a red linen wrapper with a gold border, with a box like a lady's workbox, covered with beads, by her side. Speke highly approved of her cookery, the meats being served on plantain leaves, with little flat round napkins of damp fibre to clean the fingers; but affection for him seemed to be made the excuse for a most unusual amount of dissipation in the way of pombé-drinking. The little mbugu cups being dismissed with contempt, a large trough of the precious liquor was brought and set before the queen. She drank from it like a pig, with her head in the trough, as well as the ministers; and if any was spilt in the process, the Wakungu present licked it up from the ground, and considered themselves honoured by doing so. During one long interview she changed her dress several times, and the intervals of feasting were filled up by music and conversation on all imaginable topics. At last the queen and councillors began to sing in chorus, joined by a jester, who kept up his character by always pitching his voice in a very dismal key; and what with drinking, shouting, and romping, the palace was turned into a pandemonium. At last the courtiers, as if a devil had possessed them, jumped up and flourished at the queen with their sticks, meaning that they were jealous of Speke, who had stolen her heart; and then the whole company, like Homeric gods, exploded in unextinguishable laughter. It must have been no small trial to the Englishman to have had to endure a frequent repetition of such jollifications; and what made the matter worse was that the favour of the queen-mother, by which he hoped to obtain the serious objects of his journey, proved rather an obstacle, by creating a most absurd jealousy between the mother and the son; and a series of tiffs and huffs, like lovers' quarrels, took place between Mtésa and Speke in consequence.

Speke was made extremely angry one day by a practical joke that was played on him by those impudent *gamins* the pages, who, while he was going to the king to get his message interpreted, let loose his Wanguana on the establishment of an officer marked out for con-

Q

fiscation, which they looted to their heart's content. As this was done apparently by the king's orders, Speke shut himself up in his hut for some days, and refused to come to court, saying he was doing penance for the sin into which his men had been betrayed, and to punish them he deprived them of their scarlet uniforms, as having disgraced the cloth of the bravest army in the world. The time wore on in little, tiresome, but amusing adventures with the king and queen-dowager, who both tried in their capricious way to spoil their guest, but inflicted at the same time all kinds of petty inconveniences on him. The king had learned to dress himself on state occasions in a fantastic Arab costume, and to sit on the chair that Speke had given him; and endeavoured to imitate him in everything, even in the manner in which he played with his ramrod. He had even taken the trouble to learn the coast language, that he might converse with him.

One day Speke was suddenly summoned to go out shooting with the king; but instead of buffaloes or hippopotami being the game, he led him to a high tree on which some vultures were perched, and some adjutants had built their nests. Speke at first demurred to shoot such ignoble game, but at last yielding, shot an adjutant in the nest, and a vulture on the wing, which fell in a garden enclosure. There was an outburst of immense enthusiasm, and the next thing was to go and see the bird. So, by the king's order, his train made straight for the spot, rushing through the court where the women were concealed for fear of the guns, trampling down newly-made fences in their hurry like elephants, and floundering through shrubs and plantains till they came on the bird. And then the women were all called up to join in the shout of wonder, and the whole company was taken in the direction of the queen's palace. On the

way Speke shot some herons in the air, a feat which
seemed incredible except by magic. The birds were all
picked up by the pages, except the unclean vulture, and
carried off in triumph to the queen ; and as kites, crows,
and sparrows still kept flying about, and the king insisted
on their being shot, all Speke's shot was soon expended.

On the 13th of March Mabruki and Bilal returned
from Usoga, having not been able to get beyond the
border, because their escort had been beaten by the
Wasoga. One of this race being an expert climber, which
the Waganda are not, was sent up the tree to get the
dead adjutant, but half-way he was attacked by a swarm
of bees, who drove him down again.

At last, by favour of the commander-in-chief, secured
by a judicious bribe, Speke got a number of huts assigned
to him in an eligible situation in full view of the palace.
The move was soon made, and the men constructed a
street of barracks, which were fitted with all convenient
offices, as sanitary rules were as stringent in Uganda as
among the most civilised nations. This step in advance
was followed in process of time by Speke obtaining introductions to and exchanging visits with the commander-in-
chief and all the high officials of Uganda. The court
executioner Kunza begged him to intercede with the king
for the life of his son, who had been condemned to death
for some trifling offence at the last levee. The appeal,
owing to his great influence with the king, was successful.
The commander-in-chief was so pleased with Speke, that
he made him the handsome but unseasonable offer of the
help of the Waganda army to dethrone Queen Victoria,
and set him up as king in her stead.

Speke had now managed to get admittance to the king
at any time by firing a gun in front of the palace, and by
a judicious return of her presents had brought the queen

also to reason, so that she desired she should always
be informed when he wished to see her. Although the
residence near the court was advantageous in some respects, in others it was found to be oppressive. The
king obtained his wives very easily ; Speke having seen
twenty undraped virgins presented to him at one levee,
the happy fathers profusely "nyanzigging" for the
honour done them, which caused Speke to burst into a
roar of laughter which infected the whole court, and
scattered etiquette to the winds. He also got rid of them
as lightly. Nearly every day since he had changed his
residence, Speke saw one, two, or three of the poor
creatures dragged away to execution, making the most
lamentable appeals as they went, and yet no one dared
lift a finger to save them. There were no marriage ceremonies in Uganda. If any officer committed a petty
offence he would send a handsome daughter as a peace-
offering, or a neighbouring king might give his daughter
as a tribute. The Wakungu themselves received their
wives from the king's hands in reward for services in war,
or, in making a successful seizure, as part of the spoil.
Women in Uganda had hardly so high a position as in
Unyamuézi, where they were regarded as valuable property to be paid a handsome price for, though some men
exchanged their daughters, and any who misbehaved could
be sold into slavery, flogged, or degraded to menial services.
Females were given away much as domestic cats are with
us. Speke was obliged to receive a present of this kind
from his friend the queen-dowager in the shape of two
very young girls, whom he immediately adopted and put
under the charge of a Wanyamuézi governess, but who
gave, nevertheless, considerable trouble, so that one of
them had soon to be dismissed in disgrace.

The king having at last succeeded in shooting a

heron (sitting) with his own hands, thought himself capable of aspiring to larger game; and after the ceremonies at the beginning of the month of April were over, which chiefly consisted in consulting the fetishes, and he and his court shaving their heads all but the cock's-comb, he suddenly sent a message to Speke that he had started after buffaloes, and expected him to join him. He was found in a plantain-garden about a mile beyond the palace, dressed in imitation of Speke, wideawake and all, the perfect picture of a black snob. It was easy to see there would be no sport, as a procession consisting of the band, the Wakungu, the pages, the two sportsmen, and the women, were not likely to find buffaloes; but it was useless to make any observation. As they went Speke gossiped and laughed with the women with an effrontery which utterly astonished Mtésa and his suite, and helped them over the logs which were put to span the water-drains with a gallantry which utterly astonished themselves. So fast, however, did they gain confidence, that on crossing one difficult place near the Murchison Creek, the king's favourite odalisque, Lubuga, held out both her hands to implore the help of the white man, a motion which was noticed by the king; but he, instead of resenting it, gave the Kamraviona a sly poke in the ribs, and told him what he had seen, as if it had been a secret or a joke. The king happened to be in high good-humour; and when he was tired, in order that he might sit like Speke on a chair, made a page kneel down on all-fours and sat on his back. As for the women, one of whom had once thrown herself flat and roared for fear of the stranger, they became by degrees so familiar and fearless that he could walk about with them arm-in-arm in the seraglio park, and indulge in pantomimic flirtations, and that to the wonder of an awe-struck public, with perfect impunity.

It seemed, after all, as if the terrible "Mrs Grundy" of Uganda was a phantom, which a little modest assurance would easily put to flight.

An incident occurred one day which peculiarly illustrated the inconsistency of the conventional notions of the country. Speke had called on the king to bring him some toddy which he had succeeded in distilling from pombé—and which, by the way, gladdened the royal heart quite as much as the lessons in shooting—when he found him holding a levee, at which one of the goats presented was a fine for no less a crime than an attempt at regicide. A youth of sixteen or seventeen, finding the king alone, had walked up to him and threatened to kill him, because, he said, he took the lives of men unjustly. His majesty, without disputing the undeniable truth of the proposition, put the muzzle of his revolver to the boy's cheek, and so, though it was not loaded, frightened him away. The culprit came and presented his goat with the usual "nyanzigs," stroking it and putting it to his face, and was then, strange to say, free to go about his business. Probably from the heinousness of the crime, it had no place in the penal law of Uganda, and the king was too complete a child to form an independent judgment on its nature.

Speke's repeated applications to the king had at last the effect of his agreeing, since the first expedition had failed, to send Budja, his ambassador, to look for Petherick in Unyoro. But his conscience telling him that Kamrasi had good reasons to be suspicious of everybody coming from Uganda, he always kept the subject at arm's-length as much as possible; and to keep Speke quiet, offered him, in case Petherick did not fetch him within four months, an estate entailed on his heirs for ever in his own dominions, amply stocked with men, women, and cattle, which would offer every inducement to his making Uganda his permanent residence. Certainly, as a plundering army now came back from Unyoro bringing great numbers of cows, women, and children—the men all having run away or been killed fighting—the prospect of being able to get from Uganda to Kamrasi's seemed visibly diminishing.

One day, when the king was in a very good temper with Speke, some thirty odd women were brought for execution, and the king begged Speke to take any one he fancied from the number. He chose one of the best-looking, and gave her to Ilmas, his valet, as his wife; but she, instead of being thankful that her life was saved, proved excessively refractory, as she was disappointed at not being married to Speke himself, and after trying to hang herself, finally ran away. It appears to be a custom in Uganda, neglected in this case, to chain up newly-caught women for two or three days, till the wildness wears away, and they get used to the house, just as some people smear butter on the paws of newly-imported kittens. Speke had now felt his way in saving lives, being afraid by any sudden act to compromise the success of the expedition; and an opportunity soon occurred of showing the moral mastery that he had obtained over Mtésa's savage and capricious nature. It was indeed the kind of ascendancy that Van Amburgh succeeded in acquiring over lions and tigers, the spell of which was liable to be broken at any moment by the beast finding, by licking a scratched finger, that his ruler had human blood in his veins, and tearing him in an ecstasy of fury.

Having been sent for to attend the king on the 23d of April on an excursion to the Nyanza, Speke found him waiting about near the Murchison Creek with his usual train, travelling like a pack of hounds, and firing his rifle occasionally to let him know his whereabouts.

He had just done a little business on the way to his pleasure; for noticing, as he passed, a woman tied by the hands to be punished, he fired at her by way of trying his gun, and anticipated the executioner.

So great had been his haste to start on this excursion, which was to last three days, that no preparation had been made by anybody, and Speke was obliged to leave all he wanted behind, though some of his traps arrived the following day. On arriving at the piece of water named by Speke after Sir Roderick Murchison, not a boat was to be found at the mooring station; but just as it was getting dark, the drums and the guns together managed to bring up about fifty large craft. They were all painted with red clay, and had from ten to thirty paddles, with long prows like the neck of a swan, decorated on the head with horns of the " nsunnu " or *Leucotis* antelope, between which was stuck upright a tuft of feathers like a grenadier's plume. These conveyed the party across the mouth of a deep rushy swamp to the royal yachting-station, the Cowes of Uganda, a short walk from the lake, and distant about five hours from the palace. After a picnic and rather uncomfortable night quarters, Speke had the honour of breakfasting with the king in the open air on roast-beef and plantain squash, folded in plantain leaves. He sometimes ate with a copper fork and picker not forked, but more usually used his hands to help him, as a dog does his paws. He would take the tough pieces from his mouth and throw them as a treat to the pages, who " nyanzigged," and seemed to enjoy them. The boys afterwards divided the relics. The king drank pombé himself as his only beverage, but was not very liberal in helping his guests to it.

The party now made for the lake. They rattled along, the poor women keeping up with the king's four-miles-an - hour strides as best they could, through plantains and shrubs, under trees as much as nine feet in diameter, until the beautiful waters were reached. The scenery was like that about Rio de Janeiro, save that its high background mountains were represented here by beautiful little hills. When the king arrived, a band of drums, playing like factory engines, brought up the boats, and the sailors as they arrived plumped over the gunwales into the water, like so many frogs at the edge of a pond, afraid of lifting their heads, lest they should be caught admiring the ladies. They were all dressed in plantain leaves, which gave them a resemblance to classical river-gods. In the arrangement of the flotilla, which was superintended by the king himself in his red coat and wideawake, Speke found himself in the same boat with the king, sitting at his feet, with three women behind, who offered cups of pombé. The hippopotami, who had formed part of the day's programme, were too shy to show themselves; so the day passed in doing nothing, the men going ashore to picnic, but forgetting to give the women anything to eat. A concert wound up the day's amusement, at which the king showed himself an accomplished musician. Finding the hippopotami still "not at home" on the following day, the king, paddling and steering in person with a pair of new white paddles, directed his course to an island sacred to the Mgussa, or Neptune of the Nyanza, and occupied by his familiar or deputy, who is the medium by which he communicates with the king. Speke felt a natural interest in meeting this presiding priest of the source of the Nile.

After a picnic, the whole party took a walk on the island, winding through the trees and picking fruit, when, by ill-luck, it occurred to one of the prettiest of the royal wives, probably having taken a lesson in gentle demeanour from Speke, to pluck a fruit and offer it to her lord and master. If a serpent had stung him it could not have stupified him more, and if he had seen a serpent at her ear, suggesting the gift of the forbidden fruit, he could not have been more wroth. The pages were instantly ordered to seize, bind her, and lead her to execution. No sooner was the order given than the whole bevy slipped their cord turbans from their heads, and threw themselves like a pack of Cupid beagles on the fairy queen, who, indignant at their presumption, kept beating off the urchins like flies, and appealing to the king. They were too many for her, however, and she was dragged away, crying on the Kamraviona and the Mzungu (white man) for help, while Lubuga, the pet, and all the other women clasped the knees of the king and implored forgiveness for their sister. The more they cried, however, the more furious he became, till he took up a heavy stick and began to belabour his victim on the head. Speke could stand this no longer, especially as the interesting victim had invoked him by name, and he rushed at the king, and, catching hold of his uplifted arm, demanded that he should spare the woman's life. Strange to say, this most unheard-of proceeding acted like a charm on the evil spirit that possessed the king, and, even highly amused, he released the woman.

Passing on through the trees of the beautiful island, they came to the hut of the Mgussa's representative. Its further end was ornamented with mystic symbols, amongst others a paddle, the badge of his office, and after a time the medium himself arrived. He was dressed in the Wichwézi fashion, with a little white goat-skin apron, and used a paddle for a mace or walking-stick. Though not old, he affected extreme old age, coughing asthmatically, glimmering with his eyes, and mumbling like a witch. After he had rested himself, with much seeming difficulty, by the symbols, he coughed for about half-an-hour: his wife came in and did likewise. The king laughed and looked at Speke, and then at these strange beings, as if to ask what he thought of them. Nothing was heard but a sort of frog's croak for water from the old woman, who croaked again, because what was brought was not of the purest, had the cup changed, wetted her lips with the second, and bolted away as she had come. Then the Mgussa motioned to the chief officers to draw up round him, and in a low tone gave them the orders of the deep, and walked away. The revelation seemed to have been unpropitious, for a return home was at once ordered. At the Cowes a number of braves, who had returned from the Unyoro war, having had great success and not lost a man, came to pay their respects to Mtésa. He told them how Bana (the master) had saved the queen's life, and they highly approved of it, saying he evidently knew what he was about, and was accustomed to administer justice in his own country. Speke accompanied the king on many more yachting excursions, on one of them seeing the island of Kitiri. The largest island, or group of islands, is Sésé, near the mouth of the Katonga, where another priest of Neptune is stationed.

At the beginning of the month of May a great event took place at court—the reception of the victorious army. In front of the king, in form of a hollow square, sat the lately returned officers—the nobles distinguished by leopard-cat skins and dirks, the commoners by coloured mbugus and cow or antelope skin cloaks, but all their faces and arms were painted red, black, or smoke-colour. Within the square in front of the king were placed, in three rows, the offensive and defensive arms of Uganda as the martial symbols. The great war-drum, covered with a leopard-skin, and placed on a large carpet of the same, was placed in advance. Behind this, on a rack of iron,

hung the common implements of war, such as spears, of
which two were of copper, the rest of iron, and shields of
wood and leather; whilst behind, with great taste and
effect, was arranged a sort of trophy of the various charms
useful in discomfiting enemies.   On a line with the king,
again, and outside the square, were placed the arms of the
household, a handsome French-made copper kettle-drum,
with brass bells on the outer edge hanging from copper
wires, two new spears, a painted leather shield, and various magic wands, spread on a carpet of leopard-skins.
The whole pageant gave an impression of barbaric magni-
ficence.   The ceremony consisted in each commanding
officer in turn giving account of the conduct of his regimental subalterns.   To the worthy, the king, who listened
attentively, awarded pombé; to the unworthy, death.
After each sentence there was a hubbub, as the struggling wretch was bundled away, bound hands and head
together.

On the 11th of May, Speke had the satisfaction of
receiving letters from Grant, having had at various
times more or less authentic news of him.   It was arranged that he should come by the lake, but his convoy
had been afraid of the dangers of the voyage, and brought
him by land, and he was now at the house of Maula.
Three days afterwards the Unyoro deputation returned,
attended by four men sent by Kamrasi, headed by one
Kidgwiga.   It now transpired that Mtésa had followed
Speke's advice to try gentle means with Kamrasi, by
sending a hongo instead of an army; and two elephant
tusks were sent in return.   Kidgwiga said that Petherick's
party had not reached Unyoro, but were at anchor off
Gani.   Two white men had been seen there, the one
hairy and the other smooth-faced; they had sent Kamrasi a necklace of beads, which he had duly acknowledged

The King of Uganda reviewing Colonel Congow's Regiment.—PAGE 253.

in tusks and women. Kamrasi offered to send Speke to them in boats, instead of by the dangerous route through the Kidi, which was only occasionally attempted by Wanyoro and Gani people, who dealt in cows and tippet monkey-skins, and who travelled at night, and avoided the natives as much as possible. Baraka and Ulédi, who had been sent on, were detained by Kamrasi, and not allowed to return with Mabruki and Bilal. Mabruki said that Kamrasi had received Speke's present, and then immediately ordered them to go back, remarking that the Waganda were a set of plundering blackguards.

The king had by this time very much improved in his shooting, even killing birds on the wing, and at last, on the 25th of May, to his great delight he killed in a tree his first "nundo" or adjutant. The bird stuck like a spread eagle in the upper branches, and had to be brought down by Wasoga climbers. The scene of exultation which followed beggars description, and the bird was carried before the king to be shown to all the royal family. There had been for some days past a general muster of the Uganda army; and the warriors had streamed in vast numbers, like swarms of ants, from all quarters to the palace up the straight broad roads that led to it. By this time the Colonel Congow, in full-dress uniform, had arrived in the square outside, with his regiment drawn up in review order. The king, hearing of this, at once came out with spears and shield, preceded by his adjutant, and posted himself in arms at the entrance, encircled by his squatting staff, with the dead bird placed in the middle as the centre of attraction. In front was a large parade-ground, with the Kamraviona's huts behind. The battalion, which consisted of three companies of 200 men each, being drawn up at the left extremity of the ground,

received orders to march past in single file from the right
of companies in a long trot, and re-form again at the end
of the square. The scene which ensued was inconceiv-
ably wild and fantastic. The men were nearly all naked,
with goat or cat skins hanging from their girdles, but
wore war-paint according to individual taste. One half of
the body was red or blue, the other black; but the colours
were so distributed that one (painted) stocking would be
red, the other black, while the breeches above would be
of the opposite colours, and the sleeves and waistcoat were
made to alternate in the same manner. This must somewhat have resembled the particular dress in vogue in the
fourteenth century, such as the famous three Swiss are
depicted in. Every man carried the same arms—two
spears and a shield—held as if approaching an enemy ;
and they thus moved in three lines of single rank and file,
at fifteen or twenty paces apart, with high action and long
step, the ground leg only being bent to give greater force
to the stride. The men were followed by the captain's
men, more fantastically dressed; and last came the Colonel,
looking like Robinson Crusoe, with his long white-haired
goat-skins, a fiddle-shaped leather shield tufted with hair
at its six extremities, and a magnificent helmet covered
with rich many-coloured beads, surmounted by a plume
of crimson feathers, from the middle of which rose a bent
stem, tufted with goat's hair. The companies next charged
to and fro, and finally the officers came up, pretending to
charge the king, making violent professions of loyalty,
and receiving from him the usual compliments of a reviewing officer.

Two days after the review, to Speke's inexpressible
delight, Grant arrived. He was now able to limp about
a little, and they had a hearty laugh together over his
adventures. When he left Rumanika's, his Waganda

bearers transferred his litter from their heads to their
shoulders, and rattled along with him, always keeping
his head foremost, at the rate of about six miles an
hour.   They appear on the whole to have been very careful, as any man who stumbled was reproached by his
comrades ; but they often set him down and left him for
long periods whenever plantains and plantain-wine were
abundant, and once that they might bowl rocks down
a precipice.   Each man carried on the march a small
bundle on his head, with pipes and flutes stuck in it, and
at his back a spear and shield, the latter serving as an
umbrella when rain fell.   Those who had dogs dragged
them along by a string.   After a march they always put
on their robes, and when they approached dwellings they
shouted and sang as if they were carrying a dead lion.
They made wild work with the plantains and other property of the inhabitants everywhere, living at free quarters, and eating the dinners ready cooked for other people.
Their leader was one Maribu, who had a pleasant little
wife, very attentive to Grant's wants.   The worst part of
the journey had been the crossing of the horrible rush-
drains, which, in the still inflamed condition of Grant's
leg, gave him excruciating pain.

Notwithstanding his invalid state, Grant was able to
make some observations on natural history.   The flora
along this track was not very remarkable for its variety.
The most graceful tree was the wild date-palm, growing
on the low hills in clumps of three or four.   Its crested
plumes waved in the breeze, giving almost animal life to
the silent scene.   Bird's nests or clusters of India-red fruit
hung from the branches.   There was a new sort of acacia
whose pods were broad and numerous, with fruit so abundant that it almost hid the leaves.   Not many large trees
were seen, their growth having been probably stunted by

the lichens and parasites which covered them. One flat-topped acacia was matted over with bushes of them as if they had been planted on the tops of the branches. The trunks were observed to bear most moss on the north-east side, denoting that that exposure was the dampest. The coffee-shrub was found useful as a screen from the sun. The growth of each year was marked by the knots on its branches. Two kinds of fruit were observed—one like the Indian loquot, with several stones, growing on a tree with dark foliage and dense branches, the other an underground scarlet fruit, growing in sets of five or six clustered together like bananas, and of the same size. After they were peeled, the pulp with its numerous black seeds had the refreshing taste of a lime. The Waganda carried them strung as necklaces. The stalk of this plant (an amomum) grows four feet high from a creeping knotted root, and the scarlet fruit, when ripe, peers from the ground, forcing up the soil like a mole. The green plantain is prepared by boiling, when the peel comes off, and it is eaten like mashed potatoes. It was much im-proved by being boiled with meat, and improved the meat also. The fruit furnished food as well as wine, its leaf tablecloths and plates, and its watery fibre napkins to cleanse the hands. Thread, wrappers, and strips like ribbons were taken from the trunk, and the leaves were also made into screen-fences. The plantain-orchards were seen to the greatest perfection in Uhia. The tree some-times contained two hundred large fruit, bending the stems, which had to be supported by a forked stick or ropes. The tree is cut down when the fruit is ripe, to permit the growth of the young shoot which comes from the parent root. The orchards are of bare-poled single trees, which is a better arrangement for fruit than if they grew in clusters; and should the leaf-stalk droop

King Mtesa holding a Levee.—PAGE. 267.

from the trunk, it is bandaged up to prevent the rain from beating into the heart of the tree.

At Katonga Bay Grant observed the *Trapa natans*, whose roots the Waganda eat. Its leaves looked very beautiful in the water by the side of those of the lily of the Nile. He noticed, as well as Speke, the gigantic trees in some of the dells with their deep-green foliage. Their trunks and branches were covered with parasitical plants, making a shelter for the buffalo and elephant, who, unconscious of a stage erected overhead to catch them, came there to escape the heat. He brought home some seeds of a strange-looking tree of the plantain kind, seen growing wild outside a cultivation. They were pronounced to belong to the *Ensete* of Bruce, discovered by him in Abyssinia. It had a general resemblance to the plantain, but a very stout stem and general low appearance, its shape being that of big drums placed one on the other, with gigantic single leaves growing from the sides. In 3° N. lat. this plant was again met with, growing on rocky heights. Of all the people that Grant passed he was most pleased with those of Uhia, who were exceedingly neat and clean in all their habits, and wore becoming mantles of cowskin or bark-cloth, often of a salmon colour, which contrasted well with their dark skins.

On the 28th of May the royal pages came to say that the king would receive Grant, and that he might sit on a stool in the presence. Accordingly, his present of a gun and ammunition having been graciously received, he dressed himself in his best suit—namely, white trousers, blue flannel coat, shepherd's plaid shirt, a helmet and a red turban round it. Mtésa appeared and took his seat on a bench of grass with a dog behind him; the Kamraviona sat at his feet, and several women were on his left.

R

His quick eye detected that part of Grant's hand had been cut off, and as such mutilations in Uganda are generally the consequence of some offence, he seemed puzzled, and whispered with the pages; but his mind was set at rest when Maribu informed him that the maiming was the result of a wound received in action. Other scenes followed, in which the king displayed his state, as in Speke's case. A shudder came over Grant as two women were dragged to execution, and he thought that it might have been done as a sort of compliment to his arrival.

The next day the king came in his usual bustle to return the call, dressed like a travelling monkey or a negro sailor. He wore an open coat of bed-curtain chintz, loose white trousers with a stripe of scarlet, but with naked hands and feet. He was shown to an iron chair, turned over some books in a childish manner, observed Rumanika's portrait, and then said that he expected his own to be done. His brothers—a mob of little ragamuffins—sat behind him. Several of them were handcuffed (the custom of the court), but they chatted pleasantly, tearing away at sugar-cane. Then the king rushed wildly away, the chained lads following as well as their bonds would allow them. They could only complain of their ill luck in being of such high birth, as the king himself always had gone about in chains previously to his accession. Grant was introduced by Speke to the queen-dowager, who struck him as being like a Tartar woman. She welcomed him heartily, and talked for an hour or so, fondling in her lap a sort of doll the shape and size of a hedgehog, covered with cowries and beads.

The king had become so fond of his gun that he thought and dreamed of nothing but shooting. Very early in the morning he was heard popping, with the rattle of drums that always accompanied his movements. It was hard to see him, so fully occupied was his time. He had received so many presents from Speke and Grant, had made so many promises to open the road to the north, and his pages had robbed them in his name of so much of their ammunition, that at last he became ashamed of himself, and suddenly, to their great joy, gave them permission to leave. He had become very tiresome in wanting something or other continually done for him— such as the painting of all the birds he shot—and in begging through the pages for everything they possessed. They had even had the impudence to ask for the Union-jack, the gift of Admiral Keppel. All this, added to the horrible executions and brutalities, made them feel that Uganda was by no means the paradise it had been described; and moreover, their own Seedis became very mutinous, knowing that hundreds of women and cattle were offered to the officers which they would not take, and which they themselves would gladly have accepted, while they were kept on short commons. The ammunition had been shot away to amuse Mtésa, and the men refused to march unless sufficient ball-cartridge were served out to them. In Uganda no beads were allowed to be taken by the natives, though privately provisions could be purchased with them. Cowries were a more current coin, one hundred of these shells making one string, which was equal to a bunch of a hundred plantains or the skin of a goat, and a single large gourdful of wine cost a sheet of bark-cloth.

Grant was introduced, among other high personages, to the two executioners, the one whose son Speke respited (to be put to death afterwards for another offence), and the other, an invalid, who was always carried in a litter. This man's face when he spoke was not repulsive, but when seen with a wreath of black fringe round his head, hiding

his eyes and hanging over his face, he brought to mind
a black Highland bull glowering through his forelock.
One day Grant followed a woman led by the pages; she
carried a small hoe on her head, and the cord round her
wrists in front told that she was under sentence of death.
He left her at the executioner's gardens, and as he waited
outside, no sound reached him. Only a lazy yellow-
beaked vulture, the cannibal of Uganda, sat perched on
the stump of a broken tree, while others hovered overhead contemplating some scene that was going on below!
Executions were said to be performed by cutting in
pieces with a reed-knife.

Grant was better pleased with the drill of the soldiers,
who were made to work together — as, for instance,
at stacking wood — with the industry and precision
of Roman legionaries. The Waganda were, in general,
a very clever and ingenious people. Having seen the
pictures of men and animals, they would draw the
same on their bark-cloths in black; and these bark-
cloths themselves, ranging in tint from a salmon colour
to a brick-red, were marvels of manufacture. They are
cut from several varieties of *ficus*, beaten upon a log
with a mill-headed wooden hammer, and then sewn
together into shawls or togas. The men of the expedition having worn out their clothes, were now dressed in
them like the natives. The Waganda were also very fair
cooks, cutting butcher-meat into very neat joints, wrap-
ping them in plantain-leaves, and boiling them with the
plantain itself. The Seedis lost many a good dinner
through their Mussulman prejudices. But it was as
musicians that the Waganda especially shone. They had
both wind and stringed instruments, and the sound of
drums was perpetual, the drum-call of each regiment
being different. The king's small drums were beaten so

as to swell from double piano to forte and *vice versa*. At all levees reed and bugle players attended, dancing as they played. The reeds, held like flageolets, were decorated with coloured beads, and had a sweet and pleasing sound. Sometimes the wind-instruments were joined by an enormous kettle-drum. The harmonicon was made of twelve blocks of wood, which, on being struck, gave out notes like musical glasses. They rested on trunks of plantain, and were isolated from one another by their reeds. They had also the "wanga," mentioned in the "Karagué" chapter—an elegant instrument, looking like a miniature harp when laid in the lap to be played. The queen had generally a blind harper in attendance on her. The king was an expert performer on all the instruments, and would sit for hours playing or listening. Instrumental music was more common than singing, though on a march the Waganda would sing in a quivering voice, slurring the words and notes in a manner peculiar to themseves. They possessed, too, the British butcher-boy accomplishment of whistling through their fingers, and had a curious way of snapping them like castanets when they wished to speak with emphasis.

The climate of Uganda was sultry and cloudy, and there were terrific thunderstorms occasionally, which set huts on fire, and frightened the king exceedingly. The heaviest rainfall was on the 4th of July, when 1.04 inch was registered.

Perhaps Mtésa would never, after all, have let his guests go, had not Speke known how to bring into play his jealousy of Rumanika, who had said they must be sent back safe to him. Mtésa was determined, in consequence, to forward them to Unyoro, to prevent his having his way. It was rather unfortunate that at the very time he was treating with Kamrasi, about eighty cows were driven in from Unyoro by the Waganda, showing that he was plundering him all the time. Budja was now appointed to escort them, and boats were ordered that they might go by water, but the admiral put his veto on this plan. Before they went they discharged the Wanyamuézi porters, with ivory and orders on Rumanika, and old Nasib with a handsome remuneration. Early on the 7th of July they went to bid the king farewell. Speke talked to him of future prospects of opening the country, and on other subjects which most interested him, and he replied with good feeling and taste. They then all rose with an English bow, placing the hand on the heart in saying "adieu;" and there was a complete uniformity in the ceremonial, for in whatever Speke did Mtésa imitated him. Mtésa accompanied them to the camp and had the men paraded before him, giving them good advice before parting, and charging them to follow their leaders through fire and water; then exchanging adieus once more, he led the way up the hill in gigantic strides, his pretty favourite Lubuga looking back and crying "Bana, Bana!" as she waved and beckoned with her little hands, then trotted along after her lord, the most effusive in the demonstrations of feeling which seemed to be shared more or less by all of the train, and which were repeated till they all passed out of sight over the brow.

CHAPTER V.

UNYORO.

START ON THE NORTHWARD JOURNEY—GRANT AND SPEKE DIVIDE, SPEKE MAKING FOR THE EXIT OF THE NILE AND GRANT FOR KAMRASI'S—SPEKE AT THE NILE—THE "STONES," OR RIPON FALLS —SPEKE TRIES TO GET DOWN THE NILE—THE BRITISH FLAG SURPRISED INTO PIRACY—SECOND BATTLE OF THE NILE—SPEKE RETURNS AND LOOKS FOR GRANT—GRANT MEETS HIM, HAVING BEEN DRIVEN BACK—THEY MARCH TOGETHER AGAIN FORWARD—SPORT WITH ELEPHANTS—KAMRASI'S PALACE—DESCRIPTION OF KAMRASI —LONG DETENTION WITH THE "KING OF THE BEGGARS"—SUPERSTITIONS, ETC., OF UNYORO.

SPEKE had two motives for diverging from the direct route from Karagué to Unyoro into Uganda, where he had now been, partly by compulsion, domiciled for the first six months of the year 1862. The first was that he was convinced that the Victoria Nyanza was the chief source of the Nile, and he believed that he should find its main outlet in Uganda; the second was that he was anxious to ascertain the truth of the wonderful stories he had heard about that country. This object he had completely attained by having been an eyewitness of scenes which abundantly illustrated the trite proposition, that truth is often stranger than fiction; and now a hope presented itself of realising the other by the favour of the king of Uganda. With his permission to depart, the last obstacle was cleared out of his way to his solving, as he thought, the great problem of African geography.

With Budja as general director, they started at 1 P.M. on the 7th of July on the northward journey. Though the Wanguana were still mutinous, a judicious threat of corporal punishment brought them to reason, and they marched in five successive days to a place afterwards called *Kari*, from the tragedy that took place there— thirty miles from the capital—through a fine hilly country, jungle alternating with rich cultivation. The second march, after crossing the Katawana river, with its branches flowing east into the huge rush-drain of Luajerri, carried them beyond the influence of the higher hill-system, and away from the monster grasses which characterise the border of the lake. Those villages were assigned as their night quarters, the heads of which had been seized by the king, rather than those belonging to the queen- dowager, the villagers forsaking their homes, and the escort looting wherever they went. Over each doorway of the huts Grant remarked a diamond-shaped charm of rush, hung horizontally, and generally stuck with feathers. The docile and handsome cattle in the lowlands were almost "prize" animals. They had been made hornless when young by searing with a hot iron. The general colour was grey, with black face. They had little or no hump, and were larger than the Ayrshire breed. Lanky Wahuma might be seen tending hundreds at a time. These people, unlike the Waganda, were never afraid of the caravan, which may be accounted for by their never being enslaved, although their handsome women are much sought for as wives. Mtésa had ordered sixty cattle and ten loads of butter to be sent to the expedition; but some of the first instalment of beasts, those assigned to the escort, were stolen the first night, because the precaution of tying them up had been neglected, The tracks of elephants and buffaloes were often seen on this route;

and lions were heard at night making a noise like that produced by blowing through a cow's horn, and never approaching a respectable roar. Two zebras were shot by Speke and eaten by the escort, their skins being sent as royal property to the palace. Pallah, hartebeest, and other antelopes were seen or shot, and a species new to them appeared here, the "njezza," whose horns curved over the brow. As it was a great grazing country, the natives set traps for the lion, which consisted of a number of logs raised high on end. When a goat, placed as a bait, had attracted him under them, the logs, guided by piles on either side, would fall in a mass and crush him, somewhat in the same way as the triangles of sticks and stones used to kill wild beasts in the Himalaya. Grant had a narrow escape from one of these contrivances himself, the Seedis having just called to him in time, and it actually fell on three of the cows and killed one, not very much to the regret of the beef-eaters of the escort. The Seedis being Moslems dared not touch the meat, as it had not been killed in the orthodox manner.

The natives were eager sportsmen, and snared antelopes with nets made of soft and strong fibre, generally from the aloe. They had a very simple and ingenious foot-trap for buffaloes. It was usually laid at salt-licks, and consisted of two small circles of wood placed one over the other, between which a quantity of stout acacia thorns pointed to a common centre; all the parts were lashed strongly together, and the completed trap was several inches larger than the buffalo's foot. This was fitted over a hole made in the ground, and a noose, attached to a block, laid over it and concealed with earth. When the buffalo puts his foot in it the trap fastens, and the more he struggles the tighter the noose grips him. The former king of Uganda was said to have possessed

a large menagerie caught in this way.   Birds were not
numerous, the cannibal vulture of Uganda preferring,
for substantial reasons, the neighbourhood of the capital.
The only game-birds that could be found in the high
grass were guinea-fowl and florikan.   An owl of very
handsome plumage was shot, weighing six pounds.   A
new goatsucker skimmed among the plantains at night
with a very graceful flight.   The seventh pen-feathers
were double the length of the ordinary ones, the eighth
double the seventh, and the ninth 20 inches long.   The
long feathers might have the function of intercepting flies
as the birds swept along.   Bombay said it was also found
in Uhiyow.   It has since been named by Dr Sclater
"Cosmetornis Spekii."   Fish were not to be had, though

Goatsucker (Cosmetornis Spekii).

fishing-baskets made of flags or papyrus, like an Egyptian
water-jar, were constantly found in the dwellings.   They

were used in the communications made between two parallel ditches cut in a swamp.

While they were waiting for cows, the consequence of living at free quarters was illustrated by a sad occurrence. Kari, one of Speke's men, who had distinguished himself in tailoring for the king of Uganda, had been induced to go marauding with some Waganda boys to a certain village of potters, as Budja required pots for wine. When they drew near the place, the women were the only people visible, but instead of running away, they began to bawl, and brought out their husbands. The foraging party at once fled, and Kari would have escaped too, but he was slow, and his musket empty. The potters overtook him, and when he pointed his gun, which they took for a magic horn, speared him to death, and then fled. Another morning when the men went to some springs for water, some Waganda threw spears at them from an ambuscade, but this time the guns were loaded, and two of the assailants received shot-wounds. Again, the night before leaving, two huts occupied by Seedis were set on fire by bunches of burning straw set in the doorway. The inmates had to cut their way out through the sides of the huts, losing their bayonets and bark-cloths. In revenge for this the Waganda escort burnt down all the houses they had occupied. Kari's companions were sent to the palace under a charge of having led him into trouble, and a complaint was laid against the villagers, which led to the confiscation of their effects. These events were the more to be deplored, as several instances occurred in which the peasants honestly restored lost property, besides showing a disposition to hospitality. Whenever the people came on a friendly errand, they sounded a "tambisa," or stringed wanga, by way of a flag of truce.

Budja was a handsome, intelligent man ; but, as was the fashion at court, affected the haughtiness and impetuosity of Mtésa. He travelled with three wives and about twenty young squires, one of whom always looked after the ladies—a dangerous office, since another of them, for indiscreet gallantries, had been punished by the loss of both ears and some of his fingers. Such earless people had a curious appearance ; the head looking like a barber's block with holes bored in it, but the sense of hearing did not seem to be affected.

It having been now discovered that Budja was leading the expedition in too northerly a direction to enable them to see the exit of the Nile from the Nyanza, it was arranged that Grant should go on quietly to Kamrasi's with the baggage, cattle, and women, while Speke should go up the river to its point of issue, and come down again by boat as far as practicable. On the 19th of July they started on their respective journeys. Grant turned to the west to take the highroad to Kamrasi's, while Speke went east for Urondogani, the boat-station, crossing the Luajerri rush-drain, which was three miles broad. It was said to issue from the lake, and fall into the Nile at a point due south. All the way to Urondogani the country was covered with a most inviting jungle for sport, with intermediate spaces of fine grazing land. Continually losing his way from want of guides, and the wrong directions given by the ill-natured Wahuma, Speke did not reach the boating-station till the morning of the 21st.

Here he stood at last on the brink of the Nile, and nothing could surpass the beauty of the scene. It was the perfection of the kind of effect aimed at in a highly kept park, with a magnificent stream from 600 to 700 yards wide, dotted with islets and rocks—the former occupied by fishermen's huts, the latter by sterns and crocodiles basking in the sun—flowing between fine high grassy banks, with rich trees and plantains in the background, where herds of the " nsunnu " and hartebeest could be seen grazing, while hippopotami were snorting in the water, and florikan and guinea-fowl were rising underfoot. The chief officer was not at home, but they took possession of his huts and found themselves in good quarters. Delays and subterfuges, however, began, and the acting officer made difficulties, while Speke threatened to complain to the king if boats were not forthcoming. Usoga was in front of them, the very counterpart of Uganda in richness and beauty. Here the people used huge iron-headed spears with short handles, which Speke's men remarked were better fitted for digging potatoes than human bodies.

Elephants, as had been observed by their devastations, had been very numerous, till an ivory-hunting party had driven them away. Lions also were described as destructive and numerous. Antelopes were common in the jungle, and hippopotami frequented the plantain-gardens, but were seldom seen on land, though sometimes heard. Speke hit a buck nsunnu antelope on the hither side of the river, but he was driven off by the rabble of spectators rushing upon him. A chase ensued, and the game was tracked by the blood, when a pongo (bush-boc) was flushed, and divided the party. Then another buck nsunnu turned up, who was killed at once, and a third buck was wounded and tracked till dark. Several birds were shot on the way home, including a specimen of the *Cosmetornis Spekii*. He found that the antelope that he had killed had been disputed by lions, but his men, who stood more in awe of man than the wild beasts, succeeded in bringing it home. Being still disappointed of boats, Speke amused himself in shooting, being accompanied on one occasion by one of the women of the station, with all of whom he had already become a favourite. She followed him for some way till she came to a white-ant hill, and the temptation to stop and eat the white ants as they ran out of it overcame her sporting propensities.

On the 25th he marched up the Nile to the Isamba rapids. Nango, the district officer, an old friend, entertained him here. He said that he kept off with charms the elephants who threatened his plantains, for if they once got among them they would never leave the garden till they had cleared it. At this place some falls of the Nile were seen, very beautiful, but confined. The river ran deep between its banks, which were covered with fine grass, soft cloudy acacias, and lilac convolvuli, whilst here and there, where landslips had occurred above the rapids, bared places of red earth could be seen; there, too, the waters dammed up looked like a huge, sullen, and dark mill-pond, where two crocodiles were laving about, on the look-out for prey. From the high banks a line of sloping wooded islets were seen athwart the stream, which caused both dam and rapids. The whole scene was more fairy-like than anything supposed to be possible outside a theatre—just the place which, if the stream were bridged across, would be selected for an adventure with brigands. These regions are infested by a small black fly, with thick shoulders and bullet-head, which torments with its sharp stings the naked arms and legs of the people to an extent which must make life miserable to them.

After a long straggling march the party reached a district which might be called a church estate, for it was dedicated in some mysterious manner to "Lubari" (Almighty), and was to a great extent exempt from the authority of the king. Budja, it now transpired, had an objection to lead the expedition this way, lest he should

The Ripon Falls—the Nile flowing out of Victoria Nyanza.—PAGE 271

compromise himself with the spiritual authorities.   At last, by much exertion, over hills and through huge grasses, and plantations where elephants had eaten all that was eatable, and destroyed the rest with their trunks, Speke arrived at the end of his excursion—the farthest point ever visited on the same parallel of latitude as King Mtésa's palace, and just forty miles to the east of it. He was fully rewarded for his trouble, for the "Stones," as the Waganda called the falls, formed by far the most interesting scene he had looked upon in Africa. Yet the beauty of the place did not quite realise his expectations; for the broad surface of the lake was shut out from view by a spur of hill, and the falls, about 12 feet deep, and 400 or 500 feet broad, were broken by rocks. Still it was a scene that might attract for hours together. The roar of the waters—the thousands of passenger-fish, leaping at the falls with all their might—the Wasoga and Waganda fishermen coming out in boats, and posting themselves with rod and hook on all the rocks — hippopotami and crocodiles dozing on the water—the ferry at work above the falls, and cattle driven down to drink at the margin of the lake—with the small hills, grassy at top, with trees in the folds and gardens on the lower slopes,—made a picture of surpassing interest, heightened by the feeling that the great object of the expedition had now been accomplished.

Speke had no doubt that the Victoria Nyanza is the great source of the world-famous Nile. He mourned, however, over the delays which prevented him from going to see the north-east corner of the lake, where it was connected with that other lake to which the Waganda went for their salt, and from which another river was said to flow to the north, making Usoga an island. He was assured that there was as much water on the eastern side

of the lake as on the western—if anything, rather more.
Supposing, according to his conviction, the top head of
the Nile to lie at the southern end, close to 3° S. lat., the
Nile would have, in direct measurement, a length of more
than 2300 miles, passing over thirty-four degrees of latitude, or more than one-eleventh of the earth's circumfer-
ence. From that southern point to this issue of the Nile
round the west, the Kitangulé is the only feeder of importance ; and, according to the account of the Arabs, nothing
larger than a rivulet runs into the lake on its eastern side.
As for the salt lake, this was a name given by the natives
to all lakes on whose banks salt is found. Dr Krapf, when
he obtained a sight of the snowy Kenia, heard from the
natives that there was a salt lake northward of it, and also
that a river ran from the Kenia towards the Nile. This
would suggest some connection between his river and the
salt lake Speke heard of, and between Speke's salt lake
and his, which he heard was called Baringo, but not, as
Speke considered, affect the fact of the head of the Nile
being in 3° S. lat., where in 1858 he had seen the south-
ernmost point of the Victoria Nyanza. He named the
"Stones" Ripon Falls, after the President of the Geographical Society when the expedition was got up; and
the arm of water from which the Nile issued, Napoleon
Channel, as a compliment to the French Geographical
Society, who had awarded him their gold medal. Speke
did not think it of much consequence that the volume of
the Kitangulé appeared to be as large as that of the Nile,
as the former was a slow, and the latter a rapid river.

After sketching the falls, he found that he had not much
to do, in consequence of the impracticability of Kasoro (the
Cat) his guide, and amused the people by putting a bullet
through the ferry-boat on the Usoga side 500 yards off,
while Bombay shot with his carbine a crocodile that he

Nsunnu Antelope—Uganda.—PAGE 273.

caught napping. Still contemplating the falls, and the fish flying about them, Speke thought that he only wanted a wife and family, garden and yacht, rifle and rod, to make him happy for life in this charming retirement. And it struck him that it would be just the spot for a mission, and if the missionaries introduced farming they would have hundreds of pupils. Besides the rod-and-line fishing carried on, men were observed darting pitchforks at a venture into a place over a break in the falls, which was the haunt of tired fish, while companions waited under to disengage the pinned prey.

On the 31st of July, finding the weather too cloudy for taking latitude, and Kasoro determined only to fulfil the letter of his instructions, Speke returned to the "Church Estate," sending Bombay and Kasoro to the palace for supplies and boats, and for a general order from Mtésa to go where he liked. He heard of a good deal of game, and shot, amongst other antelopes, a nsamma buck and doe—an animal much like the *Kobus ellipsiprymnus*, but without the lunated mark over the rump—and went unsuccessfully after a "rogue" elephant, who was heard every night taking his pleasure in the plantain-gardens.

Bombay and Kasoro returned to him in his old quarters at Urondogani, where he stayed till the 10th of August shooting. They had seen Mtésa, who was furious with the Sakibobo, or provincial prefect, whose orders had prevented Speke from getting boats, and only respited him from execution in consideration of a fine in kind of eighty of every species of the produce of Uganda. Four women sentenced to death were offered at this interview to Bombay for Speke; and when he declined, saying that he had no orders to receive them, the king gave him one for himself, and asked him if he would like to see the remaining three cut to pieces. Bombay, by his own account, very properly

s

declined, saying that Bana never wished him to see such cruel sights. The women who entertained Speke so hospitably at Urondogani were mostly captured Wanyoro, who had been given to the officer Mlondo by Mtésa. They said that their lower incisor teeth had been extracted when they were young, because none of their countrymen would allow any one to drink from his cup who had not conformed with this custom, which also prevailed in Usoga.

Speke now started in five loosely-constructed boats, in company with twelve Wanguana, Kasoro and his page-followers, and a small crew, to reach Kamrasi's palace in Unyoro. The vessels were propelled with paddles, but with no regularity, the lazy crew sometimes racing, but more often resting, and letting the boats drift with the current of the Nile. The river, here lake-like, was clear in the centre, but fringed in most places with tall rush, above which the green banks sloped like park-lands. The harmony of the scene was unfortunately soon disturbed by Kasoro disgracing the Union-jack by an act of piracy. A party of Wanyoro, in twelve or fifteen canoes, had come up the river to trade with the Wasoga, and having taken in their cargo, were taking their last meal on shore before they returned to their homes. Kasoro seeing this, and quite forgetting that he was bound for the same port, before Speke knew what he was about, ordered the sailors to drive in amongst them, and, landing, set to pillaging the property of those who were shortly expected to be the hosts of the expedition. Of course, as soon as Speke knew of it, he made the boatmen disgorge their plunder, and did his best to reassure the Wanyoro, and made Kasoro promise not to repeat the feat. However, a bad impression was inevitable; and the Wanyoro preceded them down the river.

·· When they came to the frontier it would be necessary
to ask leave of Nyamyonjo, the Kamrasi's officer, to
enter Unyoro. Fancying now that Grant must have
arrived at Kamrasi's, Speke thought it best to send
Bombay with some men by land, while the rest waited
till the afternoon, as it was but one hour's journey by
water. When the frontier was passed, both sides of the
river, in Usoga as well as Unyoro, belonged to Kamrasi.
Speke flattered himself now that there was no more walking to be done (he had walked all the way from Zanzibar), and that he might float quietly down the Nile to its
mouth, for Kidgwiga had promised boats on Kamrasi's
account, to take them on to Gani, where Petherick was
believed to be waiting. In a little while an enormous
canoe, full of well-dressed and well-armed men, was seen
approaching. As Speke's party still worked on, they
turned round, as if afraid. The men paddled on; theirs
did the same; and it became quite an exciting chase, won
at length by the superior numbers of the Wanyoro. The
sun was setting as they approached Nyamyonjo's. On
the rock stood a number of warriors, jumping, jabbering,
and thrusting with spears, after the manner of the Waganda. Speke thought they were doing this by way of a
welcome, but a glance at Kasoro's glassy eyes told him
that the demonstration was one of defiance. The bank,
as they advanced, rose higher, and was crowned with huts
and plantations, before which stood groups and lines of
men, armed to the teeth. Moreover, at this juncture the
canoe they had been chasing turned broadside round, and
assumed as threatening an aspect as the crowd on shore.
Speke would not believe that they meant anything serious,
and stood up in the boat, hat in hand, to show himself.
He was within ear-shot, and called out that he was an
Englishman going to visit Kamrasi; but all he could say

276 ATTACK BY THE WANYORO.

did not produce any impression. They had heard a drum beat, they said, and that was a signal for war, so war it should be; and now on both sides of the river Kamrasi's drums rattled the alarm. To make matters worse, a second canoe full of warriors issued from the rushes behind, as if with the intention of cutting off their retreat, while the one in front kept advancing, as if to hem them in. To retreat together seemed the only chance, but it was getting dark, and the boats were badly manned. Speke gave the order to close up and retire, offering ammunition as an incentive, and all came to him but one boat, which seemed so paralysed with fright that it kept spinning round and round like a crippled duck. The Wanyoro were heard to cry out, "They are women, they are running, let us at them;" while Speke kept roaring to his men, "Keep together, come for powder," and loaded his own gun with small shot, which made Kasoro laugh, and ask if it was intended for the Wanyoro. "Yes; to shoot them like guinea-fowl," was Speke's reply. But it provoked him that the crews could not be got to keep together, and retreat with him.

One of the boats served with ammunition went as hard as it could up the stream to keep out of harm's way, and another preferred hugging the dark side of the rushes to keeping the open, which Speke desired, that he might have the full benefit of the guns. It was now getting unpleasantly dark, and they could hear the Wanyoro stealing on them, though nothing could be seen. Presently the boat that hugged the shore was attacked, spears were hurled, passing fortunately into the river instead of into the men, and hooks were thrown out to grapple the boat. Speke's compromised men cried out, "Help, Bana! they are killing us;" while he roared to his crew, "Go in, go in, and victory will be ours." The cowardly Waganda

seemed spellbound, their only action consisting in their
exclaiming, "Nyawo! Nyawo!" (mother, mother); and
there seemed to be some danger of the whole force being
cut up in detail, when the action was suddenly finished
by three shots from the grappled boat. The Wanyoro
had caught a Tartar. Two of their men fell, one killed,
the other wounded. They were heard saying that their
opponents were not Waganda, and it would be better to
leave them alone, and retired accordingly, leaving Speke
a clear passage up the river. Thus was fought and won
the second battle of the Nile in which the British flag
has figured, victory having been purchased at a cheaper
rate than it was in Aboukir Bay. But then the Wanguana gunners were not English, and the Wanyoro were
certainly not French.

During this lively episode poor Bombay had come
to grief by land. He had reached Nyamyonjo's, but
had been at once ordered off; and seeing the hostile
preparations, and hearing the fracas on the river, had
made his way back, with his escort, through the path-
less jungle, coming in lame and all over scratches. They
had now recrossed the frontier, and crowds of Waganda
assembled to celebrate the victory which their countrymen did not gain. Speke did not share their elation,
as the way by the river was now closed, and his men
refused to follow him by land to Nyamyonjo's, whom
they described as a very determined and independent
chief, who only listened to Kamrasi when it pleased himself. So with much regret he turned his back on the
Nile, and came to the Luajerri. Here to his surprise he
heard that Grant's camp was not far off. Near Kari one
of the king of Uganda's little black Mercuries came to inquire after Speke's health, and to remind him about a gun
and some brandy he had promised to send Mtésa. This

was not the first or the last message he received on the same subject.

There was now some aimless wandering in trying to find Grant, some small hills being crossed, as well as tracts of grass and jungle. The people seemed hospitable, though complaining sadly of the depredations of the king's pages. Special bomas or fences were used here to protect the villages from the depredations of lions, and the tracks of buffaloes were frequent, who were here considered sacred by the natives. Grant and Speke were both looking for each other, and passed each other once very close. At last Bombay found his way to Grant's camp with a letter from Speke, opening again the communication which had been interrupted for thirty days; and Grant answered it by walking to Speke's camp while it was still at a short distance from his own.

His tale was a disheartening one, for he told of his failure to get into Unyoro by Uganda, and how he was on his way back to try the route by Karagué. Grant had set out on the 22d of July, in a N.N.W. direction, through a country of grassy jungle, where there was much large game about, and some fine antelopes were killed—amongst them the noble "leucotis"—till he came to the boundary of Unyoro. The country became there undulating, with pretty glades, and covered with tall grass and trees. At the fourth mile in Unyoro an arch of boughs, seemingly the work of the previous day, was seen spanning the path. The Waganda suspected treachery, but Grant and the Seedis went under it, thinking it was the sign common in Unyamuézi that dwellings and water were near. Sending on here Budja, with five men, to ask permission to proceed, they were soon brought to a halt by the frontier officer, whose suspicions had been aroused by their trying to enter Unyoro in two directions, and whose answer

made Grant anxious to know what had become of Speke.
A dozen armed Unyoro, with capped spears, who paid
the camp a visit, exchanging plantains for beef and beads,
said that Speke would never be allowed to go by the
water-route.

Thus brought to a standstill in coarse wet weather, at
the end of July, on the Unyoro frontier, Grant consoled
himself by observations in natural history. One day
the camp was haunted by three differently coloured vultures. The first was the ragged-looking, wedge-headed
bird of Uganda notoriety, with plumage of a dull sepia
colour. The second, possibly its female, was a much
larger and bolder bird, of a dun colour, with a bare, dark-
grey, or black neck. The third, a very shy bird, was as
large as, and plumper than, the last, and handsomer than
either. His plumage was jet-black, with the rump, thigh-
feathers, and rear half of the wings snow-white. Grant's
hut was full of lizards, about six inches long. Two of
them were observed fighting, and chasing each other round
and round, keeping their tails averted to prevent their
being bitten off; then the larger got hold of the other's
foot, and held it most viciously, till the victim struggled
away. They lived by stalking up to flies, and suddenly
pouncing on them. At night they had the power their
victims have, of sleeping upside down on the ceiling.
After rain, when small red centipedes were on the ground,
they would make a rush at the insect, shake it as a dog
does a rat, then leave it. On examining the insect, its
head had disappeared. One night a hyena carried off
one of the fattest of the goats. This beast never attacked
the cattle, though in a perfectly open fold, as the cows
would have kicked him out of the place.

After waiting till the 8th of August, a messenger arrived
from the king of Unyoro to say, that as they had come by

two different ways, and from the upstart king of Uganda, Kamrasi would not receive them. If they choose to wait a year, and bring a recommendation from Rumanika, he would then see them with pleasure. Grant thought it best, under all the circumstances, to consent to retire within the frontier of Uganda, and there wait for Speke. But his troubles were not over there.

Two Seedis were speared by Waganda villagers while taking possession of horses. In return, four prisoners were captured; and to prevent a sudden attack, all the plantains were cut down within thirty yards of the huts. The men's wounds were slight. Some armed villagers having come in the next day to pay their respects, they were disarmed by Budja, with the assistance of Grant's men. The male prisoner of the day before, a district officer, sat in the stocks by order of the same functionary. He sat on the ground with two long sticks, forked at both ends, between his feet and hands. The neck and waist were tightly bound to a post, so that all night long the poor wretch could not lie down, nor have the use of either hands or feet. He was released, however, on condition that the actual perpetrators of the attack should be surrendered. Having remained in the same spot a long time waiting for a favourable answer from the king of Unyoro, and receiving nothing but rebuffs, Grant now determined to retrace his steps and look for Speke. When the note arrived by Bombay on the 19th of August, he had marched eight miles south, crossing a wide bog and encamping on a crest of land beyond it.

Speke concluded from Grant's account of Kamrasi's objections that he was only a nervous fidgety creature, who wanted to be reassured, and that a little further parley would set matters right, especially as both parties were now together, and in Uganda. But the difficulty

was to find an envoy to Kamrasi. Whilst they were
discussing their plans, to their delight, as if they had
been overheard, up came Speke's old friend Kidgwiga,
with Vittagura, Kamrasi's commander-in-chief, to say
that their king was very anxious for them to come on,
and the Waganda escort might come or not as they
liked. Their peaceable withdrawal from the country
had disarmed Kamrasi's scruples. They said that the
Nyanswengé — meaning, as Speke thought, Petherick—
was still at Gani; that no English or others had ever
expressed a wish to enter Unyoro, or they might have
done so; and that Baraka had left for Karagué with a present of ivory. So the march was directed to the north
again. The last village on the Uganda frontier was
reached on the 22d, and the next morning Unyoro was
re-entered. The first march was a specimen of all the
country as far as the capital, an interminable forest of
small trees, bush, and tall grass, with scanty villages, low
huts, and dirty-looking people in skins; the plantain,
sweet potato, sesamum, and millet being the chief articles
of consumption. Cows were more seldom seen than goats
and fowls, as, though numerous, they were tended in remote places by the unsociable Wahuma. No hills, except
a few scattered cones, ever cheered the eye, and the general aspect of the country was dreary, and as flat as Flan-
ders. They could not expect to see again the beauty of
Karagué and Uganda, since vegetation becomes less luxuriant as the equator is left behind, and as the distance
increases from the rain-attracting mountains.

Fortunately for their progress the frontier village could
not feed the party, as, when they had arrived at Kidgwiga's
gardens farther on, one of Mtésa's messengers dropped in,
with fifty Waganda, with all kinds of commissions for
Speke, the most important of which was to bring him back

again. Speke declined with thanks, and a present for Mtésa. On the other hand, messengers now came from Kamrasi to hasten them on. It appears that they would never have been admitted into Unyoro, in consequence of the evil reports that had been spread about—one of which was that they were cannibals, which was false, and another, that they ate butter, which was true—had not Rumanika kindly engaged to be answerable for what they did in the country.

The Wanyoro, as squalid and scantily dressed as the Wanyamuézi, now came about them, hawking ivory ornaments, bracelets, tobacco, and salt, for which they were paid in cowries. The people generally forsook the villages as they advanced, and no one paid them any attention but the head-men attached to the escort, or professed traders. Still accompanied by Budja, to whose coming on there were many objections, as the king had said some of his children died in consequence of former visits of Waganda, they found their way by the compass to a place called Kiratosi, where the people gave them a cold reception at first, having heard that their iron boxes contained each a couple of white dwarfs, sitting astraddle, back to back, who flew off to eat people whenever they got the order. By a most curious coincidence one of Speke's men, called Baruti, found a sister here.

Mtésa was most indefatigable in his exertions to make his friend "Bana" come back to him, and sent message after message, and Budja said that he must take him back; and on his definite refusal, made up his mind to return himself with the Waganda. Unfortunately, a long discussion had taken place, which was overheard by Speke's Wanguana, and its principal subject being the terrors and difficulties of the onward road, twenty-eight poltroons,

armed with twenty-two of Speke's carbines, determined to
desert and go back with the Waganda; and they were
accompanied by Manamaka, the former governess of the
young girls given by the queen-mother of Uganda. Speke
told Budja at parting that he hoped Mtésa would disarm
the deserters, and banish them to an island on the Nyanza.
His followers were now reduced to twenty men armed with
fourteen carbines. A little time elapsed, and a party of
fifty Wanyoro rushed wildly into the camp with uplifted
spears, and inquired for the Waganda. They had Kamrasi's orders to take Speke's party from them by force.
These were followed by Kajunju, an athletic officer, at the
head of 150 braves, with the plantain-leaf tied round
their heads as the military badge, and a leathern sheath
on their spear-heads, tufted with cow's-tail; but, notwithstanding their imposing appearance, they expressed their
great delight at finding the enemy had departed. This
arrival helped the expedition on to Ututi, marching for
the first time without music, as the drum is never beaten
in Unyoro except on occasions of fighting or dancing.
Wanyamuézi and Wanyoro, in addition to the twenty faithful Wanguana, carried the luggage, each manœuvring to
take the smallest article he could find.

Here news came of elephants in the neighbourhood, and
Speke and Grant prepared to attack them. A number of
Wanyoro led the way to a forest covered with tall grasses
like wild oats, and with ordinary-sized shady trees. Here
and there the mounds of white ants were seen. After a
time marks were seen on the trees as if lightning had
blasted them, and the boughs appeared wildly and wanton-
ly broken, while the grass underfoot was trodden down as
if a roller had been passed over it. All the spoors were
fresh, so that every moment they expected to see the
herd, and not a little excitement prevailed. A low sharp

whistle from a sharp-eyed native made them exchange glances. He had heard the cracking of branches, and, in fact, about three hundred yards off in the open grass, appeared the blue backs of about forty elephants. Grant had never seen such a sight, and Speke wished him to have the first shot, but another herd now appeared in a different direction, and he preferred going alone, with a single follower carrying a spare gun. Here, whichever way they looked, for three-fourths of the horizon, elephants were seen grazing quietly, perfect lords of the forest, and so unconcerned that Grant walked upright through the grass to a tree within fifty yards of twenty of them. It was a beautiful sight; all were mothers with their young, none so large as the Indian breed, but short, stumpy, compact-looking animals, with small, long, and uniform tusks. The most game point about them was a peculiar back-set of their enormous ears. While waiting to get a close shot, Grant looked round for his man with the second rifle, but he had vanished; so, levelling his Lancaster, he aimed behind the shoulder of an old female with long tusks, and fired. She merely mingled with her friends who stood around in stupid alarm. They then began approaching Grant.

He changed his position to another tree within thirty yards of a full-sized animal, whose shoulder-blades he could trace distinctly, and brought her down on her hind-quarters. Up she got, rushed in among some others, who, with tails erect, began screeching and trumpeting in great perplexity. At last some wiser head than the rest took the lead, and they all scuttled off into thicker cover. He ran after them, but the jungle got so dense that he feared to lose his way, and as he was returning to more open cover he saw a female coming towards him diagonally, and she passed so close that he saw her wink her eye; but a bullet delivered at only eleven paces behind the shoulder only frightened her into a bowling amble, with her tail half-cocked. A low whistle now announced that Speke was close by. He had had no better luck than Grant. He was attended by a gun-bearer; when, stealing along under cover of the high grass, he got close to a batch of them, and firing at the largest, sent her round roaring. The whole, in great terror, then packed together, and began sniffing the air with uplifted trunks, till, ascertaining by the smell of the powder that the enemy was in front, they rolled up their trunks and came close to the spot where Speke was lying under a mound. His scent then striking across them, they pulled up short, lifted their heads high, and looked down sideways on him and his attendant. The situation looked ugly. He could not get a fair front shot at the boss of any of them; and if he waited a moment they would have picked him up or trampled him to death: so that he let fly at their temples, and though he killed none, escaped being killed himself, for they all turned and rushed away faster than they came. He now thought it useless to go on damaging them, as the wounded could not be separated from the rest. None had been killed, though ten were fired at, and it may have been that the charge of powder was too small. Though puzzled at the report at first, they seldom went far, packed in herds, and began grazing again. When the coast was clear of elephants, the Wanyoro came up and congratulated them on their great courage. The music of elephants was heard at night, and they came on them again afterwards in the same forest, walking about as if it was a park that belonged to them.

They were now close to the palace of Kamrasi, who, like most of the African kings, was fain to show his consequence

by keeping his visitors waiting; and as he was the king
of kings in Kittara, they could not expect to be admitted
without a considerable quarantine. For a few marches
the country had now been gently undulating and evergreen, with tall grass and trees. . On the light and higher
grounds the grasses grew six feet high, with large panicles
that clung to the dress. Where the richer soil had been
washed down to the lower grounds, the vegetation was
shorter, but more luxuriant. Nothing could be more
desolate than the site of their encampment near the village
capital of Unyoro. It could only be compared to a dreary
common—not a tree or garden to relieve the eye or afford
shade from the equatorial sun. The vast plain was covered with tall grass, through which at this season they
could not walk without wading, so that they were completely hemmed in by water. The northern half of the
horizon presented a few detached hills, the most interesting being in Kidi. They sloped away to the north from
a high bluff point at their lower extremity. The huts
were within a few yards of the sluggish Kafu river, which
flows from Uganda. Its depth, its mud-coloured water,
and the tall rushes fringing it, prevented their seeing the
crocodiles with which it was said to swarm. In the third
week of October, beyond which time their stay extended,
its waters had swollen greatly, and bore with them
islands of papyrus which that stream had torn away in
its course, reminding Speke of the stories told him at
Kazé about the floating islands of the Nyanza. Several
times when a gleam of sunshine broke upon the hills
in Kidi, they could see from the height near the camp
the river Nile, looking like a mirage, but they were pro-
hibited from approaching it. The bottom of the Kafu
was pebbly, while its banks were formed of retentive
clay through which no water could percolate. The

general soil was a sort of loamy sand, which, if well drained, would make excellent land for wheat crops.

The people here were not afraid, like those in Uganda, to communicate what they knew of surrounding countries. They were told that the water-route by which they hoped to effect their junction with the party they had heard of in Gani was impracticable, and this they afterwards found to be the case, owing to the cataracts between Chopi and Madi. This intelligence, with their observation of the level nature of the ground, enabled them to map the bend of the Nile, which they were not able to visit, as it was within the province of a rebel chief. One of the king's officers had travelled to the Masai country to the east of Kamrasi's, and he said they might do the same if the king would give them a magic horn to be carried at the head of the party; they would also want six hundred iron hoes, two to be given as a present to each district chief. The same man spoke of the Luta Nzigé lake as an immense body of water to the south-west in the direction of Karagué. When they afterwards met Sir Samuel Baker on his way to it, they were in consequence able to give him a map of its general bearings. During their long detention outside the palace Kidgwiga's gossip served to while away the time. He told them that Mtésa and Kamrasi both came from the original stock of the Wahuma beyond the Kidi, and that all the tribe, while burying the vulgar dead, observed the same rites in baking and preserving royal corpses, and also kept the finger-bones and hair of the chief state officers.

A story they heard in Karagué about dogs with horns in Unyoro was confirmed by Kidgwiga, who assured them that he had seen one. After the dog died, the horn was stuffed with magic powder, and in case of war, was placed for the soldiers to step over for luck, in the same way that a child is said to be sacrificed to insure victory in Unyamuézi. Another Karagué story about the Kidi men sleeping in trees he modified by saying that it applied only to bachelors. The story may have arisen from their mounting trees at night when travelling, to get out of the way of lions.

Negotiations were carried on through Bombay to get an interview with Kamrasi, but he still procrastinated, wishing to make the favour as great as possible. At last Speke hit on the expedient of sending to tell the king, that as he was so much afraid of seeing them as white men, he and Grant had made up their minds to cut off their hair and blacken their faces, so as to make themselves presentable. The king took the threat seriously, and invited them to move their encampment into a more eligible situation nearer the palace. But it was not till they had sent him an ultimatum to the effect that they were going on to Gani, and would send his present by Bombay, that they were finally admitted, having been detained at his threshold doing nothing from the 9th to the 18th of September. Then a procession was formed to attend the king's levee. The Union-jack led the way, and they carried as presents a large assortment of the most miscellaneous articles, the most valuable being a double rifle.

At the ferry on the Kafu, which separated them from the palace, three shots were fired, when, stepping into two large canoes, they all went across the river, and found to their surprise a small hut built for their reception, low down on the opposite bank, where no strange eyes could see them. Within this, on a low wooden stool placed upon a double matting of skins—cows' below and leopards' above—on an elevated platform of grass, sat the great king Kamrasi, looking, enshrouded

in his "mbugu" dress, for all the world like a pope in
state, calm and actionless. One bracelet of fine-twisted
brass wire adorned his left wrist, but his most conspicuous
ornament was a single necklace of beads. His hair, half
an inch long, had been worked up into small knobs like
peppercorns by rubbing the hand in a circle over the
crown of the head. His eyes were long, with a gentle
expression, the face was narrow, and the nose prominent,
according to the characteristics of his race; and though
a finely-made man, considerably above six feet high, he
was not so large as Rumanika. He was fair for an
African, and seemed about forty years of age. In sitting
he would often rest his head upon his hand, with his
elbow on his knee; and, from the length of his arms, the
position did not seem constrained. According to the
custom of his country, all the lower incisors and the eye-
teeth had been removed in his youth, for which operation
the family dentist had received a hundred cows. As no
tooth-drawing instruments were seen in the country, this
might have been done by the aid of a spear-head or knife.
His forehead was disfigured by black patches, where it
had been cauterised for headache or other ailments, and
he had a similar mark on his nose, which he was very
anxious to have removed. He never seemed to wear
calico or silks, and his only garment was the salmon-
coloured gown, tied tightly round his body from the
waist to the heels. It was dotted over with small black
pieces of bark-cloth, sewn very neatly with a looping
stitch. By his side a spear rested against the wall; its
blade was neatly capped over with leather, laced like a
shoe with two long stripes from the skin of a leopard.
A cow-skin, stretched out and fastened to the roof, acted
as a canopy to prevent dust from falling, and a curtain
of mbugu concealed the lower parts of the hut, in front

T

of which, on both sides of the king, sat about a dozen of the chief men.

Speke and Grant entered and took their seats on their own iron stools, whilst Bombay placed all the presents on the ground before the throne. As no greetings were exchanged, Speke broke the death-like silence by inquiring about the king's health, and saying that he had journeyed six long years (by African computation of five months to the year) for the pleasure of this meeting, coming by Karagué instead of by the Nile, because the Bari about Gondokoro had defeated all former attempts made by white men to reach Unyoro. He proposed that his majesty should trade with England by the same route, exchanging ivory for European articles. He also advised reconciliation with Mtésa. Kamrasi, in a very quiet mild manner, instead of replying to the suggestions conveyed, alluded to the absurd stories he had heard about Speke and Grant from the Waganda, such as that they drank up lakes and rivers, which he did not believe, or his own river would have run dry during their stay; and he thought that if they did eat hills and the more succulent parts of men, their appetites must have been satisfied long before they reached Unyoro. He was glad to see that, though their hair was straight and their faces white, they had hands and feet like other men.

The presents, spread on a red blanket, were received by Kamrasi with stoical indifference, and only an occasional remark; though a pair of spectacles which Bombay put on created a titter among the courtiers. Nothing was new to him but the gun, and a chronometer which he unluckily saw Speke take out of his pocket. The officers, mistaking it for the compass, said it was the magic horn by which they found their way everywhere, and Kamrasi said he must have it, though Speke said it was the only thing with which he could not part, and offered to get him another from Gani. Changing the subject, to Speke's relief, he then asked, "Who governs England?" Answer, "A woman." "Has she any children?" "Yes," said Bombay with ready impudence, pointing to Speke and Grant, "there are two of them!" He then asked, not being able to disabuse himself of the notion that they were traders, whether they would do any business with him in cows. The interview ended as coldly as it had begun, but the king sent pombé after them, with a civil message.

Among the supplies they received the next day was a sack of salt, very white and pure, which was said to have come from an island in the Luta Nzigé, about sixty miles west from Kamrasi's Chaguzi Palace, where that lake was said to be forty or fifty miles wide. The people of the island of Gasi, a specimen of whom was seen in Karagué, sometimes came to visit Kamrasi. It was said that Ugungu, a dependency of Unyoro, was on the near side of the lake, and on the opposite Ulégga, beyond which, in 2° N. lat. and 28° E. long., was the country of Namachi, and further to the west the Wilyanwantu, or cannibals, who are said to bury cows and eat men. All these distant people paid homage to Kamrasi, though they had six degrees of longitude to travel over.

Another interview with the king sealed the fate of Speke's gold chronometer, which was worth £50, and went, chain and all, into his possession; though when he had got it he treated it as a plaything, and damaged it the first day. With all his greed, however, and scant courtesy, Kamrasi does not appear to have been an unkindly man. While his neighbour Mtésa butchered his subjects for slight breaches of etiquette, no such barbarous custom prevailed in Unyoro. Murderers only were

flogged or speared to death, and their bodies thrown into
the river Kafu.

On the 22d of September Speke managed to despatch
Bombay and Mabruki to the north with a map and a
letter for Petherick. They were allowed to carry arms,
and had an escort of five Wanyoro, five Chopi, and
five Gani men. It was arranged that after their return
a general forward move should be made. On the 25th
Speke received a notice that he was to be honoured by a
visit from the king, so he had everything made as smart
as possible, hanging the room round with maps, horns,
and skins, a large box covered with a red blanket being
placed for a throne. A guard of honour fired three shots
as he set foot on their side of the river, while Frij, with
his boatswain's whistle, piped the 'Rogue's March' as a
fitting prelude to the approach of royalty. He was
pleased on this occasion to be complimentary, and
remarked what fine men they were, as he assumed his
seat of dignity. After having been duly received, he
began begging for everything he saw, and when he got
nothing but some medicines, left in some dudgeon, and
did not send over the usual pot of pombé in the evening.
He was reported to have said that they might have given
him at least a bag of beads, when he took the trouble to
pay them a visit. Speke now thought that to cut short
future annoyances he would try a little bullying, so he
tied up a bag of the commonest beads, and sent them
to Kamrasi with a message that they were thoroughly
disgusted with everything, that the beads were for the
poor beggar who had come to their house yesterday, that
they did not desire acquaintance with beggars, and that
they had made up their minds never to call again, or
receive his bread and wine any more. Kamrasi, taken
aback at this decided message, said he meant no offence,

that he was not a poor man, as he had many cows, but
that when it was a question of beads, he could not with-
stand the temptation to beg. Two pots of pombé were
sent as a peace-offering, and the chronometer for repair,
which had been put out of order for the second time
within a few days.

Nothing could have been more filthy than the state of
the king's palace, and the lanes which led to it. The
English officers were glad that they were never expected
to go there, as without stilts and respirators it would have
been a difficult business. The royal cows were kept in the
palace enclosure, the calves actually entering the huts;
and Kamrasi, like a farmer, walked among them up to his
ankles in muck and issued his orders, personally inspect-
ing and selecting the cattle intended for his guests.

About the end of September Speke's old friends, Budja
and Kasoro, came with more messages from Mtésa, with
fifty Waganda whom Mtésa had ordered to accompany the
expedition any distance short of England. Kamrasi
put his veto on their going to Gani, so they had to
return. Mtésa was keeping the deserters in durance till
further orders, and Speke repeated his wishes concerning
them, with all kinds of civil messages. Kasoro asked
Speke at parting to send Mtésa from England "some pretty
things such as he had never seen," and carried back a tin
cartridge-box as a proof that the deputation had been
received. It now transpired that the reason why Speke
and Grant were kept under a sort of police *surveillance*
at Kamrasi's, and why he had had a palaver-house built
to receive them privately, was the extreme distrust of
his brothers, who believed them to be most dangerous
sorcerers. They had shown this by turning their heads
away when Speke was showing the inner works of his
chronometer. The trouble Kamrasi had with his brothers

seemed almost, in a purely political point of view, to justify the Uganda custom of executing all the royal princes at the king's coronation.　Three of them were in open rebellion against him, and he was always very anxious to get the assistance of Speke's musketeers in fighting them.

The king's sisters or half-sisters, instead of becoming wives of the king as in Uganda, were obliged in Unyoro to live and die in the palace in single blessedness.　Their only occupation in life consisted in drinking milk.　Each was said to consume daily the produce of from ten to twenty cows, so they became so fat that walking was out of the question, and it took eight men to lift one of them on her litter.　The king's wives were in the same "prize-animal" condition, milk being their oilcake and "Thorley's food for cattle."　One of these, however, showed a little activity one day, and was convicted of stealing beads from a box which Speke had given Kamrasi.

On the 13th of October the British officers were pained by receiving intelligence of the death of Budja.　Whether he succumbed to the constant marchings and countermarchings that Mtésa's orders inflicted on him, or was poisoned in a pot of pombé—charmed to death, as the natives said—they were not able to ascertain.

At one of Speke's interviews with Kamrasi he took the Bible with him, to explain all about the king's Ethiopian descent in connection with the current traditions, especially calling his attention to the 14th chapter of the 2d Book of Chronicles, where Zerah the Ethiopian comes to fight King Asa with a thousand thousand men, adding how in later times the Ethiopians fought the Arabs in the Somali country, and the Arabs and Portuguese in Mombas, and how they took possession of certain districts, leaving their sons to people them.　That the kings of Uganda retained so little of the Wahuma features now was owing

Kamrasi's First Lesson in the Bible.—PAGE 294.

to the constant interbreeding through Waganda mothers. Kamrasi then took the Bible in his hand and began counting all the leaves, and, concluding that each page stood for one year of time since the creation, went on till he had turned over a quarter of the sacred volume, and only shut it on Speke's assuring him that it was all lost labour unless he counted the words.

At the end of October one of Speke's men was sent with a letter to Rumanika to desire him to give half of the goods left behind to Kamrasi, and keep the other half for him; and with another letter for the consul at Zanzibar, by which the bearer and Baraka and Ulédi, who were now in Karagué, would be able to draw their pay when they got back.

On the 1st of November Bombay, of whom vague reports had come at different times, returned with Mabruki in high glee, dressed in cotton jumpers and drawers given them by the party they had found. Petherick was not there himself, but a company of two hundred Turks or Egyptians, who had orders to wait for Speke. On his arrival Speke would find Petherick's name cut in a tree, but as none of the party could read Speke's letter, they were doubtful whether it came from the person they were looking out for. Petherick had gone down the river eight days' journey, but was soon expected back. Bombay had accomplished the distance to the station in Gani and back in fourteen days of actual travelling. The next day he was sent with Speke's farewell presents to Kamrasi, including a long-coveted mosquito curtain, with a request that he might be allowed to leave. After endless trouble, Kamrasi still wishing to get more out of them, and especially to receive their help against his brothers, that king of the beggars received them in stiff state, and let them go as coldly as he had welcomed them—they feeling as glad to get away as birds released from a cage. However, he gave them ten cows at starting, and an escort of twenty-four Wanyoro, who were to bring back from Gani six carbines with ammunition promised by Speke. They wished to take with them some of his sons to be educated in England, but he said they were too small to leave home, and, in fact, mere balls of fat, and sent two orphan slave-boys instead, who, however, were not judged equally acceptable.

On the 9th of November the expedition was embarked in a canoe on the river Kafu. Although it was intended that they should be smuggled away, the banks were lined with crowds shouting and waving adieus, amongst whom was conspicuous a gaily-dressed maid of honour who had generally sat at the feet of the king, and was the only female of rank whose acquaintance they had made.

The language of the Unyoro was observed to differ but slightly from that of Karagué. It had not the mumbling sounds of the Uganda dialect, in which the consonants d, g, k, and c are dropped in pronunciation. The Seedis understood it but little when they left, and found the language of the Chopi and Gani people beyond Unyoro quite unintelligible. They said it sounded like English, but that could not have been the case, as every word was uttered with a strange guttural croak. Many of the names of the men from the coast in Speke's service were heard in Unyoro. Kamrasi himself had a namesake, a corn-dealer at Pangani. This dispersion of names was in a measure owing to the slave-trade.

Among the curiosities of Kamrasi's court was a dwarf named Kimenya, a little old man less than a yard high, who called on the British travellers with a walking-stick higher than himself, performed various antics, and begged for cowries. He was perfectly sensible, though very rest-

less under the operation of having his portrait taken.   In
contrast to this dwarf the king had a sort of giant of

Kimenya the Dwarf.

amazing size and power, though not more than six feet
high.   He was employed in carrying messages, and would
go through all the motions of a warlike attack, wielding
his spear with grace and agility, struggling with the
supposed enemy, planting his foot triumphantly on the
dead body, snorting, and finishing up by wiping his spear-
head upon the grass to free it from the imaginary blood.

A class of mendicants or gentle beggars, called Bandwa,
allied to the Wichwézi, were spread over all these kingdoms.   They adorned themselves with more trinkets than
any other caste, and generally carried in their hands an
ornamented tree-creeper.   Many of their women looked
handsome when dressed in parti-coloured skins, and wearing a small turban of black cloth.   One man wore from
the crown of his head down his back the skin of a tippet-

monkey, to which he had attached the horns of an antelope. They wandered singing from house to house, and
were occasionally very importunate. A set of them, who
seemed to possess cattle, lived near the camp in Unyoro.
The natives respected them as religious devotees, and
never refused them food. They were not exactly a hereditary caste, and admitted new members to their body
by certain ceremonies. One of them held the rank of a
captain in the army. There was a tradition that the
whole country had once been occupied by this people,
but that the greater number disappeared underground.

The Wanyoro were but poorly armed. They had no
bows and arrows, and the spear was small and weak,
with a thin six-foot shaft of ordinary wood. Bead ornaments round the neck were worn by the wealthier classes ;
others wore flattened pellets, larger than garden pease,
made of polished iron or ivory, strung round the ankles.
The huts were wretched, but this was partly in consequence of the absence of wood ; and most of those seen by
the expedition were only temporary habitations. Their
floors were never swept, but bedded with grass, which,
when it became soiled, was never removed, but left to rot,
and overlaid with fresh grass, so that vermin of every description swarmed. The fields were chiefly cultivated by
women with the hoe. No fruit of any kind was grown near
the palace. Coffee was brought from Uddu, and the vegetables grown on the spot were the same as those observed
in the last countries they had passed ; but the deficiency
of plantains was severely felt in the fare of the people.
Cowries were the chief currency, two hundred of them
buying a small bag of flour. The king used to send them
a kind of beer, made from millet, which tasted like the
dregs of a cask.

The great resort for the loungers and newsmongers

was the blacksmith's shop, an awning made of the stalks of sorghum. One lad sat on the ground and blew a double-handed and double-nosed bellows, the air through which passed through a detached tube upon the live charcoal. Two men, almost naked, squatted hammering, talking, and smoking at the same time. Their anvil was a flat boulder, and the hammers bolts of iron, the shape of large chisels. The amusements of the people were few, but the Seedis remarked that the dancing was superior to what they had been used to see at Zanzibar. The nights were often enlivened by soft-sounding duets from the harmonicum and drum played across the river.

Superstitions were rife among the people, from the king downwards. Some of Kamrasi's warriors stole some straw from a thatched house occupied by one of his enemies, in order that the owners, who lived miles away, might be subject to the supernatural powers which the king's foreign guests were supposed to exercise. When the rain-gauge disappeared one night, the king sent a one-eyed man with a cow's horn in his hand to detect the thief. The horn was capped with a rag of bark, and had an iron bell tinkling at the top. It was shaken roughly in the face of each of the Seedis as they sat down. All seemed to change colour at the suspicion, and the wizard proceeded to the spot whence the gauge had been taken. He found it lying a short way off, and the tracks of a hyena showed who had been the real culprit; but the general belief in the "black art" was not shaken.

Though snakes were not common, wooden charms were worn round the ankle as a preservative against their bites. At cross roads a dead frog or fowl was often placed, or, if the family was rich enough, a goat. The animals were split open, with some plucked grass beside

them, being laid there for the purpose of curing some
sick person. Speke was told that a Myoro woman, who
bore twins that died, kept two small pots in her house as
effigies of the children, into which she milked herself
every evening, continuing the practice for the usual five
months of suckling, in order that the spirits of the dead
should not persecute her. There appears to be a similar
custom among some North American Indian tribes. The
children themselves were buried in an earthenware beer-
pot, turned mouth downwards, and placed in the jungle
under a tree. In Unyanyémbe, in the case of the death
of one twin, the mother ties a gourd to her neck as
proxy, and puts into it a sample of everything she gives
the surviving child, to avoid the consequences of the
dead one being jealous. But if both twins die, they are
thrown into water to avert public calamities. Moreover,
in the sister-province of Ngura, all living twins were said
to be thus sacrificed.

There was a singular belief current that Kamrasi, if he
liked, could divide the waters of the lake, which Grant
thought might be some dark tradition of the Mosaic miracle.
The abundant rain which fell during their monotonous
residence was felt as a relief, as it gave them employment
in reading the rain-gauge ; and at night the insects were
interesting, especially a sort of glowworm half an inch
long, seen among the roots of grasses. If placed on the
hand or sleeve, it travelled quickly, throwing out a
flickering light at shorter intervals than the firefly, which
also abounded.

CHAPTER VI.

UNYORO TO EGYPT.

THE NILE AND ITS FLOATING ISLANDS—THE DISTRICT OF CHOPI—THE
KARUMA FALLS—PASSAGE OF THE WILDERNESS OF KIDI—THE
GANI—THE CAMP OF THE ELEPHANT-HUNTERS—MAHAMED AND HIS
"RAGGED REGIMENT"—FALORO—THE MADI—MIANI'S NAME ON A
TREE AT APUDDO—SPORTING ADVENTURES—MARCH THROUGH THE
BARI—HOSTILE DEMONSTRATIONS—GONDOKORO—MEETING WITH SIR
SAMUEL BAKER—VOYAGE DOWN THE NILE TO EGYPT, AND RETURN
TO ENGLAND.

IT was delightful to feel, as they dropped down the Kafu
in their canoe, that, with the exception of a few cataracts
and rapids, there was now communication by water all
the way to England. The Kafu was about broad enough
for two "gigs" to race abreast in; there were seldom
landing-places, and the view was screened out by rushes.
At its mouth they entered an immense canoe, and found
themselves in what at first appeared a long lake, averaging from two hundred yards broad at first to a thousand
before the day's journey ended. This was the Nile.
Grant saw it for the first time, but Speke had made its
acquaintance at Urondogani and the Ripon Falls. Both
sides were fringed with the huge papyrus rush. The left
was low and swampy, while the right rose from the water
in a gently sloping bank, covered with trees and festoons
of beautiful convolvuli. In some parts the river was so

large that they had a sea-horizon. The navigation was very exciting, as the waters struggled past myriads of moving and stationary islands, particularly where a strong head-wind blew, and hippopotami reared their heads in the water. Having passed this part, there was no perceptible current, but by watching the islands rolling round and round like a wash-tub in the water, they perceived that the stream moved about a mile an hour. These islands were perfect thickets of growing ferns, creepers, bushes, &c., hiding one-third of the stems of the lofty papyrus rush. Such masses, some of them twenty yards in length, carrying sediment with them, would not be without their influence in forming the delta of the Nile. During a smart breeze, with all their vegetation yielding and lying over to the wind, they looked like a fleet of felucca-rigged vessels racing, and continually changing their relative positions.

It was a beautifully wild picture, as the crests of the waves dashed against these islands under a black and stormy sky, and as the slender stems of the papyrus, with their feathery tops, now stood erect, now waved to and fro, or crouched before the sudden blast, as if in act to spring. By the third day all had either melted away into floating fragments, or had gone ashore and lay over as wrecks, the leaves and fronds drooping in shapeless disorder. When the river was more than five hundred yards wide, the water in the centre was quite muddy from the freshes, and that of the sides a clear brown. The greatest depth was eighteen feet, with a hard bottom; within a boat's length of the shore it shoaled to nine feet, with a bottom of mud. When it narrowed to two hundred yards within steep banks, there was no longer any impediment to landing; the water became of a uniform dark colour, and shallower, flowing with a current of about half a mile an hour. When landing to step ashore, they had to pass through a long channel of water vegetation, as the sides in the parts of greatest width were walled in by a breastwork of reeds, rushes, and convolvuli. A curious custom was observed on passing an old canoe which was laid up; the boatmen sprinkled it with water, as if to show respect to its memory. There were many fine scenes at reaches and bends of the river. One was very pleasing, where a steep double-coned hill, called Kikunguru, was seen on the right bank, the river majestically sweeping round its wooded heights. The hill was estimated to be 800 feet above the water, and was a prominent landmark. The Kidi side was undulating, wild, and uninhabited; covered with fine trees, overspread with a network of flowering creepers, then in the month of November in rich bloom, and presenting every contrast of colour. This was the hunting-ground of the Wanyoro and Kidi people.

There were some exciting chases on the river, as the escort had orders from the king to appropriate any provisions they might find on their way. The moment a canoe was sighted, the oars would be plied with redoubled energy. The "chase" would then double and race with all his might, till he found the matter hopeless, and stood up in his boat by way of striking his colours. This signal was always hailed by the pursuers with a yell of delight, who would then draw up and proceed to board, the proprietor looking helplessly on, while bark-cloth, liquor, beads, and spears became the property of the captors. But the Seedis of their own accord always made the Wanyoro restore the stolen goods to their owner, who then joined in a hearty laugh at the practical joke. The largest of the canoes could carry a ton and a half, and was hollowed out of an

immense trunk, not built of planks, like those on the
Nyanza.

Their cows had been sent on by the land route, which
was rather precarious, from the marauding propensities of the natives. Four Chopi men threw their
spears at Ulédi, who was in charge of some goats. He
could not see them coming, on account of the grass, but
he captured a spear and a stick, and, to his credit, lost
none of his herd. His gun was not loaded, and he broke
his spear in throwing it at the enemy. A thief who was
caught driving their goats into the jungle was brought
into the camp pinioned, and with a rope round his neck.
The Seedis took delight in slapping his face and "tar-
ring and feathering" him after a way of their own, by
plastering him all over with a mixture of mud, ashes,
and water. He was also bound with cords in an unmer-
ciful manner; but in the night, though the door-screen
was fastened, his comrades managed to release him.

One day the big boat gave them the slip, floating away
and leaving its paddles behind. They were then distributed into six small ones, Speke's men acting as sailors.
The river still continued beautiful, but after paddling for
some hours they found it bend considerably, and narrow
to two hundred yards, the average depth being from two
to three fathoms, so they pulled in and walked up a well-
cultivated hill to Yaragonjo's, who was the governor of
Gani, and lived in a well-fenced fortress. This person-
age, alarmed by the suddenness of the visit, did not seem
disposed to admit them; but his son, a fine young man,
more than six feet high, with his body covered with
honourable scars taken in the king's service, did the
honours, and assigned them huts where they might rest
for the night. The red hill, with its plantains and neat
habitations, and the dense grasses covering the country,

reminded them of Uganda. The inhabitants seemed to
be of sporting habits, for the huts were hung with hippo-
potamus-harpoons—barbed irons stuck loosely upon heavy
poles larger than capstan-bars, attached to strong ropes
with trimmers of pith-wood; and outside them were
trophies consisting of heads of buffaloes and hippopotami.
It must have required expert swimming to strike the
hippopotamus in the water. The rather uncomely women
wore the mbugu cut into two flounces, fastened round
the waist with a drawing-string, and gaiters consisting of
strings of small shining iron beads.

Yaragonjo having disappointed them of their relay of
boats, they had to march overland the next day six miles
to Kijumbura, where the governor provided them with fresh
craft, and they entered the district of Chopi, going down the
river with the Kikunguru cone in view. The next day Grant
had to go overland with the baggage, as only one wretched
canoe was available, and they halted at Parangoni, where
the governor, who was a relation of the king, was very
communicative. He said that the people in these parts
were a sub-tribe of the Madi, and that the reason why
the western bank of the river was preferred to the other
in travelling was that Rionga, one of the rebellious
brothers who lived down the river, was always on the
look-out to kill the king's allies. He told them about a
certain governor of Ururi in Unyoro who covered his
children with bead ornaments, and threw them into the
water to test their legitimacy, in the reverse manner of
the ordeal formerly applied to witches in Europe. If they
sank, they were immediately lowered in his estimation,
but if they floated, he acknowledged them.

Here some Kidi men, who were going to visit Kamrasi,
came into the camp to have a stare at the white men. Out
of respect to the king, they wore a minimum of clothes,

U

being accustomed to eschew them altogether. Some wore
strange wigs, made like a sailor's "sou'-wester," from the
hair of some straight-haired race, as no negro wool would
be long enough.

Porters were now procured with difficulty, and only by
seizing their cattle or women as hostages. Nor was it easier
to procure the forty guards whom Kidgwiga had the king's
orders to impress. This rendered it necessary to make a zigzag route from village to village in order to obtain relays.
But, however troublesome to get together, these unwilling
recruits were polite enough on the road; when any obstacle
occurred, slapping the thigh with the hand to warn those
behind them to look out. One day during the voyage on
the Nile, besides living hippopotami, crocodiles, and gulls,
some dead fish had been observed floating, which, though
stale, were eagerly eaten by the boatmen. They were
about seven pounds' weight, the shape of a stumpy cod-
fish, but with a well-forked tail, above which was a small
rounded fleshy fin, like that seen on salmon or trout.
Where the banks were high and wooded, monkeys were
sometimes seen jumping about, which did not seem shy,
even in the neighbourhood of habitations. They were
grey, with long tails, white beards and eyebrows, black
faces and ears. The largest birds were the Batteleur
eagle and the Buceros; the former, as seen soaring and
circling in the sky, resembles a great bat. It has a black
body, with wings white underneath. The buceros is a
large black bird, walking awkwardly about cultivations,
having short legs, and its three toes nearly of equal
length.

The people on the land marches were civil and hospitable, but naturally objected to the houses being taken
possession of by the escort without their leave; and indeed the Wanyoro plundered as unscrupulously as the

Waganda. But in populous districts the people all came to see the convoy, and led the way in a shouting and saluting crowd. Some of the men got fuddled on their good wine in the middle of a march, and the natives tried to revive them by applications of water. They actually wished to carry one "incapable," and never tried to rob him of his clothes or gun, which he kept fiercely brandishing.

Grant was surprised by the quantity of brass-wire worn on the arms of some of the women. This, being an imported product, was more fashionable than copper. It came into the country as the result of the ivory-trade carried on with the people of Usui, at the mart of Karagué. The dwellings were detached grass huts, generally in plantain orchards, arranged in three sides of a square, with charmed poles outside. A storehouse on piles in the central space contained the grain, hoes, &c. The bark-cloth tree, which they had not seen for months, was abundant here, but of small size. To get salt, the people had recourse to a flat linear-leaved rush on the bank of the river, some of whose leaves were fourteen feet long. They burnt it, washed the ashes, and used the saline water thus obtained to boil their potatoes or plantains. Door-screens, resembling a wattled hurdle, are made from the papyrus. Strips from its stems, bleached white, are made into beautiful fish-creels, while its pith is converted into wrappers, or covers for jars of wine. The pith-wood supplied floats, door-bolts, or oval shields. Another useful plant was the universal bottle-gourd.

They found fresh eggs placed in forks of trees and in the ceilings of huts, as medicine or Mganga (religion). It was thought unlucky to throw away the heaps of hippopotamus spoils which lay outside the houses, and a beautiful convolvulus (*Argyreia* sp.), with immense mauve flowers, was planted near to honour them. This plant, held in the hunter's hand, was believed to bring certain sport. The millstone in these parts was a slab of the brick-red rough-grained granite seen along the pathways, or of hornblende, imbedded in and edged with clay. Any round stone was used to rub down the grain.

The country passed through was healthy enough when it sloped to the Nile with an eastern aspect, but Speke and Grant both suffered from sick headaches from exposure to the heat in the open canoe ; and the burning glass of the river became so monotonous that they were glad to come to cataracts, and have to proceed by land. On the eighth and ninth days from the time they embarked they both had attacks of fever, sickness, and dysentery. The ground on the line of march on the 19th of November was highly cultivated, and intersected by a deep branching ravine, through which water ran. A common plant observed was the sand-paper tree, whose leaves, as rough as a cat's tongue, are used for polishing clubs and spear-handles.

After a severe day of illness during the march, Grant arrived in camp at dusk exhausted, and found Speke also laid up, but in a position where the delightful sound of a cataract was audible on both sides. When morning came, after a night of fever, vermin, and mosquitoes, the noble sight of the Karuma Falls quite revived them. Suddenly, in a deep ravine one hundred yards below, they saw the formerly placid river, up which vessels of moderate size might float two or three abreast, changed into a turbulent torrent. There were three cataracts on less than a mile of the river, and each had a music of its own. Seated upon the rocks of the central fall, they were strongly impressed with its grandeur. The cloudy sky tinted the river a mossy brown, and the water was broken into white foam by a fall of six feet through three chan-

nels worn in the rock. On the centre block a hut had
been daringly placed, in commemoration of some event.
Below the falls, upon an island, other huts were erected,
uninhabited, and approachable only with difficulty. They
might have been placed there as stores for grain, where
they were safe from the depredations of the Kidi. The
trees upon the island had their branches connected by
cords, on which were strung wings and feathers of birds,
giving it the appearance of a charmed spot.

The Karuma Falls, Kidi.

Looking up the river from this fall, there was a long
reach, broken by foam in two places; but the enchant-
ment of the scene consisted in the view of the steep
banks, densely covered with foliage, forming a frame to
the picture, and recalling the wildest scenes on the Scot-

tish rivers. Just below the falls, where the water eddied among rushes, several baskets were seen hanging from trees, whose object was to contain fowls as a bait for hippopotami, or as an inducement for them to come under a trap placed not far off. Across their track a cord was placed, twined with creepers, and over this a short log, shod with iron, was hung from a bough. On the cord being touched, the weight fell upon the animal, transfixing him till the villagers might come for water.

The so-called Karuma Falls were a mere sluice or rush of water between high syenitic stones, falling in a long slope down a ten-feet drop. The others were of minor importance; but one within ear-shot, down the river, was said to be very grand. It was believed that Karuma, the familiar of a certain great spirit, placed the stones that break the current; and as a reward for his doing so, his master allowed the rapids to be called by his name. At the great falls below, as Kidgwiga informed them, the king had caused the heads of a hundred prisoners taken in the war with Rionga to be cut off, and thrown into the river.

During their detention at Karuma Falls, Grant was aroused one day from his siesta by a great tumult outside the tent. Two hostile parties had collected for a fight, the Seedis on one side, with their firearms, and the natives on the other. A gun going off in a distant part of the camp caused the parties to disperse. A woman was said to have been at the bottom of it, but no harm ensued, and such scenes of excitement were of common occurrence.

The local governor called on the 22d with a large retinue, attended by a harpist, and bringing provisions. He had been very generous to Bombay on his journey to Gani. The interview was not over when it was reported that a large party of travellers were walking down the opposite side of the river. Through the grass they could see a line of people moving along, each with a load on his head, and some wearing white skin coverings. They were Kidi going to assist Rionga against the very governor with whom the officers of the expedition were conversing, and they marched along with perfect security, as a rapid river separated the belligerents, too wide for an arrow to reach across it.

Speke's party crossed the next day to the place where they had been seen, and the whole day was consumed in the passage, the fare for the whole being a cow, with a present to the chief officer. The ferry-boats were very rotten, and obliged to be caulked with papyrus roots. Three men paddled with spoon-shaped sticks, who worked hard to pass the three hundred yards of stream, or they might have missed the landing-place, or even have been carried down the cataract. After crossing, they encamped for the night a mile from the falls on the Kidi side, in the midst of a tropical forest, where they passed a stormy and soaking night. There they waited till noon the next day for the forty porters promised by Kamrasi, of whom only twenty-five arrived, making the party seventy-eight in all. They marched across swamps, and through thick jungle and long grasses, wet, and labouring hard. The forest was only occasionally broken by a serpentine bog, along which the only path was a gutter, with grass eight feet high, meeting so close from the sides that they had to force a way through it.

At last they were rewarded by a striking view. The jungle had thinned, and they found themselves unexpectedly standing on the edge of a plateau, to the west of which for an interminable distance lay a low, flat, grass country, yellowed by the sun, with a few shrubs or trees scattered over its surface, while from fifteen to twenty miles in the rear, to the north-west, stood conspicuous the hill of Kisuga, said to be situated in Chopi, not far from the residence of the rebel princes. Grant was satisfied by his observations that, the route which they pursued being the chord of the arc of the Nile, there could be no hilly obstacle to the flow of that river from the point where they ferried it to that where they afterwards reached it again, ninety miles further north. This view was only seen for a short time, and then they dived through the jungle again with the same treadmill process. No trees were to be seen by raising the head; the man in front was generally hidden, and if any one walked at ease without stooping, the sharp grasses went into the eyes and nose, producing momentary blindness or drawing blood; and if the eyes and ears were not kept open so as to be aware of a hole, rock, or log ahead, there was danger of tripping and stumbling most distressingly. Several times the way was lost, but little Luendo, the guide, would jump on an ant-mound, take his bearings, and put them right again. In going through bogs he saved his sandals by slinging them on his wrists; but the Europeans, whose march was nearly at an end, and who had a prospect of replenishing their wardrobes, became extravagant, and walked through everything as they were, the sand getting into their shoes, and the grass cutting their shoes or gaiters. Whenever a pool was reached the younger Wanyoro would jump in it, and splash about like so many schoolboys or frogs, while the older stagers sat on the bank enjoying the sight, smoking, or cutting up their meat with their spear-heads.

When they arrived in camp, huts or arbours were constructed to sleep in. Those left by previous wayfarers were sometimes found with fires still burning, and they were told that the people of Chopi and Kidi came there for sport. A buffalo which Speke shot afforded much excitement. On his wounding him, the natives with

uplifted spears made at the animal, who charged and
scattered them like flies. At last he was shot, and pierced
to death as he wallowed in the water. Not an inch of
him was wasted, the Wanyoro, though they had loads to
carry, bringing in all the flesh as food. Many of their
spears had been bent or broken, showing the softness of
the iron. The people of Chopi were said to spear the
buffalo whenever they could catch him asleep. After this
elephants and hartebeest were seen, and the lion was heard.
On the 27th the guide showed them, from an ant-hill, Wiré
and the hill of Kisuga behind, the same plains of grass to
the west, to the north-east the jungles of Kidi, and to the
north, over downs of grass, the tops of some hills which
marked the neighbourhood of the village of Koki, the
second of the name. They set fire to the grass to telegraph
their approach, that the people might have pombé ready
for them, as Bombay was said to have got it there.

The next day they worked through another ten miles
of the same obstacles, and got near Koki in Gani; and on
the 29th of November the party stood on the surface of a
rock large enough to hold a garrison. In front of this was
another height with houses upon it. As they approached
the habitations of conical huts, groups of stark-naked
men, perched like monkeys on the granite blocks, anxiously awaited their arrival. Speke's party walked in
Indian file, led by Luendo sounding his horn as a sign
that the visit was friendly, and then halted under a tree,
waiting permission to approach the village, which was at
the northernmost limit of the original kingdom of Kittara.
By-and-by two naked striplings, with faces made ghastly
with white ashes, came madly rushing down the hill
with spears balanced, and pulled up beside them. These
Picts of the south had two coats of paint on their bodies,
purple and ash-colour, the latter veined as a painter

imitates mahogany, which gave them the grotesque look of clowns at a fair. They were soon joined by other painted people, no two being coloured alike, and one dandy of violent taste being vermilion all over. Even the boys affected gay colours, and dressed their heads with single feathers of jays, floating like a vane in the wind. Brightly-polished iron rings were worn round the thick part of the arm ; a pendant of iron wire hung from the under lip ; they had all heavy ear-rings of copper or brass, and bamboo-handled spears in their hands.

Bombay and Mabruki, who were already known to them, were welcomed with " Verembé," in a guttural voice. These people have always the power of offering a seat to strangers, for, like civilised artists, they always carry their camp-stools about with them. Instead of adopting the convenient but somewhat quaint custom of the herdsmen of Appenzell, who strap their one-legged milking-stools to their persons in such a manner that they appear to have tails, these people carry their seats on their shoulders. Having mounted the side of the rocky height to its top, the party came on a flat cleared place, surrounded by huts of bamboo and grass. In the centre stood a single bark-cloth tree, with two idol-huts of grass, and horns of wild animals on the ground, near its trunk.

Chongi, the governor, a very old man, advanced with other elders and women, carrying a white chicken, some " mwengé," or millet-beer, and a handful of a plant with a white flower. He took the fowl by one leg, and swayed it to and fro close to the ground as the ac-companiment of a harangue, and then passed it to his chief officer, who repeated the ceremony. He then took the gourd and the plant, and used the mwengé as holy water to sprinkle Luendo, the rest of the party, and then the magic house ; and, lastly, this politest of savages bade them be seated on a cow-skin under the bark-cloth tree, while he gave them a jorum of pombé, with many apologies that his stores, reduced by dearth, could afford them no better cheer.

The first impression of the little community was pleasing. The beehive huts were clean swept, and the stores of grain were raised on rough pillars of granite, which looked like small Druidical stones. The stores themselves were enormous cylinders of mud and wattle, covered with a removable lid of grass. A rough ladder or stick with forks enabled the women to get to the top when they wanted to take out grain. The men of this nation wore only ornaments, and the women only a fringe from the waist in front, and a pendant of chickweed, renewed every day, or of leathern thongs, behind. Their ankles were adorned with heavy fetters of iron, and they wore a few beads round their necks; but their plumage was not to be compared with the gay colours of the *beaux*, who might be seen sitting on the rocks in the shade of trees, dressing each other's hair with shells, beads, and feathers, or turning it up into queues covered with fine wire. This, with the decorative painting of their persons, appeared to be their chief business in life, and they were generally seen posing in some theatrical attitude. The women, for convenience, carried their infants on their backs, with gourds over the head and shoulders as a screen from the sun, which is said to be also a custom of the Watuta. The skin of a cow or goat placed on the clean mud floor of the huts formed the only bed of these people, and they dispensed with all covering. The door was so low that no stranger could enter except on hands and knees, but the people, from practice and natural suppleness, entered them walking, by bending the body like acrobats to within two feet of the ground.

The bamboo was observed to be growing here, a plant which they had missed since passing the seventh degree of south latitude, and many of the trees were identified with those in Unyamuézi.   Bruce's *ensete*, a great attraction to goats, was again found here, as well as many undescribed species of plants.   The people, notwithstanding their un-civilised exterior, were found to be remarkably civil.   This was in part owing to Chongi having enjoined this conduct in an address to the villagers, before Speke's party arrived. The beer of the country, which considerably affected Bom-bay and all others who indulged in it, was strong and agreeably bitter, made from "marwa"—millet roasted, pounded, soaked, sun-dried, and boiled.   It was pleasanter to drink lukewarm than when quite cool.

The other grains were sesamum, Hibiscus, and *Hyptis spicigera*, which was first seen here, the natives eating its seeds roasted, or making oil of them.   They made a dish resembling spinach of the *Crotolania glauca*, found abundantly in the fields.   The plantain had dis-appeared, and the maize and ground-nut, procurable as far as Unyoro, had become rare.   The cattle and crops were both poor.   The cattle were not driven, but induced to proceed by a man walking alongside and holding one horn and the tail.   The other domestic animals were stupid-looking, long-tailed sheep, with reddish-brown hair, and goats which jumped about the rocks, feeding on the leaves of the Indian jujube tree; and dogs were sometimes met with.

The country of the Gani properly extends from this point to the Asua river, whilst the Madi occupy the westward district to the Nile, which is far out of sight. There are no powerful chiefs, but each village appoints its own governor.   The tree-clad granitic hills brought to mind the familiar features of Unyamuézi, and contrasted strangely with the enormous "pampas" around. From this Koki in Gani they saw the hills behind which Petherick was believed to be lying with his vessels, and also a nearer hill where the advanced post of his elephant-hunters was said to be awaiting the arrival of the expedition. In the language of these parts none of those prefixes were found which distinguish locality, a people, or an individual, in the languages nearer the coast. The simple words Chopi, Kidi, Gani, Madi, Bari, were used in all the three applications. The sound of the words was thought to resemble the speech of the Tibet Tartars.

They halted two days to take in stores, as it was said that Petherick's Wichwézi, or "vagabonds," as the natives termed them, had eaten up all the country round about them, and in order that they might get guides, who knew a shorter route than that Bombay took, to the elephant-hunters' camp. They only got half-way there on the 2d of December, as the difficulties with occasional porters obliged them to swerve continually from the direct route and visit the more populous parts. At one village the good-natured people, as soon as they came, spread a skin, put a stool upon it, and placed in front two pots of pombé. At another, where they encamped for the night, however, the people were all afraid of them at first; but the chief man, being at last reassured, made many apologies for allowing them to dine without a drop of his beer, and said that he was, after all, very glad to see them. In the morning he actually brought them hot water to wash with!

In two hours after commencing the march on December 3d they came to the palace of a chief named Piéjoko, where half the men insisted on stopping, while Speke and Grant, being eager to meet Petherick's expedition, pushed on, and as the sun was setting, came in sight of what they thought

there must be some letters." He said that he had none, but only directions to convey them to Gondokoro as Debono's Vakil (or agent), and that his business in this place was to collect ivory while waiting for them. Speke then asked, "How is it that Petherick has not come? is he married?" "Yes, he is married; and he and his wife ride fore-and-aft on the same animal at Khartum." "Well, then, where is the tree you told Bombay you would point out to us with Petherick's name on it?" "Oh, that is on the way to Gondokoro. It was not Petherick who wrote the name, but some one else, who told me to look for your coming this way. We do not know his name, but he said you would know it at once if it were pointed out to you." It now transpired that Mahamed had sent with beads to Kamrasi two Madi men, who had always been supposed to have been messengers from Petherick. The European officers greatly enjoyed the novel scene that surrounded them now. In comparison with their own dilapidated condition, every one seemed well dressed; and they looked with delight on articles such as shoes, bedsteads, and crockery, which they had not seen for more than two years. For the Wanyoro the great sight was to see Mahamed shaved, as he sat on a low stool with a white napkin on his chest, while a boy, having strapped the razor with the rapidity of lightning, passed the instrument at a frightful pace over his head and beard, handing his master a gilt looking-glass when the operation was completed.

Mahamed's excellent dinner in the Turkish style had to be eaten without knives or forks, but that did not matter, as after it the long unknown luxury of soap to wash the hands was only the more appreciated.

The settlement of these "Toorkees" or Turks, as the miscellaneous ruffians composing Mahamed's regiment were called by the natives, though there was not one thoroughbred Turk among them, lay at the foot of small well-wooded granitic hills, with plenty of running water, in a situation perfectly healthy and beautiful. They were all married, on shorter or longer leases, to the women of the country, whom they had decently dressed in cloth and beads, and who had brought them numerous families. These women were very industrious. They might be seen in the morning doing work the reverse of cleaning door-steps, but analogous, by covering the space before the huts with a preparation of cow-dung. They nursed and tended their children with the greatest care, washing them daily with warm water, and then licking their faces dry, as a bitch treats her puppies. After that process baby was smeared with vermilion pomade, and laid upon its back in the goat-skin which did duty for a cradle, the four corners of which were then knotted together, and the child slung in the hand or over the shoulder, and then sung to sleep. When the mother was otherwise busy, the goat-skin with its little tenant was hung up on a peg like a cloak. A wife of the commander went through a strange ceremony, which corresponded to "churching." She passed a handful of burning grass three times round her body from hand to hand, walked to the left of her doorway, then in front, where the process was repeated, the grass being relit for her, and then to the left again. The women of Bari tattoo various lines on their children, as marks of race or district, rubbing in a black oily paste. A very common brand seen about Faloro consisted of barb-like cuts on the temples pointing to the eyes.

As soon as the tail of the expedition had come in, as there was no letter from Petherick, and his own men were all getting drunk, and Kidgwiga's deserting, Speke wished to march forward at once; but this was not so

easy to be done, as all manner of difficulties were raised
by Colonel Mahamed and his people.   There was a famine
at Gondokoro; the Bari were so savage that without the
Egyptian force it would be impossible to get through them;
there was a flooded stream in the way, which could not be
crossed for a month,&c.   To try to put him in good humour,
Speke showed him all his picture-books, and reviewed
his "ragged regiment," lavishing commendation like an
officer of the line when reviewing yeomanry, and omitting
to mention that he observed that all the privates gave
orders as freely as the captains.   But Mahamed wanted
to wait till he had got his complement of ivory together,
and a sufficient number of porters; and his instances were
seconded by Speke's demoralised men, who found themselves at last in clover.   As all Kidgwiga's men had now
bolted, it was determined to send him back to Kamrasi;
and Speke gave him for the king a double gun, with
ammunition, and some rich beads from Mahamed's stores,
with a message that as soon as he had arrived at Gondokoro or Khartum he would send another white man to him,
not by the Kidi route, by which he himself had come, but
by the left bank of the Nile; on which Kidgwiga observed
that the plan would do excellently, as Kamrasi would
change his residence soon and come on the Nile, that he
might get between his brother Rionga and the guns of
the Turks.

When he was gone Speke proposed an elephant-shoot-
ing excursion, that he might see where the Nile was,
and went up with Mahamed to the top of a high rock,
whence he could see the hills he first viewed in Chopi
sweeping round from south by east to north, and mark-
ing the line of the Asua river.   He did not see the Nile
itself, but believed it at the time to be at no great
distance, as he afterwards found was the case.   On

returning he was attracted by the sound of drums to a village where a ball was going on among the natives. The whole place was alive with naked black humanity in a state of perpetual motion. Drawing near, he found the drummers standing in the centre, and next to them a deep ring of women, most of whom carried babies; and outside these again was a still deeper circle of men, some blowing horns, but most holding spears erect. To the sound of the music both these rings of opposite sexes kept jumping and sidling round and round the drummers, making the most grotesque and impudent gestures to one another.

Nothing of consequence happened now till the 14th, when eighty of Rionga's men brought in two slaves and thirty tusks as a present to Mahamed. Speke suspected that this was a bribe to induce him to fight for Rionga against Kamrasi, and his suspicions were strengthened when Mahamed came to beg of him a blanket and a musket, saying that he was going off for a few days to one of his ivory depots. The blanket was given, but the musket refused. After this, Mahamed's regiment was seen to march out with all the honours of war, accompanied by Rionga's men. Speke afterwards found that old Chongi had invited them to fight against an enemy of his in whose territory vast stores of ivory were said to be buried, while the people were immensely rich in cattle, having lifted most of poor Chongi's. From the manner in which their Egyptian taskmasters treated the Madi people, it was no wonder that they stood greatly in fear of them, and the migration of a village was almost a daily spectacle, the people pulling down their huts and carrying the frames, which looked like a giantess's crinolines, and all their other goods and chattels, to some more distant site. On Christmas-day the news was communicated by Mahamed's head wife, that the Turks had sacked and burnt three villages, and were shortly expected to return. And,

Removing a Village—Madi.

in fact, on the last day of the year, Mahamed and his triumphant army did return, laden with elephantine spoil, and driving in five slave-girls and thirty head of cattle. He had inspired such fear by his proceedings, that one day some men who had fled from a village when his party had passed it, agreeably surprised that he did not stop to plunder their homes, brought him ten fine tusks of ivory to express their gratitude. Instead of expressing his, he told them that it would do very well for the present, but he should expect more when he returned from Gondokoro.

In the course of their relations with the people, the

men of the expedition found that the women of the country were well able to take care of themselves, for they all carried a small knife in the girdle, or stuck into the rings of iron worn above the elbow. This custom was not so Amazonian as that related of the women of a cannibal race nine marches to the north-west, who carried ten small knives with leathern handles at each side of the girdle. These they held by the tips of the blades, and threw at the adversary. The informant in this case remarked that after his party had obtained sufficient ivory and wished to depart, they were told that they could not be allowed to do so, as they were food! but one shot easily dispersed the cannibals. He added that this strange race wore the skins of goats, but did not keep cattle, and he had in his possession a knife which had a round spoon as a handle to its dagger-like blade. This, he was told, was intended for gouging out eyes.

During the stay of the Turks in this place (it was now their third season), they had collected by bartering plundered cattle about one hundred large tusks and three hundred smaller ones, averaging sixteen pounds weight each. All these were easily distinguishable from the eighteen that had come from elephants shot by the party, as they were red, and blackened with fire applied by the natives in extracting the tusks from the head. In preparing for a march, sets of tusks were securely lashed together with a thong cut in a single continuous strip from the hide of a cow. One man could carry on his head fifty or sixty pounds weight; heavier burdens were carried on a pole slung between two men.

A common disease among the natives here was a large permanent swelling below the knee-cap of one leg, or both, to which grown-up women were the class most liable. Though the size of a cricket-ball, it was soft, and did not incapacitate the patient from sitting, kneeling, or walking. In December these people burn all the grass, and the black ashes fill the air until laid by rain, serving the purpose of manure for the following season. The dews were very heavy at this time of year, but after eight in the morning till late in the afternoon it was too hot to walk with comfort; and though there were no mosquitoes, the place was infested with flies, which stuck to faces and clothes during a morning walk. The small stream below the village dried up as rivulets in Europe do in summer, and during January scarcely gave sufficient water for the cattle. The country being overstocked here, the animals were poor and stunted, and many of the calves were unable to follow the herds. In the villages each animal was tethered to a peg in the ground, and, when released, all rushed to a bank of salt earth which had been scooped out by their tongues.

The vegetable products were marwa, millet, tobacco, a few sweet potatoes, and the stringy seed-vessel of a mallow, called *bamea*. The plants were many of them new and interesting. A plum-tree, having fruit larger than a green gage, was found in the woods, its leaves being fed upon by large black caterpillars, armed with rows of white porcupine-like spikes. There was a species of bush, *Protea* sp., with efflorescence spread out like a silvery sunflower, and a scaly calyx of a pink colour underneath. A tree-climber (*Landolphia florida ?*) lay with its trunk winding like a huge snake, and then serving as a bridge to the stream. If traced farther, it was found to have mounted a lofty tree, and spread itself into innumerable branches, covering the highest foliage with luxuriant white flowers. The natives of Uhiyow convert its juice into playing-balls like those of India-rubber. A very handsome lily (*Crinum* sp.) was found by the bank of the stream. There were many varieties of resinous trees—*Boswellia, Balsamodendron, Khaya, Soymida,* &c. It was remarked that the "Shea-butter" trees and others of similar size sometimes had little seats placed against their trunks, while ashes of fire lay near them. This was probably a charm to bring rain or avert sickness. At the chief entrance to the village there was a slab, two feet out of the ground, with a circular hole across it, placed upright, and by it a pole with a branch of the *meelalla* palm (*Borassus*)) flying from its tip, which had some such superstitious meaning.

They had little sport at Faloro, but one bush-boc was killed, which was found feeding in the jungle of sweet pastures and shrubs by a stream. Amongst some rocks two kinds of monkey were observed—one the *Lungoor*, with black face and bushy head of hair, and the *Yanee* of the Seedis, a smaller one, red behind, and said to be so savage that he would return spears thrown at him. A kind of bustard or "cock of the woods" was occasionally marked down. When flushed, he would rise with a flurried flight and noise, make a majestic swoop over the woods, and disappear in low ground, or alight, folding his wings, in some cultivated spot. He was a noble bird, with rich game plumage, nearly as large as a vulture. Quail and guinea-fowl were also seen, but as shot had grown scarce they were not disturbed. A few rooks were seen, with strange short tails, which took swift, cutting flights from tree to tree, calling like crows, and cleverly evading the darts made at them by kites.

Their patience being exhausted in waiting for Mahamed, Speke and Grant, with their remaining Seedis carrying the loads, left Faloro on the 11th of January 1863, marching over long downs of grass, where antelopes were seen feeding, to the village of Panyoro, where they were hospitably received after the inhabitants had recovered from their first fright. The next day some of Mahamed's men overtook them, saying they had his orders to go with them as far as Apuddo, where they must wait for him. They arrived within sight of the Nile the next day at Paira. In appearance it was a noble stream, flowing on a flat bed from west to east; and immediately beyond it were the Jbl Kuku

The Nile and Jbl Kuku.

hills, rising to a height of 2000 feet above the river. Round their north-east bluff end the Nile made a majestic sweep from west to north, and the scene down the stream from this point resembled the romantic Pass of Glencoe in Scotland. The next day's march parallel to the river brought them to the central portions of Eastern Madi. At this place the Turks killed a crocodile and ate him, much to the astonishment of Speke's men. The teeth, resembling the long incisors of a sheep, were kept to be made into necklaces by the Madi. A nest of ninety-nine

eggs of this creature was found on another occasion buried
a foot underground in the sandy bed of a stream. They
were longer and larger than those of a turkey, pure white,
and uniformly shaped at both ends, with one-third an air-
chamber. Their taste was not quite approved of by the
English officers.

When they reached Apuddo, Speke went at once to
see the tree where the name had been cut that they
had heard so much of. The person who did it was described as being much like Speke, and as having come
thus far two years before with Mahamed, when he returned, alarmed at the reports he heard of the people to
the southward, and not wishing to remain a whole rainy
season at Faloro. There was certainly a mark on the
rind something like " MI," but the bark in healing had
almost obliterated it. It was afterwards discovered to
have been the work of the Venetian traveller Miani.
They had to wait about Apuddo until the 31st of January
for the rest of Mahamed's party. While digging for some
supposed gold-dust in the sand below the village, Grant
observed some bees alighting on the sands to enter their
burrows. They were of two sorts, green and yellow, barred
with black, the latter predominating. A few inches
underground a cocoon of the tender leaves of the *Ste-
reospermum* sp., a tree with pink-white blossom, was
found neatly wrapped round some scented substance,
with a faint taste of honey. It may have been liquid
wax, since the natives said that the bees transported this
substance to their hives. It lay in wet sand near water,
being probably placed there to preserve it from the hot
winds. In such oozy sand the people dug holes to fill
their earthen gurrahs. Strong barricades of sticks and
logs were placed round the villages here, the entrances to
which were closed at night by thorn-bushes, and even by

day it was necessary to stoop to go in. The chiefs had a mode of salutation peculiar to them, which was to take the hands of strangers, one after the other, in theirs, lift them as high as they could, and then let them drop. This custom would have been more agreeable if their hands had been cleaner.

At Apuddo the gales were hot, and powerful enough to have melted any extent of glaciers. The "Kousee" wind from the N.E., laden with dust, blew as through a funnel during the latter half of January, its violence being probably increased by the proximity of the Jbl Kuku hills. After sunset it died away, and they could then go about with comfort, and sheets of serge were found necessary to keep them warm at night. Grain was scarce and dear during this winter season, but certain large figs, though thick-skinned and full of seeds, were easily procured and palatable. No crops were seen. Even the stream which flowed past Apuddo, for three miles up its tortuous course, had not a thicket to mark its windings. The banks dropped fifteen feet sheer to its sandy bed, which was sometimes broken by grass-topped and fissured rocks, and in places by ridges, causing a rapid or waterfall. There was a calm reach for two hundred yards above this place, teeming with fish two or three feet in length.

The people lived in fortified villages of not less than two hundred souls each. On account of the neighbourhood of the Kidi, no smaller number would be considered safe. The chief of one district was seen with leprous hands and limbs. Grant thought that he might have owed his dignity to this affection, as lepers are much admired in many parts of Africa for their motley skins. Both the Bari and the Madi people wore crocodile teeth for necklaces, the pearly white of which was highly becoming to their dark complexions. And the thigh-bones of sheep and rats were also used as personal decorations suspended to the neck, as among the Zulu Kaffirs.

While at Apuddo Speke's party were quartered in the village, but the Turks remained outside, and carried off the tops of the huts to make their tents, besides taking the villagers' pots to cook their dinners, and helping themselves from their scanty stores of grain, so that the poor people were driven to live on wild berries and fruit. To make matters worse, all the village chiefs were at war with one another. One night an armed party reconnoitred the village, but feared to attack it, because Speke's guns were inside. The villagers turned out the next morning and killed two of the enemy, who vowed vengeance as soon as the guns should be gone.

Being unable to get a guide to go on with, Speke went out shooting. The antelopes were numerous, but too wild to be approached. On his homeward path, however, some natives who were on the look-out for flesh observed in the distance three buffaloes feeding on the top of a roll of high ground. While stalking up to them he came on another trio, whom he fired at at a venture as they lay in the grass. They joined the others, and, as he was busy loading, all six came charging upon him. He fully expected to be tossed or trampled to death, but they changed their minds and scampered off when within a few yards of him. The next day Grant killed a fine buck *nsamma*, and Speke went again after the six buffaloes, one of which he thought was hurt.

After walking up a long slope for three miles to the east, he found himself at once in view of the Nile on the one hand and the long-heard-of Asua on the other, backed by hills even higher than the Jbl Kuku range. But at that moment five buffaloes, five giraffes, two elands, and several other antelopes, called his attention from geography to game. The place looked like a park, and he began with stalking towards the elands, but the gawky giraffes always got in the way, and drove everything away but two of the buffaloes. He went at them with his only rifle, leaving the servants and savages behind. The beasts were feeding composedly in the open grass, so he stole up to within forty yards, and then, in a naked patch of ground, waiting his opportunity, put a ball in the shoulder of the larger one. Both bulls charged in an instant, but they pulled up on the same bare space where he was, sniffing and tossing their horns, and looking about for the enemy, who had thrown himself flat on the ground. This *tableau* lasted for twenty minutes or so; one of the buffaloes stood bleeding at the mouth, and with a broken hind-leg, the bullet having traversed his body, while the friend kept turning round and round looking for the aggressor, who was anxiously watching him, and deliberately loading. When ready, Speke took a sight at the sound one, but was nearly betrayed by the snapping of the cap, for they both stared at the spot where he lay—the sound one making vigorous demonstrations, but the wounded one only bleeding considerably. Some minutes more of suspense passed, and then they walked away, and he was able to breathe freely. They could not be followed up that evening, as darkness set in. He sprang, however, the next day, a herd of fifty or more buffaloes in the same place, and as his wounded one pulled up for a charge, he succeeded in knocking him over. The poor villagers were most grateful for the beef, as the only present they were accustomed to from strangers was a good thrashing.

The next day Speke shot a rhinoceros, who seemed inclined to dispute the right of way. It was not eaten, for the natives had grown nice, and voted the flesh unclean.

He was prevented from getting a shot at some buffaloes which he saw, by an antelope scaring them away by getting up in front.   Before the 30th of the month three more antelopes had been killed.   The sum of the sport for three of those days had been rhinoceros, buffalo, hartebeest, nsunnu, killed ; and elephant, giraffe, eland, pig, leucotis antelope, and other smaller species seen.   The long-necked giraffes, whose golden black-spotted skins looked beautiful in the morning sun, could always see the sportsman in such open cover, and then they went off like camels, lashing their sides with their tails; and the hartebeest had a provoking habit of permitting approach within three or four hundred yards, then cantering off and stopping to stare again.

Mahamed arrived on the last day of January, but he wanted a great number of porters to carry his property and plunder, and these could only be obtained by putting the screw severely on the village chiefs.   On the 1st of February 1863 they marched in a caravan of no less than three hundred souls from the camp of Apuddo in the direction of Gondokoro.   In a little time they came on the Nile, running like a fine Highland stream between the gneiss and mica-schist hills of Kuku, and followed it down to its junction with the Asua.   It was a most interesting march.

The noble stream was seen now and then breaking into foam upon hidden rocks, or running at about four miles an hour, past islands so laden with trees and aquatic undergrowth that it was only possible to catch occasional glimpses of the opposite bank or the river itself.   They saw on the hither side several species of acacia, the double black-thorned and the white, with other trees in lilac bloom, wild figs, &c.   If the thorny scrub had been cleared away, it would have looked like a paradise.   When the

first gap in the thicket enabled them to get a draught of
the tempting water, they exclaimed, "Awangeh! Awangeh!" (old friend) as they recognised their acquaintance of
Uganda. From the rocky bank on which they then sate
the views were of the greatest interest. At their feet, by
the side of a foaming rapid, fish rose like porpoises, showing their backs in a whirling black pool, where reeds,
rushes, branches, and leaves floated about in a manner
that would have puzzled an ordinary fly-fisher. The
shore was covered with fish-scales, and the remains of
fires showed that the natives had been enjoying a picnic.
Looking across, a densely-wooded island hid the other
branch of the river. For a quarter of a mile here no boat
could live at any season, and it would have been impossible to stem the strong flow of the vast torrent. Down
stream the river lay in a deep, one-sided gorge, the left
bank being formed by the Jbl Kuku in a straight escarpment some two thousand feet high. These hills were
bleak and barren, diminishing in size and breaking into
cones as they receded into the blue distance to the north.
The river was not so full as at the Karuma Falls, yet, according to Dr Knopflecher, the founder of the Gondokoro
Mission, it ought to have been in flood about this time, as
it reached its lowest level at Gondokoro in the middle of
January. It seemed as if Speke's party had actually out-
stripped the stream; yet, considering the delays, this is
difficult to imagine, unless, as Speke thought, the Luta
Nzigé has been a backwater to the Nile. They left the
river again as it arched round by the west, and reached the
Asua. The ford was about fifty yards across, waist-deep
in the strong middle current, and the sharp slippery rocks
were painful to bare feet. Speke did not think this river
could come from the Nyanza, as the waters appeared to
be falling, and were little discoloured. In December, as

judged by the old water-marks, it must have been a furious impassable torrent.

All the inhabitants had fled in terror from a village called Madi—Madi being the name of the country; and such occurrences were more painful to the feelings of the British travellers than all the fleecings they had undergone in Usui. Sometimes the people retaliated on their oppressors, for one night four Bari men and a slave-girl slipt off with a hundred of the plundered cattle. Their path lay now along the top of vertical strata, pointing to the north-west, of a slaty blue rock, cloven into loose squares and oblongs, with quartz veins. Grant diverged one day to have another look at the Nile, and found it running calmly for two miles in a reach eighty yards across, unbroken by rock or cataract, between banks at a dead level, with some barren hills rising abruptly at a little distance. The level was dotted with fig, palm, plum, and jujube trees, the soil being in parts under cultivation. The people had a scooped log as a ferry-boat, and they also crossed on sheaves of jowari straw, a practice commonly observed farther down. The civilised custom of establishing separate hospitals for the sick outside the villages was observed here in the heart of Africa. The huts, too, were very clean, and the abundance of bamboos supplied the materials for comfort. The floors were made of hard red clay, and the thresholds were tesselated with fragments of earthenware. Bamboos on movable bars prevented cattle from entering the houses.

The march now continued over rolling ground, covered in some places with bush-jungle, in others with villages, where there were some fine trees resembling oaks. Upon the grass tops of the huts in the village of Barwudi numbers of univalve shells lay bleaching, of the large spiral species seen five degrees south of the equator. The natives cut them into circles the size of shirt-buttons, and string hundreds of them together to be worn as ornaments round the waist. These pieces were the coinage of the country. At Mugi, the frontier station of Madi, they found ostrich-eggs used in a similar manner. Here, during the two days' halt, the shock of an earthquake was felt. The value of labour was estimated here in cows, the porters being paid a small cow each for a journey of four marches, and expected to carry a return load. The hire was always paid in advance, and the cows which constituted it were tied up in a safe place till the journey was over.

The country was populous; but in February, though displaying pretty undulating downs dotted with tamarind and fig trees, and though the double-coned hills had woody tops, there was a general parched appearance, and the brooks were dry, so that during several marches the only obtainable water was got by digging in their beds. The wild fruits, and especially the fig, furnished, however, an occasional refreshment. One of the Cucurbitaceæ, the size of a fowl's egg, was gathered by the natives, who dried and ate its yellow rind. The grain was stored as before on the tops of piles or pillars of stone outside the houses, which were very inviting to the marauding Turks. The country was too open and populous for sport, but the men seen on the route often wore ornaments of boar's tusks, which, tied with a thong above the elbows, looked very jaunty on their well-formed arms. Their spears were some inches taller than a man could stretch, with bamboo handles and well-made iron blades. Each was shod with a point of iron, or the end was made like the loaded end of an Indian hog-spear. Their iron appeared to be manufactured on the spot. An earthenware beer-strainer was observed amongst the otherwise rude crock-

ery.   They had the perennial cotton-bush growing eight
feet high, close to the houses, without irrigation, and the
pods were now ripening.   Three or four bushes gave
enough cotton for a family.   The women dyed it brown,
and made waistbelts of the stuff, and tails of the fibre.
The men practised archery a good deal, placing a number
of the seed-vessels of the *Kigelia pinnata* on end, and
aiming at them at forty or fifty yards.

They heard at Mugi the good news that three white
men had just arrived in vessels at Gondokoro, but received at the same time the less agreeable intelligence, that
the Bari, whose country they were now entering, hearing
of the advance of the expedition, and despairing of being
able to kill them with spears, had determined to poison
all the waters.   Notwithstanding this, all business having
been settled, they marched, with the additional porters, a
thousand strong, on February 12th into the Bari country.
Mahamed would not allow the villages to be occupied, for
fear that the Bari should kill them in the night, but insisted on all sleeping in one great camp.   The country,
still flanked on the right by hills, was undulating and
prettily wooded.   The inhabitants fled from the villages,
excepting a few of the boldest men, who remained and
gazed at the caravan.   The villages at all the halting-
places were sacked.

On the 14th they came again in sight of the Nile, and
put up at a station called Doro, near the well-known
hill Rijeb, where Nile voyagers delight in cutting their
names.   The country continued the same, but as the
grass became daily shorter and finer, the men declared
it was a sign they were approaching England.   One evening after they had settled down for the night, and the
Turks had finished plundering the nearest villages, they

heard two guns fired, and the whole place immediately afterwards was alive with Bari. Their war-drums were beaten as a signal of attack, and those of the villages around responded. The Turks grew somewhat nervous at this, and as darkness began to close in, sent out patrols in addition to their nightly watches. The savages next tried to steal in upon the camp, but were soon dismayed by the patrols cocking their guns. Finding themselves baffled, they then collected in hundreds in front, set fire to the grass, and marched up and down, brandishing lighted grass in their hands, howling like demons, and swearing they would annihilate the party in the morning. This night, however, passed without anything more serious than this demonstration.

That part of the Bari country which they passed over was about forty miles across, a series of gentle downs sloping to the Nile a few miles on the left. When the ripe grass was set on fire it blazed furiously in the wind, but on a still night it burned quietly, and with a brilliance which allowed them to dine by the light as well as if they had sat near the foot-lights of a theatre. The umbrageous trees scattered over the landscape made it look like an English park, the palms and tropical genera being absent. They had to cross a multitude of the rocky channels of rivulets, with water at most knee-deep, which in the period of rains must have been nearly impassable. Shy as the Bari were, they were able to observe one specimen in a man who joined them. He was tall, erect, and thin, naked from head to foot, but gave himself all the airs of an exquisite, as his body was smeared over with red clay pomade. Above each elbow he wore a massive ring of ivory, and carried on one shoulder, after the Gani fashion, a little stool of one piece of dark wood, and in his rope-sash there was stuck a charm like five fingers. This man had no weapons. He received a goat with a kid for a fine tusk which he brought in. The women were more difficult to observe. They wore a long apron of leather to the knees, and a separate broader one behind, both covered with clay, but did not seem to possess ornaments. That this people, who for thirty years had been within reach of the Austrian Mission, should still be so wild, is accounted for by the aggressions of the ivory-traders, which cause them to regard all strangers, whether white or coloured, as enemies. A favourite posture with the few individuals who stopped to look at the army passing, was to stand on one leg, resting the foot of the other on it above the knee. This would be most uncomfortable to any European but a professional tumbler. One body of them stood till they saw white faces, and then ran wildly away. They appeared to have made the threatened attempt to poison the streams by placing in them large branches of the *Euphorbia antiquorum* under stones, but the water when tried did not seem any the worse, and produced no ill effects. Two porters were wounded on the march by the arrows of the Bari; and they showed such a front on the occasion of Grant's umbrella being accidentally left behind, that although thirty men went back for it, it was judged most prudent to leave it as a trophy in the hands of the enemy.

By daylight on the 15th of February, after the night which had been made hideous by alarms, the party moved off in a compact mass, and were not molested, though they passed villages, outcropping rocks, and jungle of low trees, all favouring attack. The features of the country changed from highland to lowland as they advanced. As far as the eye could reach, there lay to the north a dreary plain, dotted with the Punjab *madar* growing upon firm and heavy sand.

As they approached Gondokoro, N. lat. 4° 54′ 5″ and E. long. 31° 46′ 9″, a white speck was pointed out as the church which belonged to the Austrian Mission, which had now been given up. The sight of the masts of Nile boats now wound their excitement to the highest pitch, and the brief delay was irritating to the English officers, when the Turks drew up at the distance of a mile from the place to fire a salute. When they had arrived, they at once entered the first respectable-looking hut, and inquired for Petherick, and were informed that a white man had been there only a few minutes before. They went in quest of the person referred to, and soon had the happiness to see a sturdy English figure approaching. With a hearty cheer they waved their hats and rushed into the arms, not of Petherick but of Baker, the elephant-hunter of Ceylon, who had bravely come in search of them with three well-appointed vessels. From him they learnt all the news which had been accumulating during their long banishment from civilised society,—the sad death of H.R.H. the Prince Consort of England, the outbreak of the American civil war, &c. &c.

Petherick, while waiting for a vessel to be built, had lost the north winds at 7° N. lat., and was gone overland to his trading depot at Nyambara. Baker offered Speke and Grant his boats to take them to Khartum, but proposed himself to push on with Mahamed, and survey the country they had not seen, especially the Luta Nzigé lake, about which they had heard so much. It is well known that he was eminently successful, and that his lake now figures by the side of Speke's as the Albert Nyanza.

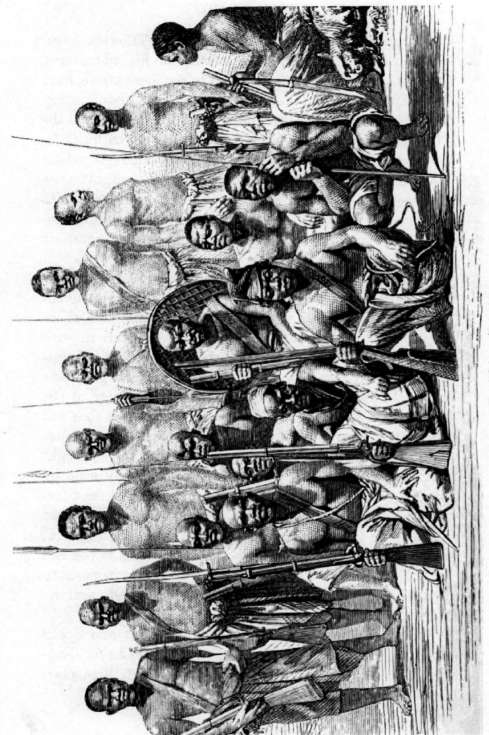

Speke's "Faithfuls."—PAGE 341

During their residence at Gondokoro, Petherick afterwards came in and gave an account of his adventures, saying that he had never expected to see them arrive, from the accounts he had heard. All was now plain sailing. Baker's boats were well found, and they slipped down the Nile to Khartum, where they met with an enthusiastic reception from the European residents, amongst whom was Mr De Bono, the ivory-trader, whose outpost they had met with, and the Baroness Von Capellan, who, with Madame Tinne and her daughter (at that time unfortunately absent on a collateral expedition), had come up the Nile to look for them.

From this point to Alexandria Captain Grant's narrative is replete with interesting observations. Few adventures were met with worthy to be compared with those they had passed through, though those they fell in with would have made a mere Nile voyage extremely interesting. The Nile is now as familiar to African travellers as the Rhine to European tourists. The passage of the Nubian Desert with camels from Berber, where they cut off a great elbow of the Nile, was perhaps the most exciting part of the homeward journey. They were brought from Aswan to Cairo by a steamer obligingly sent by his Highness Ismail Pasha, Viceroy of Egypt, and received by him with all possible distinction. They arrived at Cairo on the 25th of May 1863. The eighteen faithful men and four women who accompanied them to the end of the journey parted with them with every demonstration of affectionate regret, and were forwarded, well rewarded, to Zanzibar.

On the 4th of June 1863 Captains Grant and Speke sailed together in the Pera, Captain Jamieson, for England, where they arrived after an absence of three years and fifty-one days. The fatal accident which terminated Captain Speke's career in England, in the prime of his life and at the zenith of his glory, was attended with the solitary consolation, that after so long and perilous a wandering it was his lot to sleep with his fathers.

THE END.

PRINTED BY WILLIAM BLACKWOOD AND SONS, EDINBURGH.

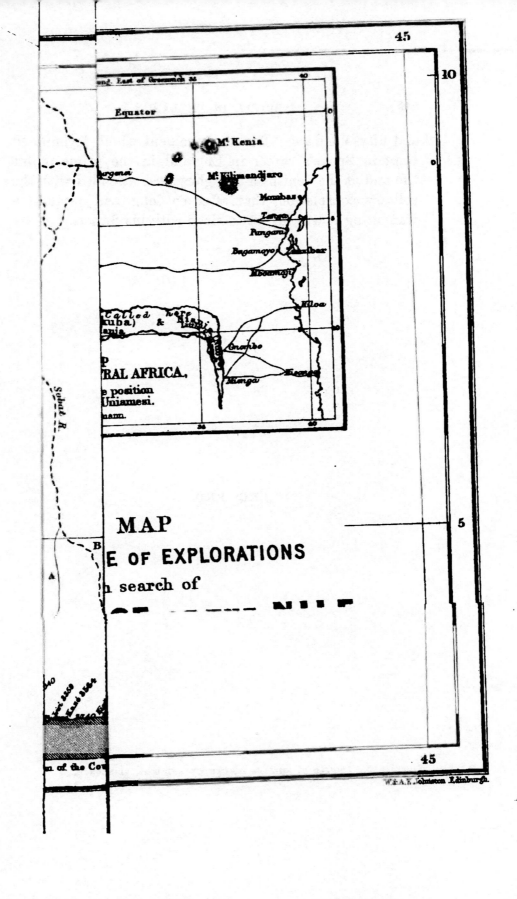

45

10

Long. East of Greenwich 35

Equator

Mt Kenia

Mt Kilimandjaro

Mombas

Tanga

Pangani

Bagamoyo Zanzibar

Kisamaji

Kiloa

(Called here

(Kuba) & Nyassi

Uenia

Quanbo

P

RAL AFRICA.

e position

Uniamesi.

nann.

Kianga

Kwea

Sobat R.

MAP

E OF EXPLORATIONS

h search of

5

A B

n of the Cou

45

W. & A. K. Johnston, Edinburgh.

THE HANDY HORSE-BOOK;

OR, PRACTICAL INSTRUCTIONS IN RIDING, DRIVING, AND THE GENERAL CARE AND MANAGEMENT OF HORSES. By a CAVALRY OFFICER. A New Edition, with Six Engravings, 4s. 6d.

"As cavalry officer, hunting horseman, coach proprietor, whip, and steeplechase rider, the author has had long and various experience in the management of horses, and he now gives us the cream of his information."—*Athenæum.*

"He propounds no theories, but embodies in simple untechnical language what he has learned practically."—*Sporting Gazette.*

PHYSIOLOGY AT THE FARM, IN REARING AND

FEEDING THE LIVE STOCK. By WILLIAM SELLER, M.D. F.R.S.E., and HENRY STEPHENS, F.R.S.E. Octavo, 16s.

CATTLE AND CATTLE-BREEDERS.

By WILLIAM M'COMBIE, Tillyfour. *Contents*—I. The Feeding of Cattle, &c. II. Reminiscences. III. The Cattle Trade, then and now. IV. Black polled Aberdeen and Angus Cattle and Shorthorns. V. Hints on the Breeding and Care of Cattle. Price 5s.

HANDY BOOK OF METEOROLOGY.

By ALEXANDER BUCHAN, Secretary of the Scottish Meteorological Society. Crown 8vo, 4s. 6d.

"A very handy book this, for in its small compass Mr Buchan has stored more and later information than exists in any volume with which we are acquainted."—*Symons's Meteorological Magazine.*

GEOLOGY FOR GENERAL READERS.

A SERIES OF POPULAR SKETCHES IN GEOLOGY AND PALÆONTOLOGY. By DAVID PAGE, LL.D. F.R.S.E. F.G.S. Second Edition, containing several New Chapters. Price 6s.

"Few of our handbooks of popular science can be said to have greater or more decisive merit than those of Mr Page on Geology and Palæontology. They are clear and vigorous in style, they never oppress the reader with a pedantic display of learning, nor overwhelm him with a pompous and superfluous terminology; and they have the happy art of taking him straightway to the face of nature herself, instead of leading him by the tortuous and bewildering paths of technical system and artificial classification."—*Saturday Review.*

"This is one of the best of Mr Page's many good books. It is written in a flowing popular style. Without illustration or any extraneous aid, the narrative must prove attractive to any intelligent reader."—*Geological Magazine.*

HANDY BOOK OF THE FLOWER GARDEN,

BEING PLAIN PRACTICAL DIRECTIONS FOR THE PROPAGATION, CULTURE, AND ARRANGEMENT OF PLANTS IN FLOWER-GARDENS ALL THE YEAR ROUND; embracing all classes of Gardens, from the largest to the smallest; with Engraved Plans, illustrative of the various systems of Grouping in Beds and Borders. By DAVID THOMSON, Archerfield Gardens, Author of a 'Practical Treatise on the Culture of the Pine-Apple.' In crown 8vo.

ON THE TREATMENT OF OUR DOMESTICATED DOGS.

By "MAGENTA," Author of the 'Handy Horse Book.' [*In the Press.*

VOLS. III. and IV. of

MR KINGLAKE'S HISTORY OF THE INVASION OF
THE CRIMEA. With numerous Maps, Plans, and Diagrams.

[*In the Press.*

LAKE VICTORIA:
A NARRATIVE OF EXPLORATIONS IN SEARCH OF THE SOURCE OF THE NILE. Compiled from the Memoirs of Captains SPEKE and GRANT. By GEORGE C. SWAYNE, M.A., Late Fellow of Corpus Christi College, Oxford. Crown 8vo, with Engravings, price 7s. 6d.

THE LIFE OF ST COLUMBA,
APOSTLE OF CALEDONIA. Reprinted from the 'Monks of the West.' By the COUNT DE MONTALEMBERT. Crown, 3s. 6d.

MEMOIR OF WILLIAM E. AYTOUN, D.C.L.,
Author of 'Lays of the Scottish Cavaliers,' &c. By THEODORE MARTIN. With Portrait. Post 8vo, 12s.

"This biography is quite a model in its way, and a delightful relief after much that has been done of late years in a similar line. Good taste, right feeling, and a generous but seldom excessive appreciation of the subject, mark the work."—*Manchester Guardian.*

THE PUBLIC SCHOOLS:
WINCHESTER — WESTMINSTER — SHREWSBURY — HARROW — RUGBY. Notes of their History and Traditions. By the Author of 'ETONIANA.' Crown 8vo, 3s. 6d.

ON PRIMARY INSTRUCTION IN RELATION TO EDU-
CATION. By SIMON S. LAURIE, A.M., Author of 'Philosophy of Ethics,' &c. Crown 8vo, 4s. 6d.

CAPTAIN SHERARD OSBORN'S WORKS.
Uniform Edition. In 3 vols. Sold separately.

Vol. I. STRAY LEAVES FROM AN ARCTIC JOURNAL; OR, EIGHTEEN MONTHS IN THE POLAR REGIONS IN SEARCH OF SIR JOHN FRANKLIN, IN THE YEARS 1850-51. THE CAREER, LAST VOYAGE, AND FATE OF SIR JOHN FRANKLIN. 5s.

Vol. II. THE DISCOVERY OF A NORTH-WEST PASSAGE BY H.M.S. INVESTIGATOR, CAPTAIN R. M'CLURE, DURING THE YEARS 1850-54. 5s.

Vol. III. QUEDAH; OR, STRAY LEAVES FROM A JOURNAL IN MALAYAN WATERS. - A CRUISE IN JAPANESE WATERS. THE FIGHT OF THE PEIHO IN 1859. 7s. 6d.

MEMOIR OF SIR WILLIAM HAMILTON, BART.
Professor of Logic and Metaphysics in the University of Edinburgh. By PROFESSOR VEITCH, of the University of Glasgow. [*In the Press.*

LECTURES ON THE EARLY GREEK PHILOSOPHY,

AND OTHER PHILOSOPHIC REMAINS OF PROFESSOR FER-RIER OF ST ANDREWS. Edited by Sir ALEX. GRANT and Pro-fessor LUSHINGTON. 2 vols. post 8vo, 24s.

" These lectures, in so far as they treat of Greek philosophy down to Plato, have been carefully elaborated, and are of much value—of higher value, indeed, than any writings on the same sub-ject in the English language; and in point of clearness, depth, and resolute search after truth, and tenacious hold of it when found, we doubt if they are surpassed in any language. . . . For our part, we do not know any philosophical writings so fascinating to a young student of philoso-phy as these early pages."—*Scotsman.*

THE WORKS OF SIR WILLIAM HAMILTON, BART.,

Professor of Logic and Metaphysics in the University of Edinburgh.

LECTURES ON METAPHYSICS. Edited by the Rev. H. L. MANSEL, B.D. LL.D., Waynflete Professor of Moral and Metaphysical Phi-losophy, Oxford; and JOHN VEITCH, M.A., Professor of Logic and Rhetoric in the University of Glasgow. Third Edition. 2 vols. 8vo, 24s.

LECTURES ON LOGIC. Edited by the Same. Second Edition. 2 vols. 8vo, 24s.

DISCUSSIONS ON PHILOSOPHY AND LITERATURE, EDUCA-TION AND UNIVERSITY REFORM. Third Edition. 8vo, price 21s.

MR WORSLEY'S TRANSLATION OF HOMER INTO

ENGLISH VERSE IN THE SPENSERIAN STANZA.

ODYSSEY, 2 vols., 18s. ILIAD, Books I.-XII., 10s. 6d.

COMPLETION OF MR WORSLEY'S TRANSLATION OF THE ILIAD.
BY PROFESSOR CONINGTON.

THE ILIAD OF HOMER.

Books XIII. to XXIV. Translated into English Verse in the Spen-serian Stanza. By JOHN CONINGTON, M.A., Corpus Professor of Latin in the University of Oxford.

FAUST: A DRAMATIC POEM.

By GOETHE. Translated into English Verse by THEODORE MARTIN. Second Edition, post octavo, price 6s.

"The best translation of ' Faust ' in verse we have yet had in England."—*Spectator.*
"Mr Theodore Martin's translation is unquestionably the best in the language, and will give to English readers a fair idea of the greatest of modern poems."—*Press.*

CATALOGUE

OF

MESSRS BLACKWOOD AND SONS'

PUBLICATIONS.

◆

HISTORY OF EUROPE,

From the Commencement of the French Revolution in 1789 to the Battle of Waterloo. By Sir ARCHIBALD ALISON, Bart., D.C.L.

A NEW LIBRARY EDITION (being the Tenth), in 14 vols. demy 8vo, with Portraits, and a copious Index, £10, 10s.

ANOTHER EDITION, in crown 8vo, 20 vols., £6.

A PEOPLE'S EDITION, 12 vols., closely printed in double columns, £2, 8s., and Index Volume, 8s.

"An extraordinary work, which has earned for itself a lasting place in the literature of the country, and within a few years found innumerable readers in every part of the globe. There is no book extant that treats so well of the period to the illustration of which Mr Alison's labours have been devoted. It exhibits great knowledge, patient research, indefatigable industry, and vast power."—*Times, Sept. 7, 1860.*

CONTINUATION OF ALISON'S HISTORY OF EUROPE,

From the Fall of Napoleon to the Accession of Louis Napoleon. By Sir ARCHIBALD ALISON, Bart., D.C.L. In 9 vols., £6, 7s. 6d. Uniform with the Library Edition of the previous work.

A PEOPLE'S EDITION, in 8 vols., closely printed in double columns, £1, 14s.

EPITOME OF ALISON'S HISTORY OF EUROPE.

For the Use of Schools and Young Persons. Fifteenth Edition, 7s. 6d., bound.

ATLAS TO ALISON'S HISTORY OF EUROPE;

Containing 109 Maps and Plans of Countries, Battles, Sieges, and Sea-Fights. Constructed by A. KEITH JOHNSTON, F.R.S.E. With Vocabulary of Military and Marine Terms. Demy 4to. Library Edition, £3, 3s.; People's Edition, crown 4to, £1, 11s. 6d.

LIVES OF LORD CASTLEREAGH AND SIR CHARLES

STEWART, Second and Third Marquesses of Londonderry. From the Original Papers of the Family, and other sources. By Sir ARCHIBALD ALISON, Bart., D.C.L. In 3 vols. 8vo, £2, 5s.

ANNALS OF THE PENINSULAR CAMPAIGNS.

By Capt. THOMAS HAMILTON. A New Edition. Edited by F. HARD-MAN, Esq. 8vo, 16s.; and Atlas of Maps to illustrate the Campaigns, 12s.

A VISIT TO FLANDERS AND THE FIELD OF WATERLOO.

By JAMES SIMPSON, Advocate. A Revised Edition. With Two Coloured Plans of the Battle. Crown 8vo, 5s.

WELLINGTON'S CAREER:

A Military and Political Summary. By LIEUT.-COL. E. BRUCE HAMLEY, Professor of Military History and Art at the Staff College. Crown 8vo, 2s.

THE STORY OF THE CAMPAIGN OF SEBASTOPOL.

Written in the Camp. By LIEUT.-COL. E. BRUCE HAMLEY. With Illustrations drawn in Camp by the Author. 8vo, 21s.

"We strongly recommend this 'Story of the Campaign' to all who would gain a just comprehension of this tremendous struggle. Of this we are perfectly sure, it is a book unlikely to be ever superseded. Its truth is of that simple and startling character which is sure of an immortal existence; nor is it paying the gallant author too high a complement to class this masterpiece of military history with the most precious of those classic records which have been bequeathed to us by the great writers of antiquity who took part in the wars they have described."—The Press.

THE INVASION OF THE CRIMEA:

Its Origin, and Account of its Progress down to the Death of Lord Raglan. By ALEXANDER WILLIAM KINGLAKE, M.P. Vols. I. and II., bringing the Events down to the Close of the Battle of the Alma. Fourth Edition. Price 32s.

TEN YEARS OF IMPERIALISM IN FRANCE.

Impressions of a "Flâneur." Second Edition. In 8vo, price 9s.

"There has not been published for many a day a more remarkable book on France than this, which professes to be the impressions of a Flaneur. . . . It has all the liveliness and sparkle of a work written only for amusement; it has all the solidity and weight of a State paper; and we expect for it not a little political influence as a fair, full, and masterly statement of the Imperial policy—the first and only good account that has been given to Europe of the Napoleonic system now in force."—Times.

FLEETS AND NAVIES.

By CAPTAIN CHARLES HAMLEY, R.M. Originally published in 'Blackwood's Magazine.' Crown 8vo, 6s.

HISTORY OF GREECE UNDER FOREIGN DOMINATION.

By GEORGE FINLAY, LL.D., Athens—viz :

GREECE UNDER THE ROMANS. B.C. 146 to A.D. 717. A Historical View of the Condition of the Greek Nation from its Conquest by the Romans until the Extinction of the Roman Power in the East. Second Edition, 16s.

HISTORY OF THE BYZANTINE EMPIRE, A.D. 716 to 1204; and of the Greek Empire of Nicæa and Constantinople, A.D. 1204 to 1453. 2 vols., £1, 7s. 6d.

MEDIÆVAL GREECE AND TREBIZOND. The History of Greece, from its Conquest by the Crusaders to its Conquest by the Turks, A.D. 1204 to 1566; and the History of the Empire of Trebizond, A.D. 1204 to 1461. 12s.

GREECE UNDER OTHOMAN AND VENETIAN DOMINATION. A.D. 1453 to 1821. 10s. 6d.

HISTORY OF THE GREEK REVOLUTION. 2 vols. 8vo, £1, 4s.

"His book is worthy to take its place among the remarkable works on Greek history, which form one of the chief glories of English scholarship. The history of Greece is but half told without it."—London Guardian.

THE NATIONAL CHARACTER OF THE ATHENIANS.

By JOHN BROWN PATTERSON. Edited from the Author's revision, by PROFESSOR PILLANS, of the University of Edinburgh. With a Sketch of his Life. Crown 8vo, 4s. 6d.

STUDIES IN ROMAN LAW.

With Comparative Views of the Laws of France, England, and Scotland. By LORD MACKENZIE, one of the Judges of the Court of Session in Scotland. 8vo, 12s. Second Edition.

"We know not in the English language where else to look for a history of the Roman law so clear, and, at the same time, so short. . . . More improving reading, both for the general student and for the lawyer, we cannot well imagine; and there are few, even among learned professional men, who will not gather some novel information from Lord Mackenzie's simple pages."—London Review.

THE EIGHTEEN CHRISTIAN CENTURIES.

By the REV. JAMES WHITE. Fourth Edition, with an Analytical Table of Contents, and a Copious Index. Post 8vo, 7s. 6d.

THE MONKS OF THE WEST,

From St Benedict to St Bernard. By the COUNT DE MONTALEMBERT. Authorised Translation. 5 vols. 8vo, £2 12s. 6d.

HISTORY OF FRANCE,

From the Earliest Period to the Year 1848. By the REV. JAMES WHITE. Author of 'The Eighteen Christian Centuries.' School Edition. Post 8vo, 6s.

"An excellent and comprehensive compendium of French history, quite above the standard of a school-book, and particularly well adapted for the libraries of literary institutions."—*National Review.*

LEADERS OF THE REFORMATION:

LUTHER, CALVIN, LATIMER, and KNOX. By the REV. JOHN TULLOCH, D.D., Principal, and Primarius Professor of Theology, St Mary's College, St Andrews. Second Edition, crown 8vo, 6s. 6d.

ENGLISH PURITANISM AND ITS LEADERS:

CROMWELL, MILTON, BAXTER, and BUNYAN. By the REV. JOHN TULLOCH, D.D. Uniform with the 'Leaders of the Reformation.' 7s. 6d.

HISTORY OF THE FRENCH PROTESTANT REFUGEES.

By CHARLES WEISS, Professor of History at the Lycée Buonaparte. Translated by F. HARDMAN, Esq. 8vo, 14s.

HISTORY OF THE CHURCH OF SCOTLAND,

From the Reformation to the Revolution Settlement. By the Very REV. JOHN LEE, D.D., LL.D., Principal of the University of Edinburgh. Edited by the Rev. WILLIAM LEE. 2 vols. 8vo, 21s.

HISTORY OF SCOTLAND FROM THE REVOLUTION

To the Extinction of the last Jacobite Insurrection, 1689-1748. By JOHN HILL BURTON, Esq., Advocate. 2 vols. 8vo, reduced to 15s.

LIVES OF THE QUEENS OF SCOTLAND,

And English Princesses connected with the Regal Succession of Great Britain. By AGNES STRICKLAND. With Portraits and Historical Vignettes. Post 8vo, £4, 4s.

"Every step in Scotland is historical; the shades of the dead arise on every side; the very rocks breathe. Miss Strickland's talents as a writer, and turn of mind as an individual, in a peculiar manner fit her for painting a historical gallery of the most illustrious or dignified female characters in that land of chivalry and song."—*Blackwood's Magazine.*

MEMORIALS OF THE CASTLE OF EDINBURGH.

By JAMES GRANT, Esq. A New Edition. In crown 8vo, with 12 Engravings, 3s. 6d.

MEMOIRS OF SIR WILLIAM KIRKALDY OF GRANGE,

Governor of the Castle of Edinburgh for Mary Queen of Scots. By JAMES GRANT, Esq. Post 8vo, 10s. 6d.

MEMOIRS OF SIR JOHN HEPBURN,

Marshal of France under Louis XIII., &c. By JAMES GRANT, Esq. Post 8vo, 8s.

WORKS OF THE REV. THOMAS M'CRIE, D.D.

A New and Uniform Edition. Edited by Professor M'CRIE. 4 vols. crown 8vo, 24s. Sold separately—viz. :

LIFE OF JOHN KNOX. Containing Illustrations of the History of the Reformation in Scotland. Crown 8vo, 6s.

LIFE OF ANDREW MELVILLE. Containing Illustrations of the Ecclesiastical and Literary History of Scotland in the Sixteenth and Seventeenth Centuries. Crown 8vo, 6s.

HISTORY OF THE PROGRESS AND SUPPRESSION OF THE REFORMATION IN ITALY IN THE SIXTEENTH CENTURY. Crown 8vo, 4s.

HISTORY OF THE PROGRESS AND SUPPRESSION OF THE REFORMATION IN SPAIN IN THE SIXTEENTH CENTURY. Crown 8vo, 3s. 6d.

THE BOSCOBEL TRACTS;
Relating to the Escape of Charles the Second after the Battle of Worcester, and his subsequent Adventures. Edited by J. HUGHES, Esq., A.M. A New Edition, with additional Notes and Illustrations, including Communications from the Rev. R. H. BARHAM, Author of the 'Ingoldsby Legends.' In 8vo, with Engravings, 16s.

"'The Boscobel Tracts' is a very curious book, and about as good an example of single subject historical collections as may be found. Originally undertaken, or at least completed, at the suggestion of the late Bishop Copplestone, in 1827, it was carried out with a degree of judgment and taste not always found in works of a similar character."—*Spectator.*

LIFE OF JOHN DUKE OF MARLBOROUGH.
With some Account of his Contemporaries, and of the War of the Succession. By SIR ARCHIBALD ALISON, Bart., D.C.L. Third Edition. 2 vols. 8vo, Portraits and Maps, 30s.

THE NEW 'EXAMEN;'
Or, An Inquiry into the Evidence of certain Passages in 'Macaulay's History of England' concerning—THE DUKE OF MARLBOROUGH—THE MASSACRE OF GLENCOE—THE HIGHLANDS OF SCOTLAND—VISCOUNT DUNDEE—WILLIAM PENN. By JOHN PAGET, Esq., Barrister-at-Law. In crown 8vo, 6s.

"We certainly never saw a more damaging exposure, and it is something worth notice that much of it appeared in 'Blackwood's Magazine' during the lifetime of Lord Macaulay, but he never attempted to make any reply. The charges are so direct, and urged in such unmistakable language, that no writer who valued his character for either accuracy of fact or fairness in comment would let them remain unanswered if he had any reason to give."—*Gentleman's Magazine.*

AUTOBIOGRAPHY OF THE REV. DR CARLYLE,
Minister of Inveresk. Containing Memorials of the Men and Events of his Time. Edited by JOHN HILL BURTON. In 8vo. Third Edition, with Portrait, 14s.

"This book contains by far the most vivid picture of Scottish life and manners that has been given to the public since the days of Sir Walter Scott. In bestowing upon it this high praise, we make no exception, not even in favour of Lord Cockburn's 'Memorials'—the book which resembles it most, and which ranks next to it in interest."—*Edinburgh Review.*

MEMOIR OF THE POLITICAL LIFE OF EDMUND BURKE.
With Extracts from his Writings. By the REV. GEORGE CROLY, D.D. 2 vols. post 8vo, 18s.

CURRAN AND HIS CONTEMPORARIES.
By CHARLES PHILLIPS, Esq, A.B. A New Edition. Crown 8vo, 7s. 6d.

"Certainly one of the most extraordinary pieces of biography ever produced. . . . . . No library should be without it."—*Lord Brougham.*
"Never, perhaps, was there a more curious collection of portraits crowded before into the same canvas."—*Times.*

MEMOIR OF MRS HEMANS.
By her SISTER. With a Portrait. Fcap. 8vo, 5s.

LIFE OF THE LATE REV. JAMES ROBERTSON, D.D.,
F.R.S.E., Professor of Divinity and Ecclesiastical History in the University of Edinburgh. By the REV. A. H. CHARTERIS, M.A., Minister of New-abbey. With a Portrait. 8vo, price 10s. 6d.

ESSAYS; HISTORICAL, POLITICAL, AND MISCELLANEOUS.
By SIR ARCHIBALD ALISON, Bart. 3 vols. demy 8vo, 45s.

ESSAYS IN HISTORY AND ART.
By R. H. PATTERSON. Viz.:
COLOUR IN NATURE AND ART—REAL AND IDEAL BEAUTY—SCULPTURE—ETHNOLOGY OF EUROPE—UTOPIAS—OUR INDIAN EMPIRE—THE NATIONAL LIFE OF CHINA—AN IDEAL ART-CONGRESS—BATTLE OF THE STYLES—GENIUS AND LIBERTY—YOUTH AND SUMMER—RECORDS OF THE PAST: NINEVEH AND BABYLON—INDIA: ITS CASTES AND CREEDS—"CHRISTOPHER NORTH:" IN MEMORIAM. In 1 vol. 8vo, 12s.

NORMAN SINCLAIR.
By W. E. AYTOUN, D.C.L., Author of 'Lays of the Scottish Cavaliers,' &c. &c. In 3 vols. post 8vo, 31s. 6d.

THE OLD BACHELOR IN THE OLD SCOTTISH VILLAGE.
By THOMAS AIRD. Fcap. 8vo, 4s.

SIR EDWARD BULWER LYTTON'S NOVELS.
Library Edition. Printed from a large and readable type. In Volumes of a convenient and handsome form. 8vo, 5s. each—viz.:

THE CAXTON NOVELS, 10 Volumes :

The Caxton Family. 2 vols.	What will he do with it ?
My Novel. 4 vols.	4 vols.

HISTORICAL ROMANCES, 11 Volumes :

Devereux. 2 vols.	The Siege of Grenada. 1 vol.
The Last Days of Pompeii. 2 vols.	The Last of the Barons. 2 vols.
Rienzi. 2 vols.	Harold. 2 vols.

ROMANCES, 5 Volumes :

The Pilgrims of the Rhine. 1 vol.	Eugene Aram. 2 vols.
	Zanoni. 2 vols.

NOVELS OF LIFE AND MANNERS, 15 Volumes :

Pelham. 2 vols.	Ernest Maltravers — Second Part (i.e. Alice.) 2 vols.
The Disowned. 2 vols.	
Paul Clifford. 2 vols.	
Godolphin. 1 vol.	Night and Morning. 2 vols.
Ernest Maltravers—First Part. 2 vols.	Lucretia. 2 vols.

"It is of the handiest of sizes; the paper is good ; and the type, which seems to be new, is very clear and beautiful. There are no pictures. The whole charm of the presentment of the volume consists in its handiness, and the tempting clearness and beauty of the type, which almost converts into a pleasure the mere act of following the printer's lines, and leaves the author's mind free to exert its unobstructed force upon the reader."—*Examiner.*
" Nothing could be better as to size, type, paper, and general get-up."—*Athenæum.*

JESSIE CAMERON: A HIGHLAND STORY.
By the LADY RACHEL BUTLER. Second Edition. Small 8vo, with a Frontispiece, 2s. 6d.

SOME PASSAGES IN THE LIFE OF ADAM BLAIR,
And History of Matthew Wald. By the Author of 'Valerius.' Fcap. 8vo, 4s. cloth.

CAPTAIN CLUTTERBUCK'S CHAMPAGNE:
A West Indian Reminiscence. Post 8vo, 12s.

SCENES OF CLERICAL LIFE.
The Sad Fortunes of Amos Barton—Mr Gilfil's Love-Story—Janet's Repentance. By GEORGE ELIOT. 2 vols. fcap. 8vo, 12s.

ADAM BEDE.
By GEORGE ELIOT. 2 vols. fcap. 8vo, 12s.

THE MILL ON THE FLOSS.
By GEORGE ELIOT. 2 vols. fcap. 8vo, 12s.

SILAS MARNER: THE WEAVER OF RAVELOE.
By GEORGE ELIOT. Fcap. 8vo, 6s.

THE NOVELS OF GEORGE ELIOT.
Cheap Edition, complete in 3 vols., price 6s. each—viz.:
ADAM BEDE.
THE MILL ON THE FLOSS.
SCENES OF CLERICAL LIFE, and SILAS MARNER.

ANNALS OF THE PARISH, AND AYRSHIRE LEGATEES.
By JOHN GALT. Fcap. 8vo, 4s. cloth.

SIR ANDREW WYLIE.
By JOHN GALT. Fcap. 8vo, 4s. cloth.

THE PROVOST, AND OTHER TALES.
By JOHN GALT. Fcap. 8vo, 4s. cloth.

THE ENTAIL.
By JOHN GALT. Fcap. 8vo, 4s. cloth.

THE YOUTH AND MANHOOD OF CYRIL THORNTON.
By CAPTAIN HAMILTON. Fcap. 8vo, 4s. cloth.

LADY LEE'S WIDOWHOOD.
By LIEUT.-COL. E. B. HAMLEY. Crown 8vo, with 13 Illustrations by the
Author. 6s.

THE LIFE OF MANSIE WAUCH,
Tailor in Dalkeith. By D. M. MOIR. Fcap. 8vo, 3s. cloth.

NIGHTS AT MESS, SIR FRIZZLE PUMPKIN, AND OTHER
TALES. Fcap. 8vo, 3s. cloth.

KATIE STEWART: A TRUE STORY.
By MRS OLIPHANT. Fcap. 8vo, with Frontispiece and Vignette. 4s.

PEN OWEN.
Fcap. 8vo, 4s. cloth.

PENINSULAR SCENES AND SKETCHES.
Fcap. 8vo, 3s. cloth.

REGINALD DALTON.
By the Author of 'Valerius.' Fcap. 8vo, 4s. cloth.

LIFE IN THE FAR WEST.
By G. F. RUXTON, Esq. Second Edition. Fcap. 8vo, 4s.

TOM CRINGLE'S LOG.
A New Edition. With Illustrations by STANFIELD, WEIR, SKELTON, WALKER,
&c., Engraved by WHYMPER. Crown 8vo, 6s.
"Everybody who has failed to read 'Tom Cringle's Log' should do so at once. The 'Quarterly Review' went so far as to say that the papers composing it, when it first appeared in 'Blackwood,' were
the most brilliant series of the time, and that time one unrivalled for the number of famous magazinists
existing in it. Coleridge says, in his 'Table Talk,' that the 'Log' is most excellent; and these verdicts
have been ratified by generations of men and boys, and by the manifestation of Continental approval
which is shown by repeated translations. The engravings illustrating the present issue are excellent."—
Standard.

TOM CRINGLE'S LOG.
Fcap. 8vo, 4s. cloth.

THE CRUISE OF THE MIDGE.
By the Author of 'Tom Cringle's Log.' Fcap. 8vo, 4s. cloth.

CHAPTERS ON CHURCHYARDS.
By MRS SOUTHEY. Fcap. 8vo, 7s. 6d.

THE SUBALTERN.
By the Author of the 'The Chelsea Pensioners.' Fcap. 8vo, 3s. cloth.

CHRONICLES OF CARLINGFORD: SALEM CHAPEL.
Second Edition. Complete in 1 vol., price 5s.

" This story, so fresh, so powerfully written, and so tragic, stands out from among its fellows like a piece of newly-coined gold in a handful of dim commonplace shillings. Tales of pastoral experience and scenes from clerical life we have had in plenty, but the sacred things of the conventicle, the relative position of pastor and flock in a Nonconforming ' connection,' were but guessed at by the world outside, and terrible is the revelation."—*Westminster Review.*

CHRONICLES OF CARLINGFORD: THE RECTOR, AND THE DOCTOR'S FAMILY. Post 8vo, price 4s. *THE PERPETUAL CURATE.* Complete in one vol. 8vo, price 6s.

TALES FROM BLACKWOOD.
Complete in 12 vols., bound in cloth, 18s. The Volumes are sold separately, 1s. 6d. ; and may be had of most Booksellers, in Six Volumes, handsomely half-bound in red morocco.

CONTENTS.

VOL. I. The Glenmutchkin Railway.—Vanderdecken's Message Home.—The Floating Beacon.—Colonna the Painter.—Napoleon.—A Legend of Gibraltar.—The Iron Shroud.

VOL. II. Lazaro's Legacy.—A Story without a Tail.—Faustus and Queen Elizabeth.—How I became a Yeoman.—Devereux Hall.—The Metempsychosis.—College Theatricals.

VOL. III. A Reading Party in the Long Vacation.—Father Tom and the Pope.—La Petite Madelaine. — Bob Burke's Duel with Ensign Brady. — The Headsman : A Tale of Doom.—The Wearyful Woman.

VOL. IV. How I stood for the Dreepdaily Burghs.—First and Last.—The Duke's Dilemma : A Chronicle of Niesenstein.—The Old Gentleman's Teetotum.—" Woe to us when we lose the Watery Wall."—My College Friends : Charles Russell, the Gentleman Commoner.—The Magic Lay of the One-Horse Chay.

VOL. V. Adventures in Texas.—How we got Possession of the Tuileries.—Captain Paton's Lament.—The Village Doctor.—A Singular Letter from Southern Africa.

VOL. VI. My Friend the Dutchman.—My College Friends—No. II. : Horace Leicester.—The Emerald Studs.—My College Friends—No. III. : Mr W. Wellington Hurst.—Christine : A Dutch Story.—The Man in the Bell.

VOL. VII. My English Acquaintance.—The Murderer's Last Night.—Narration of Certain Uncommon Things that did formerly happen to Me, Herbert Willis, B.D.—The Wags.—The Wet Wooing : A Narrative of '98.—Ben-na-Groich.

VOL. VIII. The Surveyor's Tale. By Professor Aytoun.—The Forrest Race Romance.—Di Vasari : A Tale of Florence. — Sigismund Fatello. — The Boxes.

VOL. IX. Rosaura : A Tale of Madrid.—Adventure in the North-West Territory.—Harry Bolton's Curacy.—The Florida Pirate.—The Pandour and his Princess.—The Beauty Draught.

VOL. X. Antonio di Carara.—The Fatal Repast.—The Vision of Cagliostro.—The First and Last Kiss.—The Smuggler's Leap.—The Haunted and the Haunters.—The Duellists.

VOL. XI. The Natolian Story-Teller.—The First and Last Crime.—John Rintoul.—Major Moss.—The Premier and his Wife.

VOL. XII. Tickler among the Thieves !—The Bridegroom of Barna.—The Involuntary Experimentalist.—Lebrun's Lawsuit.—The Snowing-up of Strath Lugas.—A Few Words on Social Philosophy.

THE WONDER-SEEKER ;
Or, The History of Charles Douglas. By M. FRASER TYTLER, Author of ' Tales of the Great and Brave,' &c. A New Edition. Fcap. 8vo, 3s. 6d.

VALERIUS: A ROMAN STORY.
Fcap. 8vo, 3s. cloth.

THE DIARY OF A LATE PHYSICIAN.
By SAMUEL WARREN, D.C.L. 1 vol. crown 8vo, 5s. 6d.

TEN THOUSAND A-YEAR.
By SAMUEL WARREN, D.C.L. 2 vols. crown 8vo, 9s.

NOW AND THEN.
By SAMUEL WARREN, D.C.L. Crown 8vo, 2s. 6d.

THE LILY AND THE BEE.
By SAMUEL WARREN, D.C.L. Crown 8vo, 2s.

MISCELLANIES.
By SAMUEL WARREN, D.C.L. Crown 8vo, 5s.

WORKS OF SAMUEL WARREN, D.C.L.
Uniform Edition. 5 vols. crown 8vo. 24s.

WORKS OF PROFESSOR WILSON.
Edited by his Son-in-law, Professor FERRIER. In 12 vols. crown 8vo, £2, 8s.
Illustrated with Portraits on Steel.

RECREATIONS OF CHRISTOPHER NORTH.
By PROFESSOR WILSON. In 2 vols. crown 8vo, 8s.

THE NOCTES AMBROSIANÆ.
By PROFESSOR WILSON. With Notes and a Glossary. In 4 vols. crown 8vo, 16s.

LIGHTS AND SHADOWS OF SCOTTISH LIFE.
By PROFESSOR WILSON. Fcap. 8vo, 3s. cloth.

THE TRIALS OF MARGARET LYNDSAY.
By PROFESSOR WILSON. Fcap. 8vo, 3s. cloth.

THE FORESTERS.
By PROFESSOR WILSON. Fcap. 8vo, 3s. cloth.

TALES.
By PROFESSOR WILSON. Comprising 'The Lights and Shadows of Scottish Life;' 'The Trials of Margaret Lyndsay;' and 'The Foresters.' In 1 vol. crown 8vo, 4s. cloth.

ESSAYS, CRITICAL AND IMAGINATIVE.
By PROFESSOR WILSON. 4 vols. crown 8vo, 16s.

TONY BUTLER.
Originally published in 'Blackwood's Magazine.' 3 vols. post 8vo, £1, 11s. 6d.

THE BOOK-HUNTER, ETC.
By JOHN HILL BURTON. New Edition. In crown 8vo, 7s. 6d.

"A book pleasant to look at and pleasant to read—pleasant from its rich store of anecdote, its geniality, and its humour, even to persons who care little for the subjects of which it treats, but beyond measure delightful to those who are in any degree members of the above-mentioned fraternity."—*Saturday Review.*

"We have not been more amused for a long time: and every reader who takes interest in typography and its consequences will say the same, if he will begin to read; beginning, he will finish, and be sorry when it is over."—*Athenæum.*

"Mr Burton has now given us a pleasant book, full of quaint anecdote, and of a lively bookish talk. There is a quiet humour in it which is very taking, and there is a curious knowledge of books which is really very sound."—*Examiner.*

HOMER AND HIS TRANSLATORS,
And the Greek Drama. By PROFESSOR WILSON. Crown 8vo, 6s.

"But of all the criticisms on Homer which I have ever had the good fortune to read, in our own or any language, the most vivid and entirely genial are those found in the 'Essays, Critical and Imaginative,' of the late Professor Wilson."—*Mr Gladstone's Studies on Homer.*

THE SKETCHER.
By the REV. JOHN EAGLES. Originally published in 'Blackwood's Magazine.' 8vo, 10s. 6d.

"This volume, called by the appropriate name of 'The Sketcher,' is one that ought to be found in the studio of every English landscape-painter. . . . . More instructive and suggestive readings for young artists, especially landscape-painters, can scarcely be found."—*The Globe.*

ESSAYS.
By the REV. JOHN EAGLES, A.M. Oxon. Originally published in 'Blackwood's Magazine.' Post 8vo, 10s. 6d.

CONTENTS:—Church Music, and other Parochials.—Medical Attendance, and other Parochials.—A few Hours at Hampton Court.—Grandfathers and Grandchildren.—Sitting for a Portrait.—Are there not Great Boasters among us?—Temperance and Teetotal Societies.—Thackeray's Lectures: Swift.—The Crystal Palace.—Civilisation: The Census.—The Beggar's Legacy.

ESSAYS; HISTORICAL, POLITICAL, AND MISCELLANEOUS.
By SIR ARCHIBALD ALISON, Bart., D.C.L. Three vols., demy 8vo, 45s.

LECTURES ON THE POETICAL LITERATURE OF THE
PAST HALF-CENTURY. By D. M. MOIR. Third Edition. Fcap. 8vo, 5s.

"Exquisite in its taste and generous in its criticisms."—*Hugh Miller.*

LECTURES ON THE HISTORY OF LITERATURE,
Ancient and Modern. From the German of F. SCHLEGEL. Fcap., 5s.

"A wonderful performance—better than anything we as yet have in our own language."—*Quarterly Review.*

THE GENIUS OF HANDEL,
And the distinctive Character of his Sacred Compositions. Two Lectures. Delivered to the Members of the Edinburgh Philosophical Institution. By the VERY REV. DEAN RAMSAY, Author of 'Reminiscences of Scottish Life and Character.' In crown 8vo, 3s. 6d.

BLACKWOOD'S MAGAZINE,
From Commencement in 1817 to December 1861. Numbers 1 to 554, forming 90 Volumes. £31, 10s.

INDEX TO THE FIRST FIFTY VOLUMES OF BLACKWOOD'S
MAGAZINE. 8vo, 15s.

LAYS OF THE SCOTTISH CAVALIERS,

And other Poems. By W. EDMONDSTOUNE AYTOUN, D.C.L., Professor of Rhetoric and English Literature in the University of Edinburgh. Eighteenth Edition. Fcap. 8vo, 7s. 6d.

"Professor Aytoun's 'Lays of the Scottish Cavaliers'—a volume of verse which shows that Scotland has yet a poet. Full of the true fire, it now stirs and swells like a trumpet-note—now sinks in cadences sad and wild as the wail of a Highland dirge."—*Quarterly Review.*

BOTHWELL : A POEM.

By W. EDMONDSTOUNE AYTOUN, D.C.L. Third Edition. Fcap. 8vo, 7s. 6d.

"Professor Aytoun has produced a fine poem and an able argument, and 'Bothwell' will assuredly take its stand among the classics of Scottish literature."—*The Press.*

THE BALLADS OF SCOTLAND.

Edited by Professor AYTOUN. Third Edition. 2 vols. fcap. 8vo, 12s.

"No country can boast of a richer collection of Ballads than Scotland, and no Editor for these Ballads could be found more accomplished than Professor Aytoun. He has sent forth two beautiful volumes which range with 'Percy's Reliques'—which, for completeness and accuracy, leave little to be desired—which must henceforth be considered as the standard edition of the Scottish Ballads, and which we commend as a model to any among ourselves who may think of doing like service to the English Ballads."—*Times.*

POEMS AND BALLADS OF GOETHE.

Translated by Professor AYTOUN and THEODORE MARTIN. Second Edition. Fcap. 8vo, 6s.

"There is no doubt that these are the best translations of Goethe's marvellously-cut gems which have yet been published."—*Times.*

THE BOOK OF BALLADS.

Edited by BON GAULTIER. Ninth Edition, with numerous Illustrations by DOYLE, LEECH, and CROWQUILL. Gilt edges, post 8vo, 8s. 6d.

FIRMILIAN; OR, THE STUDENT OF BADAJOS.

A Spasmodic Tragedy. By T. PERCY JONES. In small 8vo, 5s.

"Humour of a kind most rare at all times, and especially in the present day, runs through every page, and passages of true poetry and delicious versification prevent the continual play of sarcasm from becoming tedious."—*Literary Gazette.*

POETICAL WORKS OF THOMAS AIRD.

Fourth Edition. In 1 vol. fcap. 8vo, 6s.

POEMS.

By the LADY FLORA HASTINGS. Edited by her SISTER. Second Edition, with a Portrait. Fcap., 7s. 6d.

THE POEMS OF FELICIA HEMANS.

Complete in 1 vol. royal 8vo, with Portrait by FINDEN. Cheap Edition, 12s. 6d. *Another Edition*, with MEMOIR by her SISTER. Seven vols. fcap., 35s. *Another Edition*, in 6 vols., cloth, gilt edges, 24s.

The following Works of Mrs HEMANS are sold separately, bound in cloth, gilt edges, 4s. each :—
RECORDS OF WOMAN. FOREST SANCTUARY. SONGS OF THE AFFECTIONS. DRAMATIC WORKS. TALES AND HISTORIC SCENES. MORAL AND RELIGIOUS POEMS.

THE ODYSSEY OF HOMER.

Translated into English Verse in the Spenserian Stanza. By PHILIP STANHOPE WORSLEY, M.A., Scholar of Corpus Christi College. 2 vols. crown 8vo, 18s.

"Mr Worsley,—applying the Spenserian stanza, that beautiful romantic measure, to the most romantic poem of the ancient world—making the stanza yield him, too (what it never yielded to Byron), its treasures of fluidity and sweet ease—above all, bringing to his task a truly poetical sense and skill,—has produced a version of the 'Odyssey' much the most pleasing of those hitherto produced, and which is delightful to read."—*Professor Arnold on Translating Homer.*

POEMS AND TRANSLATIONS.
By PHILIP STANHOPE WORSLEY, M.A., Scholar of Corpus Christi College, Oxford. Fcap. 8vo, 5s.

POEMS.
By ISA. In small 8vo, 4s. 6d.

POETICAL WORKS OF D. M. MOIR.
With Portrait, and Memoir by THOMAS AIRD. Second Edition. 2 vols. fcap. 8vo, 12s.

LECTURES ON THE POETICAL LITERATURE OF THE
PAST HALF-CENTURY. By D. M. MOIR (Δ). Second Edition. Fcap. 8vo, 5s.
" A delightful volume."—*Morning Chronicle.*
" Exquisite in its taste and generous in its criticisms."—*Hugh Miller.*

THE COURSE OF TIME: A POEM.
By ROBERT POLLOK, A.M. Twenty-fourth Edition. Fcap. 8vo, 5s.
" Of deep and hallowed impress, full of noble thoughts and graphic conceptions—the production of a mind alive to the great relations of being, and the sublime simplicity of our religion."—*Blackwood's Magazine.*

AN ILLUSTRATED EDITION OF THE COURSE OF TIME.
In large 8vo, bound in cloth, richly gilt, 21s.
" There has been no modern poem in the English language, of the class to which the 'Course of Time' belongs, since Milton wrote, that can be compared to it. In the present instance the artistic talents of Messrs FOSTER, CLAYTON, TENNIEL, EVANS, DALZIEL, GREEN, and WOODS, have been employed in giving expression to the sublimity of the language, by equally exquisite illustrations, all of which are of the highest class."—*Bell's Messenger.*

POEMS AND BALLADS OF SCHILLER.
Translated by Sir EDWARD BULWER LYTTON, Bart. Second Edition. 8vo, 10s. 6d.

ST STEPHEN'S;
Or, Illustrations of Parliamentary Oratory. A Poem. *Comprising*—Pym—Vane—Strafford—Halifax—Shaftesbury—St John—Sir R. Walpole—Chesterfield — Carteret — Chatham — Pitt — Fox — Burke—Sheridan—Wilberforce—Wyndham—Conway—Castlereagh—William Lamb (Lord Melbourne)—Tierney — Lord Grey — O'Connell — Plunkett—Shiel—Follett—Macaulay—Peel. Second Edition. Crown 8vo, 5s.

LEGENDS, LYRICS, AND OTHER POEMS.
By B. SIMMONS. Fcap., 7s. 6d.

SIR WILLIAM CRICHTON—ATHELWOLD—GUIDONE:
Dramas by WILLIAM SMITH, Author of 'Thorndale,' &c. 32mo, 2s. 6d.

THE BIRTHDAY, AND OTHER POEMS.
By MRS SOUTHEY. Second Edition, 5s.

ILLUSTRATIONS OF THE LYRIC POETRY AND MUSIC
OF SCOTLAND. By WILLIAM STENHOUSE. Originally compiled to accompany the 'Scots Musical Museum,' and now published separately, with Additional Notes and Illustrations. 8vo, 7s. 6d.

PROFESSOR WILSON'S POEMS.
Containing the 'Isle of Palms,' the 'City of the Plague,' 'Unimore,' and other Poems. Complete Edition. Crown 8vo, 4s.

POEMS AND SONGS.
By DAVID WINGATE. Second Edition. Fcap. 8vo, 5s.
" We are delighted to welcome into the brotherhood of real poets a countryman of Burns, and whose verse will go far to render the rougher Border Scottish a classic dialect in our literature."—*John Bull.*

THE PHYSICAL ATLAS OF NATURAL PHENOMENA.

By ALEXANDER KEITH JOHNSTON, F.R.S.E., &c., Geographer to the Queen for Scotland. A New and Enlarged Edition, consisting of 35 Folio Plates, and 27 smaller ones, printed in Colours, with 135 pages of Letterpress, and Index. Imperial folio, half-bound morocco, £8, 8s.

" A perfect treasure of compressed information."—*Sir John Herschel.*

THE PHYSICAL ATLAS.

By ALEXANDER KEITH JOHNSTON, F.R.S.E., &c. Reduced from the Imperial Folio. This Edition contains Twenty-five Maps, including a Palæontological and Geological Map of the British Islands, with Descriptive Letterpress, and a very copious Index. In imperial 4to, half-bound morocco, £2, 12s. 6d.

" Executed with remarkable care, and is as accurate, and, for all educational purposes, as valuable, as the splendid large work (by the same author) which has now a European reputation."—*Eclectic Review.*

A GEOLOGICAL MAP OF EUROPE.

By SIR R. I. MURCHISON, D.C.L., F.R.S., &c., Director-General of the Geological Survey of Great Britain and Ireland; and JAMES NICOL, F.R.S.E., F.G.S., Professor of Natural History in the University of Aberdeen. Constructed by ALEXANDER KEITH JOHNSTON, F.R.S.E., &c. Four Sheets imperial, beautifully printed in Colours. In Sheets, £3, 3s.; in a Cloth Case, 4to, £3, 10s.

GEOLOGICAL AND PALÆONTOLOGICAL MAP OF THE

BRITISH ISLANDS, including Tables of the Fossils of the different Epochs, &c. &c., from the Sketches and Notes of Professor EDWARD FORBES. With Illustrative and Explanatory Letterpress. 21s.

GEOLOGICAL MAP OF SCOTLAND.

By JAMES NICOL, F.R.S.E., &c., Professor of Natural History in the University of Aberdeen. With Explanatory Notes. The Topography by ALEXANDER KEITH JOHNSTON, F.R.S.E., &c. Scale, 10 miles to an inch. In Cloth Case, 21s.

INTRODUCTORY TEXT-BOOK OF PHYSICAL GEOGRAPHY.

By DAVID PAGE, F.R.S.E., &c. With Illustrations and a Glossarial Index. Crown 8vo, 2s.

INTRODUCTORY TEXT-BOOK OF GEOLOGY.

By DAVID PAGE, F.R.S.E., F.G.S. With Engravings on Wood and Glossarial Index. Seventh Edition, 2s.

" It has not often been our good fortune to examine a text-book on science of which we could express an opinion so entirely favourable as we are enabled to do of Mr Page's little work."—*Athenæum.*

ADVANCED TEXT-BOOK OF GEOLOGY,

Descriptive and Industrial. By DAVID PAGE, F.R.S.E., F.G.S. With Engravings and Glossary of Scientific Terms. Fourth Edition, revised and enlarged, 7s. 6d.

" It is therefore with unfeigned pleasure that we record our appreciation of his ' Advanced Text-Book of Geology.' We have carefully read this truly satisfactory book, and do not hesitate to say that it is an excellent compendium of the great facts of Geology, and written in a truthful and philosophic spirit."—*Edinburgh Philosophical Journal.*

HANDBOOK OF GEOLOGICAL TERMS, GEOLOGY, AND

PHYSICAL GEOGRAPHY. By DAVID PAGE, F.R.S.E. F.G.S. Second Edition, crown 8vo, 7s. 6d.

THE PAST AND PRESENT LIFE OF THE GLOBE:

Being a Sketch in Outline of the World's Life-System. By DAVID PAGE, F.R.S.E., F.G.S. Crown 8vo, 6s. With Fifty Illustrations, drawn and engraved expressly for this Work.

" Mr Page, whose admirable text-books of geology have already secured him a position of importance in the scientific world, will add considerably to his reputation by the present sketch, as he modestly terms it, of the Life-System, or gradual evolution of the vitality of our globe. In no manual that we are aware of have the facts and phenomena of biology been presented in at once so systematic and succinct a form, the successive manifestations of life on the earth set forth in so clear an order, or traced so vividly from the earliest organisms deep-buried in its stratified crust, to the familiar forms that now adorn and people its surface."—*Literary Gazette.*

THE GEOLOGICAL EXAMINATOR:
A Progressive Series of Questions adapted to the Introductory and Advanced Text-Books of Geology. Prepared to assist Teachers in framing their Examinations, and Students in testing their own Progress and Proficiency. By DAVID PAGE, F.R.S.E., F.G.S. Third Edition, 1s.

THE GEOLOGY OF PENNSYLVANIA:
A Government Survey; with a General View of the Geology of the United States, Essays on the Coal-Formation and its Fossils, and a Description of the Coal-Fields of North America and Great Britain. By Professor HENRY DARWIN ROGERS, F.R.S., F.G.S., Professor of Natural History in the University of Glasgow. With Seven large Maps, and numerous Illustrations engraved on Copper and on Wood. In 3 vols. royal 4to, £8, 8s.

SEA-SIDE STUDIES AT ILFRACOMBE, TENBY, THE
SCILLY ISLES, AND JERSEY. By GEORGE HENRY LEWES. Second Edition. Crown 8vo, with Illustrations, and a Glossary of Technical Terms, 6s. 6d.

PHYSIOLOGY OF COMMON LIFE.
By GEORGE HENRY LEWES, Author of 'Sea-side Studies,' &c. Illustrated with numerous Engravings. 2 vols., 12s.

CHEMISTRY OF COMMON LIFE.
By Professor J. F. W. JOHNSTON. A New Edition. Edited by G. H. LEWES. With 113 Illustrations on Wood, and a Copious Index. 2 vols. crown 8vo, 11s. 6d.

NOMENCLATURE OF COLOURS,
Applicable to the Arts and Natural Sciences, to Manufactures, and other Purposes of General Utility. By D. R. HAY, F.R.S.E. 228 Examples of Colours, Hues, Tints, and Shades. 8vo, £3, 3s.

NARRATIVE OF THE EARL OF ELGIN'S MISSION TO
CHINA AND JAPAN. By LAURENCE OLIPHANT, Private Secretary to Lord Elgin. Illustrated with numerous Engravings in Chromo-Lithography, Maps, and Engravings on Wood, from Original Drawings and Photographs. Second Edition. In 2 vols. 8vo, 21s.
"The volumes in which Mr Oliphant has related these transactions will be read with the strongest interest now, and deserve to retain a permanent place in the literary and historical annals of our time."—Edinburgh Review.

RUSSIAN SHORES OF THE BLACK SEA
In the Autumn of 1852. With a Voyage down the Volga and a Tour through the Country of the Don Cossacks. By LAURENCE OLIPHANT, Esq. 8vo; with Map and other Illustrations. Fourth Edition, 14s.

EGYPT, THE SOUDAN, AND CENTRAL AFRICA:
With Explorations from Khartoum on the White Nile to the Regions of the Equator. By JOHN PETHERICK, F.R.G.S., Her Britannic Majesty's Consul for the Soudan. In 8vo, with a Map, 16s.

NOTES ON NORTH AMERICA:
Agricultural, Economical, and Social. By Professor J. F. W. JOHNSTON. 2 vols. post 8vo, 21s.
"Professor Johnston's admirable Notes . . . The very best manual for intelligent emigrants, whilst to the British agriculturist and general reader it conveys a more complete conception of the condition of these prosperous regions than all that has hitherto been written."—Economist.

A FAMILY TOUR ROUND THE COASTS OF SPAIN AND
PORTUGAL during the Winter of 1860-1861. By LADY DUNBAR, of Northfield. In post 8vo, 5s.

THE ROYAL ATLAS OF MODERN GEOGRAPHY.

In a Series of entirely Original and Authentic Maps. By A. KEITH JOHNSTON, F.R.S.E., F.R.G.S., Author of the 'Physical Atlas,' &c. With a complete Index of easy reference to each Map, comprising nearly 150,000 Places contained in this Atlas. Imperial folio, half-bound in russia or morocco, £5, 15s. 6d. (Dedicated by permission to Her Majesty.)

"No one can look through Mr Keith Johnston's new Atlas without seeing that it is the best which has ever been published in this country."—*The Times.*

"Of the many noble atlases prepared by Mr Johnston and published by Messrs Blackwood & Sons, this Royal Atlas will be the most useful to the public, and will deserve to be the most popular."—*Athenæum.*

"We know no series of maps which we can more warmly recommend. The accuracy, wherever we have attempted to put it to the test, is really astonishing."—*Saturday Review.*

"The culmination of all attempts to depict the face of the world appears in the Royal Atlas, than which it is impossible to conceive anything more perfect."—*Morning Herald.*

"This is, beyond question, the most splendid and luxurious, as well as the most useful and complete, of all existing atlases."—*Guardian.*

"There has not, we believe, been produced for general public use a body of maps equal in beauty and completeness to the Royal Atlas just issued by Mr A. K. Johnston."—*Examiner.*

"An almost daily reference to, and comparison of it with others, since the publication of the first part some two years ago until now, enables us to say, without the slightest hesitation, that this is by far the most complete and authentic atlas that has yet been issued."—*Scotsman.*

"Beyond doubt the greatest geographical work of our time."—*Museum.*

INDEX GEOGRAPHICUS:

Being an Index to nearly ONE HUNDRED AND FIFTY THOUSAND NAMES OF PLACES, &c.; with their LATITUDES and LONGITUDES as given in KEITH JOHNSTON'S 'ROYAL ATLAS;' together with the COUNTRIES and SUBDIVISIONS OF THE COUNTRIES in which they are situated. In 1 vol. large 8vo., 21s.

A NEW MAP OF EUROPE.

By A. KEITH JOHNSTON, F.R.S.E. Size, 4 feet 2 inches by 3 feet 5 inches. Cloth Case, 21s.

ATLAS OF SCOTLAND.

31 Maps of the Counties of Scotland, coloured. Bound in roan, price 10s. 6d. Each County may be had separately, in Cloth Case, 1s.

KEITH JOHNSTON'S SCHOOL ATLASES:—

GENERAL AND DESCRIPTIVE GEOGRAPHY, exhibiting the Actual and Comparative Extent of all the Countries in the World, with their present Political Divisions. A New and Enlarged Edition. With a complete Index. 26 Maps. Half-bound, 12s. 6d.

PHYSICAL GEOGRAPHY, illustrating, in a Series of Original Designs, the Elementary Facts of Geology, Hydrology, Meteorology, and Natural History. A New and Enlarged Edition. 19 Maps, including coloured Geological Maps of Europe and of the British Isles. Half-bound, 12s. 6d.

CLASSICAL GEOGRAPHY, comprising, in Twenty-three Plates, Maps and Plans of all the important Countries and Localities referred to by Classical Authors; accompanied by a pronouncing Index of Places, by T. HARVEY, M.A. Oxon. A New and Revised Edition. Half-bound, 12s. 6d.

ASTRONOMY. Edited by J. R. HIND, Esq., F.R.A.S., &c. Notes and Descriptive Letterpress to each Plate, embodying all recent Discoveries in Astronomy. 18 Maps. Half-bound, 12s. 6d.

ELEMENTARY SCHOOL ATLAS OF GENERAL AND DESCRIPTIVE GEOGRAPHY for the Use of Junior Classes. A New and Cheaper Edition. 20 Maps, including a Map of Canaan and Palestine. Half-bound, 5s.

"They are as superior to all School Atlases within our knowledge, as were the larger works of the same Author in advance of those that preceded them."—*Educational Times.*

"Decidedly the best School Atlases we have ever seen."—*English Journal of Education.*

"The best, the fullest, the most accurate and recent, as well as artistically the most beautiful atlas that can be put into the schoolboy's hands."—*Museum, April 1863.*

A MANUAL OF MODERN GEOGRAPHY:

Mathematical, Physical, and Political. Embracing a complete Development of the River-Systems of the Globe. By the REV. ALEX. MACKAY, F.R.G.S. With Index. 7s. 6d., bound in leather.

THE BOOK OF THE FARM.

Detailing the Labours of the Farmer, Farm-Steward, Ploughman, Shepherd, Hedger, Cattle-man, Field-worker, and Dairymaid, and forming a safe Monitor for Students in Practical Agriculture. By HENRY STEPHENS, F.R.S.E. 2 vols. royal 8vo, £3, handsomely bound in cloth, with upwards of 600 Illustrations.

"The best book I have ever met with."—*Professor Johnston.*

"We have thoroughly examined these volumes; but to give a full notice of their varied and valuable contents would occupy a larger space than we can conveniently devote to their discussion; we therefore, in general terms, commend them to the careful study of every young man who wishes to become a good practical farmer."—*Times.*

"One of the completest works on agriculture of which our literature can boast."—*Agricultural Gazette.*

THE BOOK OF FARM IMPLEMENTS AND MACHINES.

By JAMES SLIGHT and R. SCOTT BURN. Edited by HENRY STEPHENS, F.R.S.E. Illustrated with 876 Engravings. Royal 8vo, uniform with the 'Book of the Farm,' half-bound, £2, 2s.

THE BOOK OF FARM BUILDINGS:

Their Arrangement and Construction. By HENRY STEPHENS, F.R.S.E., and R. SCOTT BURN. Royal 8vo, with 1045 Illustrations. Uniform with the 'Book of the Farm.' Half-bound, £1, 11s. 6d.

THE BOOK OF THE GARDEN.

By CHARLES M'INTOSH. In 2 large vols. royal 8vo, embellished with 1353 Engravings.

Each Volume may be had separately—viz.:

I. ARCHITECTURAL AND ORNAMENTAL.—On the Formation of Gardens— Construction, Heating, and Ventilation of Fruit and Plant Houses, Pits, Frames, and other Garden Structures, with Practical Details. Illustrated by 1073 Engravings, pp. 766. £2, 10s.

II. PRACTICAL GARDENING.—Directions for the Culture of the Kitchen Garden, the Hardy-fruit Garden, the Forcing Garden, and Flower Garden, including Fruit and Plant Houses, with Select Lists of Vegetables, Fruits, and Plants. Pp. 868, with 279 Engravings. £1, 17s. 6d.

"We feel justified in recommending Mr M'Intosh's two excellent volumes to the notice of the public."—*Gardeners' Chronicle.*

PRACTICAL SYSTEM OF FARM BOOK-KEEPING:

Being that recommended in the 'Book of the Farm' by H. STEPHENS. Royal 8vo, 2s. 6d. Also, SEVEN FOLIO ACCOUNT-BOOKS, printed and ruled in accordance with the System, the whole being specially adapted for keeping, by an easy and accurate method, an account of all the transactions of the Farm. A detailed Prospectus may be had from the Publishers. Price of the complete set of Eight Books, £1, 4s. 6d. Also, A LABOUR ACCOUNT OF THE ESTATE, 2s. 6d.

"We have no hesitation in saying that, of the many systems of keeping farm accounts which are now in vogue, there is not one which will bear comparison with this."—*Bell's Messenger.*

AINSLIE'S TREATISE ON LAND-SURVEYING.

A New and Enlarged Edition. Edited by WILLIAM GALBRAITH, M.A., F.R.A.S. 1 vol. 8vo, with a Volume of Plates in Quarto, 21s.

"The best book on surveying with which I am acquainted."—*W. RUTHERFORD, LL.D., F.R.A.S., Royal Military Academy, Woolwich.*

THE FORESTER:

A Practical Treatise on the Planting, Rearing, and Management of Forest Trees. By JAMES BROWN, Wood Manager to the Earl of Seafield. Third Edition, greatly enlarged, with numerous Engravings on Wood. Royal 8vo, 30s.

"Beyond all doubt this is the best work on the subject of Forestry extant."—*Gardeners' Journal.*

"The most useful guide to good arboriculture in the English language."—*Gardeners' Chronicle.*

HANDBOOK OF THE MECHANICAL ARTS,

Concerned in the Construction and Arrangement of Dwellings and other Buildings ; Including Carpentry, Smith-work, Iron-framing, Brick-making, Columns, Cements, Well-sinking, Enclosing of Land, Road-making, &c. By R. SCOTT BURN. Crown 8vo, with 504 Engravings on Wood, 6s. 6d.

PROFESSOR JOHNSTON'S WORKS:—

EXPERIMENTAL AGRICULTURE. Being the Results of Past, and Suggestions for Future, Experiments in Scientific and Practical Agriculture. 8s.

ELEMENTS OF AGRICULTURAL CHEMISTRY AND GEOLOGY. Eighth Edition, 6s. 6d.

A CATECHISM OF AGRICULTURAL CHEMISTRY AND GEOLOGY. Fifty-seventh Edition. Edited by Dr VOELCKER. 1s.

ON THE USE OF LIME IN AGRICULTURE. 6s.

INSTRUCTIONS FOR THE ANALYSIS OF SOILS. Fourth Edition, 2s.

THE RELATIVE VALUE OF ROUND AND SAWN TIMBER,

Shown by means of Tables and Diagrams. By JAMES RAIT, Land-Steward at Castle-Forbes. Royal 8vo, 8s. half-bound.

THE YEAR-BOOK OF AGRICULTURAL FACTS.

1859 and 1860. Edited by R. SCOTT BURN. Fcap. 8vo, 5s. each. 1861 and 1862, 4s. each.

ELKINGTON'S SYSTEM OF DRAINING:

A Systematic Treatise on the Theory and Practice of Draining Land, adapted to the various Situations and Soils of England and Scotland, drawn up from the Communications of Joseph Elkington, by J. JOHNSTONE. 4to, 10s. 6d.

JOURNAL OF AGRICULTURE, AND TRANSACTIONS OF
THE HIGHLAND AND AGRICULTURAL SOCIETY OF SCOTLAND.

OLD SERIES, 1828 to 1843, 21 vols. . . .	£3 3 0
NEW SERIES, 1843 to 1851, 8 vols. . . .	2 2 0

THE RURAL ECONOMY OF ENGLAND, SCOTLAND, AND

IRELAND. By LEONCE DE LAVERGNE. Translated from the French. With Notes by a Scottish Farmer. In 8vo, 12s.

" One of the best works on the philosophy of agriculture and of agricultural political economy that has appeared."—*Spectator.*

DAIRY MANAGEMENT AND FEEDING OF MILCH COWS:

Being the recorded Experience of MRS AGNES SCOTT, Winkston, Peebles. Second Edition. Fcap., 1s.

ITALIAN IRRIGATION:

A Report addressed to the Hon. the Court of Directors of the East India Company, on the Agricultural Canals of Piedmont and Lombardy ; with a Sketch of the Irrigation System of Northern and Central India. By LIEUT.-COL. BAIRD SMITH, C.B. Second Edition. 2 vols. 8vo. with Atlas in folio, 30s.

THE ARCHITECTURE OF THE FARM:

A Series of Designs for Farm Houses, Farm Steadings, Factors' Houses, and Cottages. By JOHN STARFORTH, Architect. Sixty-two Engravings. In medium 4to, £2, 2s.

" One of the most useful and beautiful additions to Messrs Blackwood's extensive and valuable library of agricultural and rural economy."—*Morning Post.*

THE YESTER DEEP LAND-CULTURE:

Being a Detailed Account of the Method of Cultivation which has been successfully practised for several years by the Marquess of Tweeddale at Yester. By HENRY STEPHENS, Esq., F.R.S.E., Author of the ' Book of the Farm.' In small 8vo, with Engravings on Wood, 4s. 6d.

A MANUAL OF PRACTICAL DRAINING.
By HENRY STEPHENS, F.R.S.E., Author of the 'Book of the Farm.'
Third Edition, 8vo, 5s.

A CATECHISM OF PRACTICAL AGRICULTURE.
By HENRY STEPHENS, F.R.S.E., Author of the 'Book of the Farm,' &c.
In crown 8vo, with Illustrations, 1s.

HANDY BOOK ON PROPERTY LAW.
By LORD ST LEONARDS. The Seventh Edition. To which is now added
a Letter on the New Laws for obtaining an Indefeasible Title. With a Portrait of the Author, engraved by HOLL. 3s. 6d.
"Less than 200 pages serve to arm us with the ordinary precautions to which we should attend in selling, buying, mortgaging, leasing, settling, and devising estates. We are informed of our relations to our
property, to our wives and children, and of our liability as trustees or executors, in a little book for the
million,—a book which the author tenders to the *profanum vulgus* as even capable of 'beguiling a few
hours in a railway carriage.'"—*Times.*

THE PLANTER'S GUIDE.
By SIR HENRY STEUART. A New Edition, with the Author's last Additions
and Corrections. 8vo, with Engravings, 21s.

STABLE ECONOMY:
A Treatise on the Management of Horses. By JOHN STEWART, V.S.
Seventh Edition, 6s. 6d.
"Will always maintain its position as a standard work upon the management of horses."—*Mark Lane
Express.*

ADVICE TO PURCHASERS OF HORSES.
By JOHN STEWART, V.S. 18mo, plates, 2s. 6d.

A PRACTICAL TREATISE ON THE CULTIVATION OF THE
GRAPE VINE. By WILLIAM THOMSON, Gardener to His Grace the
Duke of Buccleuch, Dalkeith Park. Fifth Edition. 8vo, 5s.
"When books on gardening are written thus conscientiously, they are alike honourable to their author
and valuable to the public."—*Lindley's Gardeners' Chronicle.*
"Want of space prevents us giving extracts, and we must therefore conclude by saying, that as the
author is one of the very best grape-growers of the day, this book may be stated as being the key to his
successful practice, and as such, we can with confidence recommend it as indispensable to all who wish
to excel in the cultivation of the vine."—*The Florist and Pomologist.*

THE CHEMISTRY OF VEGETABLE AND ANIMAL PHYSI-
OLOGY. By DR J. G. MULDER, Professor of Chemistry in the University
of Utrecht. With an Introduction and Notes by Professor JOHNSTON. 22
Plates. 8vo, 30s.

THE MOOR AND THE LOCH.
Containing Minute Instructions in all Highland Sports, with Wanderings
over Crag and Correi, Flood and Fell. By JOHN COLQUHOUN, Esq.
Third Edition. 8vo, with Illustrations, 12s. 6d.

SALMON-CASTS AND STRAY SHOTS:
Being Fly-Leaves from the Note-Book of JOHN COLQUHOUN, Esq.,
Author of 'The Moor and the Loch,' &c. Second Edition. Fcap. 8vo, 5s.

COQUET-DALE FISHING SONGS.
Now first collected by a North-Country Angler, with the Music of the Airs.
8vo, 5s.

THE ANGLER'S COMPANION TO THE RIVERS AND LOCHS
OF SCOTLAND. By T. T. STODDART. With Map of the Fishing Streams
and Lakes of Scotland. Second Edition. Crown 8vo, 3s. 6d.
"Indispensable in all time to come, as the very strength and grace of an angler's tackle and equipment
in Scotland, must and will be STODDART'S ANGLER'S COMPANION."—*Blackwood's Magazine.*

RELIGION IN COMMON LIFE:

A Sermon preached in Crathie Church, October 14, 1855, before Her Majesty the Queen and Prince Albert. By the Rev. JOHN CAIRD, D.D. Published by Her Majesty's Command. Bound in cloth, 8d. Cheap Edition, 3d.

SERMONS.

By the Rev. JOHN CAIRD, D.D., Professor of Divinity in the University of Glasgow, and one of Her Majesty's Chaplains for Scotland. In crown 8vo, 5s. This Edition includes the Sermon on 'Religion in Common Life,' preached in Crathie Church, Oct. 1855, before Her Majesty the Queen and the late Prince Consort.

"They are noble sermons; and we are not sure but that, with the cultivated reader, they will gain rather than lose by being read, not heard. There is a thoughtfulness and depth about them which can hardly be appreciated, unless when they are studied at leisure; and there are so many sentences so felicitously expressed that we should grudge being hurried away from them by a rapid speaker, without being allowed to enjoy them a second time."—*Fraser's Magazine.*

THE BOOK OF JOB.

By the late Rev. GEORGE CROLY, LL.D., Rector of St Stephen's, Walbrook. With a Memoir of the Author by his Son. Fcap. 8vo, 4s.

LECTURES IN DIVINITY.

By the late Rev. GEORGE HILL, D.D., Principal of St Mary's College, St Andrews. Stereotyped Edition. 8vo, 14s.

"I am not sure if I can recommend a more complete manual of Divinity."—*Dr Chalmers.*

THE MOTHERS LEGACIE TO HER UNBORNE CHILDE.

By Mrs ELIZABETH JOCELINE. Edited by the Very Rev. Principal Lee. 32mo, 4s. 6d.

"This beautiful and touching legacie."—*Athenæum.*
"A delightful monument of the piety and high feeling of a truly noble mother."—*Morning Advertiser.*

ANALYSIS AND CRITICAL INTERPRETATION OF THE HEBREW TEXT OF THE BOOK OF GENESIS.

Preceded by a Hebrew Grammar, and Dissertations on the Genuineness of the Pentateuch, and on the Structure of the Hebrew Language. By the Rev. WILLIAM PAUL, A.M. 8vo, 18s.

PRAYERS FOR SOCIAL AND FAMILY WORSHIP.

Prepared by a COMMITTEE OF THE GENERAL ASSEMBLY OF THE CHURCH OF SCOTLAND, and specially designed for the use of Soldiers, Sailors, Colonists, Sojourners in India, and other Persons, at Home or Abroad, who are deprived of the Ordinary Services of a Christian Ministry. *Published by Authority of the Committee.* Third Edition. In crown 8vo, bound in cloth, 4s.

PRAYERS FOR SOCIAL AND FAMILY WORSHIP.

Being a Cheap Edition of the above. Fcap. 8vo, 1s. 6d.

THE CHRISTIAN LIFE,

In its Origin, Progress, and Perfection. By the Very Rev. E. B. RAMSAY, LL.D., F.R.S.E., Dean of the Diocese of Edinburgh. Crown 8vo, 9s.

THEISM: THE WITNESS OF REASON AND NATURE TO AN ALL-WISE AND BENEFICENT CREATOR.

By the Rev. JOHN TULLOCH, D.D., Principal and Professor of Theology, St Mary's College, St Andrews; and one of Her Majesty's Chaplains in Ordinary in Scotland. In 1 vol. 8vo, 10s. 6d.

ON THE ORIGIN AND CONNECTION OF THE GOSPELS OF MATTHEW, MARK, AND LUKE;

With Synopsis of Parallel Passages, and Critical Notes. By JAMES SMITH, Esq. of Jordanhill, F.R.S., Author of the 'Voyage and Shipwreck of St Paul.' Medium 8vo, 16s.

INSTITUTES OF METAPHYSIC: THE THEORY OF KNOW-ING AND BEING. By JAMES F. FERRIER, A.B. Oxon., Professor of Moral Philosophy and Political Economy, St Andrews. Second Edition. Crown 8vo, 10s. 6d.

"We have no doubt, however, that the subtlety and depth of metaphysical genius which his work betrays, its rare display of rigorous and consistent reasonings, and the inimitable precision and beauty of its style on almost every page, must secure for it a distinguished place in the history of philosophical discussion."—*Tulloch's Burnett Prize Treatise.*

LECTURES ON METAPHYSICS.
By SIR WILLIAM HAMILTON, Bart., Professor of Logic and Metaphysics in the University of Edinburgh. Edited by the Rev. H. L. MANSEL, B.D., LL.D., Waynflete Professor of Moral and Metaphysical Philosophy, Oxford; and JOHN VEITCH, M.A., Professor of Logic, Rhetoric, and Metaphysics, St Andrews. Third Edition. 2 vols. 8vo, 24s.

LECTURES ON LOGIC.
By SIR WILLIAM HAMILTON, Bart. Edited by Professors MANSEL and VEITCH. In 2 vols., 24s.

THORNDALE; OR, THE CONFLICT OF OPINIONS.
By WILLIAM SMITH, Author of 'A Discourse on Ethics,' &c. Second Edition. Crown 8vo, 10s. 6d.

"The subjects treated of, and the style—always chaste and beautiful, often attractively grand—in which they are clothed, will not fail to secure the attention of the class for whom the work is avowedly written. . . . It deals with many of those higher forms of speculation characteristic of the cultivated minds of the age."—*North British Review.*

GRAVENHURST; OR, THOUGHTS ON GOOD AND EVIL.
By WILLIAM SMITH, Author of 'Thorndale,' &c. In crown 8vo, 7s. 6d.

"One of those rare books which, being filled with noble and beautiful thoughts, deserves an attentive and thoughtful perusal."—*Westminster Review.*

A DISCOURSE ON ETHICS OF THE SCHOOL OF PALEY.
By WILLIAM SMITH, Author of 'Thorndale.' 8vo, 4s.

ON THE INFLUENCE EXERTED BY THE MIND OVER THE BODY, in the Production and Removal of Morbid and Anomalous Conditions of the Animal Economy. By JOHN GLEN, M.A. Crown 8vo, 2s. 6d.

DESCARTES ON THE METHOD OF RIGHTLY CONDUCT-ING THE REASON, and Seeking Truth in the Sciences. Translated from the French. 12mo, 2s.

DESCARTES' MEDITATIONS, AND SELECTIONS FROM HIS PRINCIPLES OF PHILOSOPHY. Translated from the Latin. 12mo, 3s.

SPECULATIVE PHILOSOPHY:
An INTRODUCTORY LECTURE delivered at the Opening of the Class of Logic and Rhetoric in the University of Glasgow, Nov. 1, 1864. By JOHN VEITCH, M.A., Professor of Logic and Rhetoric in the University of Glasgow. 1s.

CORNELIUS O'DOWD UPON MEN AND WOMEN, AND OTHER THINGS IN GENERAL. Originally published in 'Blackwood's Magazine.' 3 vols. crown 8vo, 31s. 6d.

"The flashes of the author's wit must not blind us to the ripeness of his wisdom, nor the general playfulness of his O'Dowderies allow us to forget the ample evidence that underneath them lurks one of the most earnest and observant spirits of the present time."—*Daily Review.*
"In truth one of the most delightful volumes of personal reminiscence it has ever been our fortune to peruse."—*Globe.*

THE INCREASE OF FAITH.

Contents—1. Of the Nature of Faith. 2. Of the Aspirations of the Believer for Increase of Faith. 3. That Faith is capable of Increase. 4. Of Faith's Increase: What it is. 5. Of Faith as the Gift of God. 6. Of the Means of Faith's Increase. 7. Of the Hindrances to Faith's Increase. 8. Of the Assurance of Grace and Salvation. 9. Of Faith made Perfect. Price 3s. 6d.

NATURAL THEOLOGY:

AN INQUIRY INTO THE FUNDAMENTAL PRINCIPLES OF RELIGIOUS, MORAL, AND POLITICAL SCIENCE. By W. R. PIRIE, D.D., Professor of Divinity and Church History in the University of Aberdeen.

EUCHOLOGION; OR, BOOK OF PRAYERS:

Being Forms of Worship issued by the Church Service Society. Price 6s. 6d.

THE FATHERHOOD OF GOD,

CONSIDERED IN ITS GENERAL AND SPECIAL ASPECTS, AND PARTICULARLY IN RELATION TO THE ATONEMENT; WITH A REVIEW OF RECENT SPECULATIONS ON THE SUBJECT. By THOMAS J. CRAWFORD, D.D., Professor of Divinity in the University of Edinburgh. Second Edition, revised and enlarged, with a Reply to the Strictures of Dr Candlish. Price 7s. 6d.

THE RESURRECTION OF JESUS CHRIST:

With an Examination of the Speculations of Strauss in his 'New Life of Jesus,' and an Introductory View of the present position of Theological Inquiry in reference to the Existence of God, and the Miraculous Evidence of Christianity. By ROBERT MACPHERSON, D.D., Professor of Theology in the University of Aberdeen. Price 9s.

PRAYERS FOR SOCIAL AND FAMILY WORSHIP.

For the use of Soldiers, Sailors, Colonists, Sojourners in India, and other Persons, at home and abroad, who are deprived of the ordinary services of a Christian Ministry; also, Prayers and Thanksgivings on particular occasions. Third Edition, crown octavo, 4s. Cheap Edition, 1s. 6d. Another Edition, on toned paper, 2s. 6d.

FAMILY PRAYERS,

As authorised by the General Assembly of the Church of Scotland; to which is prefixed a Pastoral Letter from the General Assembly on Family Worship. Price 4s. 6d. Also a People's Edition, 2s.

Lightning Source UK Ltd.
Milton Keynes UK
30 September 2010

160595UK00007B/117/P